BUSINESS AS MISSION:

FROM IMPOVERISHED TO EMPOWERED

OTHER TITLES IN THE EMS SERIES:

BUSINESS AS MISSION:

FROM IMPOVERISHED TO EMPOWERED

Edited by
Tom Steffen & Mike Barnett

Evangelical Missiological Society Series
Number 14

EMS Series No. 14

Cover design: Bill Bangham with photograph by Scott Lashinsky

Published by William Carey Library

1605 E. Elizabeth St.

Pasadena, California 91104

www.WCLBooks.com

William Carey Library is a Ministry of the
U.S. Center for World Mission, Pasadena, California.

ISBN: 0-87808-388-X

Printed in the United States of America

This book is dedicated to

those businesspersons who wish to

glorify God and expand his Kingdom through

starting and multiplying businesses

(Great Commission Companies)

for the benefit of those residing in

the least reached and least resourced

parts of the world.

Contents

II. MISSIOLIGICAL FOUNDATIONS

III. CASE STUDIES

Author Profiles

Dwight Baker is associate director of the Overseas Ministries Study Center in New Haven, Connecticut, and is associate editor of the International Bulletin of Missionary Research. Previously he served for seven years at the U.S. Center for World Mission in Pasadena, California, where he was director of the World Christian Foundations study program.

David Befus started many of the Opportunity International programs in Latin America, and also helped World Vision develop its micro-finance programs in Latin America, Africa, and Eastern Europe. He has been the President of Latin America Mission since 1999, and has written a book for missions on the implementation of economic development programs entitled *Kingdom Business*.

Michael Cooper is Assistant Professor of Biblical Studies and Christian Ministries at Trinity International University. Prior to coming to Trinity, he spent 13 years on the mission field in Central and Eastern Europe. He has published and lectured on topics involving the history of missions and its contemporary relevance in mission practice. His current research interest is in the missionary efforts of the early and medieval church and the revival of Pagan religions in Western society.

Meg Crossman is a missions mobilizer and is the editor of *Worldwide Perspectives* missions course from the William Carey Library. She has directed Perspectives Partnership since 1996 and is Director Emeritus of Worldwide Perspectives since 2004.

Jay Gary is president of ChristianFutures.com, a network of scholars and ministry leaders that focus on the future of faith in a changing society. He is best known among mission leaders as the lead developer of the Perspectives Study Program and the AD 2000 movement. His latest project was creating

11

a Masters degree of Strategic Foresight for mid-career ministry and business professionals at Regent University's School of Leadership Studies.

Norm Ewert teaches economics at Wheaton College focusing on macroeconomics, economic development, and small-scale enterprise and development. He also has been involved with the Human Needs and Global Resources program at the College.

Carla Hausman graduated with a BA in anthropology and is now working towards her MA in ICS. She hopes to someday teach anthropology in higher education.

Neal Johnson has served as west coast Regional Director for the Fellowship of Companies for Christ International (FCCI), a niche ministry to Christian business owners and CEOs. Most recently, he joined Belhaven College in Jackson, Mississippi, as the founding Dean and Executive Director of a Center for Marketplace Missions. His dissertation from Fuller Seminary's School of World Mission entitled, *God's Mission To, Within and Through the Marketplace* illustrates his passion for Christ in the global marketplace.

Joseph Kilpatric is the director of the School of Business Administration and professor of business administration at Toccoa Falls College in Toccoa Falls, Georgia. Previously, he served as a missionary in Belgium, Hong Kong, and Miami, FL, as well as a missions administrator and publisher. He holds a B.S. degree in accounting, an MBA degree, and a doctorate in international business administration.

Patrick Lai and his family have lived and worked in the 10/40 Window for 23 years. They served for four years as regular missionaries and 19 years as tentmakers. The Lord has enabled his team to plant two churches and begin several for profit businesses. Patrick has degrees in Business, an MDiv., and a doctorate in Intercultural Studies. He has written numerous articles on tentmaking and lectures around the world on using business as missions for Christ.

João Mordomo is co-founder and executive director of a not-for-profit organization based in south Brazil dedicated to training and sending Brazilian cross-cultural workers to the Muslim world. He serves on the Lausanne Committee for World Evangelization's Business as Mission Working Group, is professor of missions and intercultural studies at two seminaries and the author of numerous articles. He holds degrees in sociology and practical theology and is currently working on his doctorate in missiology. He and his wife and their two small children live in Paraná, Brazil.

Howard Owens is chair and assistant professor of missions and Christian education at Temple Baptist Seminary of Tennessee Temple University. He has a Ph.D. from New Orleans Baptist Theological Seminary, where he taught adjunctively in the areas of missions and evangelism. Previously he served as a church planter in Montpellier, France for twelve yeas with International Teams and earned a M.Div. from Columbia Biblical Seminary and School of Missions.

D. D. Pani (pseudonym) is a textbook author and has published a large number of international articles. Over the last three decades, Dr. Pani has spent considerable time in India. Though he and his wife are currently residents of Pennsylvania, he continues to travel extensively in the Indian subcontinent.

Steven Pointer is Professor of History at Trinity International University. He is a member of the American Society of Church History, and the Conference on Faith and History. He has published several articles and essays in the fields of American and British church history. His book *Joseph Cook, Boston Lecturer and Evangelical Apologist* was published in 1991. He pursued additional graduate study and research in France and England. His current research interest is English Puritanism.

Mans Ramstad (pseudonym) has been involved in health work in China for over ten years. He has a PhD in Public Health. He has published in the areas of missiology in the creative context and the role of holistic ministry as a missions strategy.

Steve Rundle is associate professor of economics at Biola University. He received his B.A. in economics from California State University, Northridge, and his Ph.D. in economics from Claremont Graduate University. Before entering the academic world, he served in the U.S. Marine Corps, followed by several management-level positions in the interstate trucking industry. He has authored or coauthored many journal articles and book chapters on this subject, as well as a book, *Great Commission Companies: The Emerging Role of Business in Missions* (IVP, 2003).

Sue Russell served 17 years with SIL in Malaysia working with a Tagal translation committee where she learned many of the principles in the article. She is now associate professor of anthropology at the School of Intercultural Studies, Biola University.

Mark Russell is currently a doctoral student at Asbury Theological Seminary. He has a Masters of Divinity from Trinity Evangelical Divinity School and a Bachelors of Science in International Business from Auburn University. He has lived and worked in Russia, Chile and Germany and has traveled extensively in over 50 countries on a variety of business, educational, humanitarian and religious projects. He is married to Laurie and they have two children, Noah and Anastasia.

Tom Stallter is professor of Intercultural Studies and World Mission at Grace Theological Seminary. He spent 18 years in leadership training and church development in the countries of Central African Republic and the Republic of Chad. He is co-founder and President of Love in Action International, Inc.

Sarah Vinateri graduated with a BA in anthropology. She is now preparing to work in relief and development overseas.

Bill Wagner is the Baker James Cauthen Professor of Missions at Golden Gate Baptist Theological Seminary in San Francisco. He served with the International Mission Board of the Southern Baptists for thirty-two years during which time he spent 12 years as their Consultant for Evangelism and Church Growth for Europe, Middle East, and North Africa. He is a past Vice President of the Southern Baptist Convention. Two other seminaries where he serves as professor of missions are the Evangelical Theological Faculty in Belgium and the Bible Seminary Bonn in Germany.

Ralph Winter founded the Frontier Mission Fellowship that led to the founding of the U.S. Center for World Mission and the William Carey University. He is the founder of the William Carey Library, co-founder of the American Society of Missiology, assisted in the founding of ACMC (Advancing Churches in Mission Commitment), and inaugurated the Perspectives Study Program. He served in Guatemala for ten years, helping to develop Theological Education by Extension before serving on the faculty of Fuller School of World Mission for another decade.

Introduction

"...remember the Lord your God, for it is he who gives you
the ability to produce wealth..." (Dt 8:18, NIV).

In a recent issue of *Christianity Today*, a question directly related to this volume was asked, "Do we not owe the business people in our midst solid teaching about their calling?"[1] This question deserves special attention today because the Holy Spirit continues to stir the hearts of numerous businesspersons to become involved in missions. Not just to write checks for missionaries and mission endeavors, mind you, but to personally participate in global missions through starting businesses at home and abroad. This annual volume of the Evangelical Missiological Society (EMS) originated from the IFMA/EMS annual meeting held at the Minneapolis Airport Marriot in September 22-24, 2005, and the multiple EMS regional meetings that took place during the year throughout the United States and Canada. The contributors attempt to further the discussion of the relationship between business and mission. The EMS theme for 2005 was: "Business as Mission: From Impoverished to Empowered." This volume is a collection of the papers presented at the annual and regional meetings that attempt to answer some foundational questions, such as: Is business a legitimate vehicle for missions? What are the marks of integrity in business conducted with mission objectives in a crosscultural context? Which business models make the greatest impact on the communities they serve? How can the spiritual and emotional well-being of the workers be ensured? How will training have to change for business personnel? How will training have to change for mission personnel?

"To put it bluntly," wrote Doug Pennoyer, Dean of the School of Intercultural Studies, Biola University and President of EMS, when announcing the call for BAM papers, "Business as mission (BAM) is a work in progress. It is a field that needs definition, theological clarity, and missiological focus. Our call for papers for our regional conferences is timely, and the culminating discussions and presentations at the national level puts us in a place to make a pivotal contribution in a sea of some confusion and even controversy."

For some, BAM is *the* tool God will use to reach the unreached world hostile to the gospel and the West. BAM will also provide funding for kingdom professionals who increasingly find it difficult to raise support from churches suffering from giving fatigue and/or a loss of appreciation for the Great Commission and Great Commandment. Others see BAM as one of many excellent tools that God has (again) raised up to integrate the spiritual and the social, providing businesspeople front row participation in reaching the least reached and least resourced peoples of the world. Still others prefer Business as Missions over Business as Mission.

While this volume will certainly not bring total clarity to the topic, it will provide some needed definition and precision while at the same time identify areas that will demand further discussion, clarification, and maturity. In this volume the reader will find contributors contradicting each other. While challenging, we find this healthy for the ongoing debate. We therefore intentionally include different perspectives believing that as the Holy Spirit moves his people into new, integrative directions for this age, insight will follow for the humble learner-leaders.

We have divided the book into four parts. The first part provides an overview of BAM, providing a broad-brushed sweep from the past to the present while part 2 considers missiological foundations for the movement. Part 3 presents actual case studies from different parts of the world demonstrating the hope of holistic ministry that moves people from poverty to empowerment. The last part reflects on future challenges facing BAM, from the training of business personnel to incorporate missions into their business plan, to missions people incorporating a business plan into their ministry plan. While major strides have been made in the last five years in BAM, many more remain. May God use this book to further his glory and grace through a budding movement entitled BAM so that many others may have the opportunity to move from spiritual darkness to the Light, and from impoverishment to empowerment.

Tom Steffen
Biola University
January 2006

[1] See: CT's "Views on Key Issues - Neighbor Love Inc.: Christians in Business Have an Honored Place in God's Plan," *Christianity Today,* September 2005:37.

Part 1

Overview of BAM

1

Distinctives and Challenges of Business as Mission

Neal Johnson and Steve Rundle

The speaker was in some ways a caricature of globalization — an Iranian-born citizen of Canada, educated in the U.S., and now working in China alongside her American husband. In 1993, before an audience of about 19,000 college students, "Mary" shared the following story:

> [M]y husband and I traveled to a remote place in China — we went as far as the airplane could take us, and then on by train. That evening as we strolled down the street we stopped at a little sidewalk restaurant to eat. Knowing that we were foreigners, the people eagerly crowded around us and began saying, "Coca Cola. We like Coca Cola." We asked them if they had ever heard of Jesus? After some murmuring they answered, "No, no one had ever heard that name." In anguish, I wondered why Coca Cola had gotten to this area, and after 2000 years, Jesus had not?[1]

Her story illustrates the remarkable capacity of business to reach people virtually anywhere in the world, including places where the gospel still struggles to gain a foothold. It also helps explain why well-known evangelicals such as Billy Graham, Henry Blackaby and Wayne Grudem are focusing more of their attention on the heretofore neglected role of business — and those who run them — in mission. This increased attention is part of an even broader movement, perhaps the first great missionary movement of the Twenty-First Century, in which laypeople from every profession are discovering, or rather, *rediscovering*, their role in *missio Dei*. That role goes beyond financial support, service on church committees and prayer, and extends into areas that were once thought to be the exclusive purview of professional missionaries.

Terms such as "Marketplace Ministry," "Business as Mission" and "Tentmaking" are all being used, often synonymously, to describe what in our view are separate strands, or camps, within a single movement. They are closely related in that all start by emphasizing the "priesthood of all believers" (1 Pe 2:9-10) and the idea that mission, properly understood, is something all Christians are called into. They all promote the intrinsic value of work, and claim that the distinction often made between sacred and secular vocations is not only unbiblical, but is counterproductive to the completion of the Great Commission.

However there are also important differences. For example, in addition to promoting the evangelistic potential of individual Christians in a workplace setting, as Tentmaking does, Business as Mission stresses the redemptive potential of a *business itself*; a distinction sometimes referred to as a focus on "job taking" versus "job making." The primary concern of Marketplace Ministries (also referred to as Workplace Ministries) is equipping Christian lay people to be more effective ambassadors for Christ in the workplace. While many of these organizations are now international, their principle purpose is to minister to other Christians within a mono-cultural setting. In contrast, Business as Mission stresses the strategic role of business in reaching places where Christ has never been preached (Ro 15:20). Put another way, Business as Mission (and Tentmaking) is primarily interested in the "uttermost parts of the earth," while Jerusalem is the main concern of Marketplace Ministry.

The differences are admittedly subtle, and, at times, unnecessarily divisive. Yet, as every missiologist knows, advancing the cause of Christ in foreign, less-evangelized places is a vastly different undertaking from doing it mono-culturally. Likewise, the challenges businesspeople face in these settings are in many ways quite different from those facing physicians, teachers or professional missionaries. It is therefore good to have a degree of specialization by profession, cultural or geographical orientation, and mission strategy. However, too much specialization can be counterproductive if it leads to disunity, redundancies and inefficiencies. This is a risk the movement currently faces. For example, each camp now has its own associations, conferences, advocates, models, literature, goals and leadership. There is little, if any, communication taking place between the camps, little awareness that the other camps even exist, let along what is transpiring within each camp.

This point was underscored at the 2004 Lausanne conference Pattaya, Thailand, where there was not one, but *three* different issue groups on these topics — Issue Group #11 (Marketplace Ministry), Issue Group #30 (Business as Mission), and Issue Group #10 (The Local Church and Tentmaking). For those who consider Micro-Enterprise Development to be part of this movement (not everyone does, as we will see below), a fourth issue group would be included — Issue Group #4 (Holistic Mission). While there were some opportunities at the conference for cross-communication, there was little, if any collaboration and no coordination. In the end, much of the work done by these groups was redundant, and an opportunity for each camp to discern and define their distinctive roles within the larger movement was missed.

Such confusion and competition at this early stage is predictable, and, we hope, ultimately healthy. The purpose of this chapter is to provide a basic overview of the Movement as a whole, with particular emphasis on the Business as Mission (BAM) camp. For the sake of simplicity, we will refer to the broader movement simply as "the Movement." After defining the various camps within the Movement, we will turn our attention to some of the ongoing debates within BAM circles, drawing heavily from the discussions that took place at the 2004 Lausanne conference. This will be followed by a look at some of the challenges facing this Movement, BAM in particular, and the implications for churches, educators, missiologists and business professionals.

Four Camps Within A Single Movement

This new Movement, which at its core stresses the active participation of laypeople in ministry and missions, can be divided, or more precisely, *has divided itself*, into distinct camps: Tentmaking; Marketplace Ministries; and Business as Mission. For the purposes of this essay, we include a fourth camp, Enterprise Development, which includes micro-enterprise development (MED), small- and medium-size enterprise (SME) development, and revolving loan funds. Not everyone agrees, however, that Enterprise Development — which relies heavily on charitable donations and is not particularly geared toward mobilizing laypeople into mission — fits within the Movement under discussion. But there is no denying that many people think instinctively of Enterprise Development when the term Business as Mission is used. After all, they argue, it involves business and has a missional purpose. Accordingly, no overview of this Movement would be complete in our opinion without some discussion of this approach.

Although a detailed discussion of each camp is beyond the scope of this chapter, a brief introduction to each is necessary in order to help the reader understand their nuances, and to put BAM into its broader context.

Tentmaking

We turn first to the most familiar of the four camps: Tentmaking. While there is no single, agreed upon definition of the term, for present purposes let us define a tentmaker as a mission-minded Christian who supports himself or herself in a cross-cultural mission context through a vocation such as teaching English, medical work, or working for a locally-owned or international company.

The term, and the model, originated with the Apostle Paul — the pioneer of Christian missions — who was, by trade, a tentmaker (Ac 18:3). While there is some debate as to how much tentmaking he actually did, at a minimum we know that Paul plied his trade in Corinth (1 Co 9), Ephesus (Ac 20: 34-35), and Thessalonica (1 Th 2:9, 2 Th 3:8). He received financial support from others on occasion (Php 4:15-16), but his vigorous refusal to seek such support suggests that self-support was his preferred practice (1 Co 9: 12, 15 and 18). Not that he opposed the idea of donor support. On the contrary, in the same text Paul strongly defends the right of missionaries to receive financial support from donors. Yet, he denied himself this right and preached "without charge" so as not to be seen as motivated by personal gain (1 Co 9:16-18). Supporting himself also added credibility to his message and gave him ample opportunities to model a godly work ethic and Christ-centered lifestyle. It is highly likely that he saw his day job as a central part of his ministry, as an indispensable part of his church planting strategy, and as important to his witness as his preaching.

This is not, however, the popular notion of tentmaking within the pews today. Instead, the prevailing notion is that the tentmaker's job is mainly a source of income, or a "cover" for access and ministry, rather than a legitimate ministry in its own right. Put another way, they see the job as a necessary evil rather than an indispensable part of a healthy church planting strategy. In fact, one commonly cited disadvantage of tentmaking is that the requirements of the job leave little time for ministry. Such a perspective presupposes a dichotomy between "work" and "ministry," and is based on a gross misunderstanding of the purpose and the power of tentmaking. It also creates deep ethical tensions as it encourages tentmakers to work only enough to keep their supervisors and local authorities happy. It is hard to imagine that Paul worked only for appearances sake, or that when he exhorted his followers to "imitate me" (1 Co 4:16) or to "follow us" (2 Th 3:7-9) he was encouraging deceptive practices. Nevertheless, while such practices are roundly condemned in many ministry and mission circles, they remain commonplace — and are even encouraged — among many.

Marketplace Ministries

The second camp within this Movement is referred to as Marketplace Ministries, although the term Workplace Ministries is also gaining currency. These ministries are usually para-church organizations that bring together the members of a given business community to minister to each other and to evangelize, disciple and coach others within their spheres of influence. More than 1200 such ministries are currently operating around the globe.[2] Many are local, some are regional, and a few are global in reach. But in almost all cases, the focus is on near-neighbor rather than cross-cultural outreach.

Many such ministries focus on the business owners, chief executive officers (CEOs) or other leaders who have significant authority within a corporation and, as such, help influence the corporate culture. Ministering to these leaders and equipping them to manage their companies according to biblical principles, to integrate their faith into the lifeblood of the companies, and to be a positive witness for Christ to their employees, customers, suppliers and competitors is therefore paramount. These ministries emphatically believe that a person can be both a good, successful business person, with all that implies, as well as a faithful, obedient follower of Jesus Christ. They believe that God calls people into business the same way He calls others into the pastorate. They are ardent promoters of the doctrine of the "priesthood of all believers," and as such, encourage business men and women to view the business as their ministry and their employees, coworkers, suppliers and customers as their "flock." The focus is on evangelism, discipleship and coaching, but almost never on cross-cultural outreach or church planting. The members of these ministries are, however, called to be faithful members of a local congregation.

Enterprise Development

The Enterprise Development camp is well known to most missiologists. The primary goal of enterprise development is to help the world's poorest people bootstrap themselves out of poverty by helping them create a business. Many such businesses are known as micro-enterprises. These are the smallest of businesses, designed to help poverty-stricken families become economically productive, but generally too small to employ others in the community. For example, a woman may be a skilled seamstress, but have no sewing machine and no access to capital. An organization specializing in micro-enterprise development (MED) and micro-finance might help this woman by providing a small loan — usually less than US$300 and more often in the US$50 to US$100 range — for the purpose of acquiring her equipment and/or initial inventory. When the loan is repaid the funds are recycled as seed capital for other loans. The money essentially becomes part of a permanent endowment that will be perpetually recycled to help the poor.

A variation of this approach is small- and medium size enterprise (SME) development, which targets larger businesses that have the potential for creating employment for many people in the community. These businesses, while still small, more closely resemble businesses in the developed world in that there is a semblance of a corporate structure, a payroll to be met, a variety of products or services, and so forth. Because of their location in countries that lack well-developed credit markets, these businesses (like micro-enterprises) often must turn to nontraditional sources like Non-Governmental Organizations (NGOs) for financing. Loans in the range of US$500 to US$5,000 are common, and some can reach as high as US$20,000.

In all three cases (micro-, small- and medium-sized business development), the object is to intervene in the community by providing loans to entrepreneurs and helping them set up or expand their businesses so that they can become economically self-sufficient. The mission focus is holistic, although the importance placed on the spiritual component of holistic mission varies widely from organization to organization. Some target Christian entrepreneurs only, as part of a broader strategy to build up the indigenous church. Others make loans to anyone who qualifies, hoping that the exposure to this program and the relationships it creates with Christians will lead to evangelistic and discipleship opportunities. Still others make no effort to evangelize at all, striving instead to simply address the people's economic needs.

Business as Mission

Business as Mission (BAM) is the newest camp to emerge within this Movement. The term was first coined in 1999 by a small group of people meeting in the U.K. at the Oxford Center for Mission Studies to discuss a relatively new approach to missions, one that taps the power and the redemptive potential of large, often *global*, businesses. The BAM label was one of two that were created during those meetings, the other one being "Business with a Christian Hat." The latter term, which thankfully never caught on, was meant to describe businesses that have a Christian reputation, but are not thinking or acting strategically in a global mission sense. In contrast, BAM arises out of a deep concern for the least-developed and least-reached nations of the world, especially those in the 10/40 window. Like Paul, it proceeds from a compelling desire to see the Gospel taken to places where Christ has never been preached (Ro 15:20).

The BAM label resonated within the Christian mission community and took on a life of its own. A mere five years later, major BAM events were being held on every continent and its leaders were invited to participate in the 2004 Forum of the Lausanne Committee for World Evangelization in Pattaya, Thailand. Nonetheless, an agreed upon, concise definition of BAM has been illusive. For the purposes of this discussion, we define BAM as "the utilization of for-profit businesses as instruments for global mission." A business is not likely to be an effective instrument for mission unless there are Christians managing it, so the vital role of Christian business *people* is implied in this definition.

Proponents of BAM often use adjectives like "real" and "legitimate" to describe these businesses in an effort to differentiate them from the business-as-cover strategies sometimes associated with tentmaking. Such adjectives would seem to also rule out unprofitable businesses that are sustained with the help of nonprofit-subsidized labor and/or capital, although on this matter there are differences of opinion.

BAM, like MED and SME development, is a holistic mission strategy that aims to create jobs and wealth for the local people as well as address other physical, social and spiritual needs. The approaches, however, are quite different. Enterprise Development strategies are designed explicitly to promote entrepreneurship at the local level. BAM, on the other hand, often (but not always) involves a team of *expatriate* entrepreneurs who launch and manage a business and *hire* local people. Many BAM companies — commonly referred to either as "Great Commission Companies" or "Kingdom Companies" — promote leadership training and development from within the company, with a long range goal of turning over management and possibly ownership of the company to local national employees. In some cases there is a complete exit strategy in place, while in others the owner(s) retain an equity interest to finance the development of other Great Commission Companies.

BAM-related ministry takes many forms. First, there is a recognition of the intrinsic value of the business itself, that God (and man) derives pleasure from a business that is well-run, and especially when done in such a way as to draw attention to Himself. In this way there is little difference between BAM and Marketplace Ministries. Both see business itself as an act of worship and as a legitimate calling. BAM takes this a step further, however, by making a concerted effort within the company setting to witness for Christ, both overtly and through holistic lifestyle evangelism. Examples of these efforts include such things as Bible studies, training in the areas of literacy, nutrition, sanitation, childcare, healthy living, and healthcare, as well as company-sponsored community projects that demonstrate the loving heart of Jesus. In addition, an effort is often made to leverage the business strategy itself for greater ministry impact through creative alliances with other Great Commission Companies or ministries. In short, the business is an integral part of a holistic mission strategy, one that specifically aims to meet physical as well as spiritual needs in the least-evangelized and least-developed parts of the world.

Internal Debates

Unfortunately, as more people use a label, the murkier its definition tends to become. Like "tentmaking," the term BAM now means different things depending on whom you ask. Our goal for this section is not necessarily to resolve this debate, but rather, to highlight some of the ambiguities or areas of disagreement. Recall that BAM was originally coined to describe businesses that were created specifically for the purpose of actively and holistically participating in global mission. But what exactly qualifies as a "real" business? Do businesses that are launched and/or sustained with assistance from nonprofits — for example, those staffed by donor-supported workers or financed with the help of donated funds — count? Under what conditions? Is the BAM umbrella big enough to include strategies like MED aimed at indigenous business development, or are these two distinctly different approaches to mission? And what exactly qualifies as a mission strategy? Are good deeds enough, or must BAM include verbal proclamation of the gospel? On this matter missiologists will have a strong sense of *déjà vu*, as it basically rehashes the decades-old debate about holistic mission.

What Kind of Business?

As any business person will confirm, a "real" business must succeed on its own merits. It must produce a good or service that people will buy, and generate enough revenue in the long run to cover its capital and operating costs. In other words, even though companies often rely on outside sources of capital, they must eventually generate sufficient revenue *internally* to repay the capital, as well as pay all other expenses. By contrast, the typical ministry is funded by *externally* generated income; that is, by donations. Finding ways to fund ministries with internally generated income is well outside the experience base and comfort zones of most people in traditional ministry, *but is precisely the gift that many business people have.* For those who catch a vision for BAM there is never an expectation of a donation — business people have no such preconditioning. Instead, they seek ways to harness the power of market economics for the benefit of the Kingdom.[3]

A complete discussion of the preference for donor-supported ministry, which can be traced throughout the history of the Church, is beyond the scope of this essay. Certainly there is nothing new about misgivings about commerce, and especially about the mixing of ministry and commerce. Those misgivings came to a head in the 20th Century when Christians, following the Industrial Revolution, debated with renewed vigor questions about the compatibility of Christianity and capitalism, and whether it was possible to be both a good Christian and a successful businessperson. While this debate is gradually fading into the history books, many people continue to see the pursuit of profit as inherently exploitive and antithetical to good corporate citizenship. Many still hold the view that only those profits that are donated to charities are praiseworthy. This ambivalence about profits helps explain why business remains perhaps the final frontier of Christian ministry and mission strategies. Professions such as teaching, healthcare and construction have long been accepted as having a legitimate role in mission, but there remains a strong presumption that the principle contribution a business person makes is a financial one. Put another way, business people are perceived mainly as the golden geese of Christian ministry and mission.

The lingering ambivalence about profit-making, combined with the preferential treatment the government gives to nonprofit corporations, explains why nonprofits are the organizational form of choice for most ministry leaders. The bias against profit-making also reflects a subtle, deeply-ingrained belief that nonprofit corporations are more trustworthy, and that those who work for them are less susceptible to temptations such as greed and pride. Together, these biases form an almost insurmountable philosophical and cultural barrier for most ministry leaders against any truly for-profit mission strategy. In those cases when the promotion of business is a goal of the ministry, such as MED and micro-loan programs, the programs themselves are rarely expected to become self-supporting, much less a source of income for the parent organization.

These biases — and the attempt to break through them — were at the heart of many of the debates that took place at the 2004 Lausanne conference. However, while the final document produced by the BAM issue group attempts to present a clear case that BAM is different, and that it represents a fundamentally new approach to missions, not all participants agreed on exactly where the boundaries should be drawn.[4]

Differences notwithstanding, most BAM advocates agree that what is most distinctive about BAM is its for-profit approach to mission. It represents a sharp break from the "ministry-equals-nonprofit" way of thinking, and the view, held uncritically by many Christians, that businesses are by definition greed-driven and, as such, inappropriate instruments for mission. Advocates of both Marketplace Ministries and BAM are trying to counter that view by (1) affirming the God-pleasing purpose of business, and (2) encouraging business people to *embrace* that purpose rather than treat it as something outside of the ministry domain. BAM takes this a step further by encouraging business people to look beyond their own people group and to use their creativity in ways that will advance the cause of Christ in the neediest, least-reached parts of the world. In short, BAM goes beyond "ministry" and brings business into "mission."

What Kind of Mission?

The question of what qualifies as "mission" is a familiar one to missiologists, so we will not labor long here except to put the question into a business context. On one hand, as one theologian forcefully argues, businesses themselves, by imitating the attributes of God, can glorify Him.[5] Another evangelical theologian maintains that since mission is the purpose of the Church, all Christians are missionaries by definition: the implication is that mission is undertaken in everything a Christian does — work, play, family life, and religious activities.[6] Of course, others have argued that if everything is mission, then the term is essentially meaningless.[7] Nevertheless, there are some who maintain that simply by doing business responsibly, a business person is fulfilling his or her calling, and by extension, if he or she owns the business, it would seem to qualify as a BAM business.

Others are more selective, reserving the label for only those businesses that have an obviously redemptive purpose. An interesting case in point is the story of the founding of the Guinness Brewing Company.[8] As the story is told, the company was founded by a young Irish Christian, Arthur Guinness, who was deeply concerned about his countrymen's addiction to hard liquor and the devastating impact it was having in the community. The burden he felt, his calling if you will, was to create a healthy drink that people would enjoy. The original recipe of Guinness beer was apparently so heavy, so full of iron, that a person could hardly drink more than a couple of pints, thus reducing the problem of drunkenness. It was also so full of minerals and natural ingredients that doctors prescribed it to pregnant women.

This is a fascinating story about the positive and culturally appropriate difference a Christian entrepreneur was able to make in society. But is this an example of Business as Mission? Many say yes. Guinness was led by the Spirit (no pun intended) to find a creative solution to this plague, and the sharp reduction in alcohol consumption and crime was a clear victory for the Kingdom of God. The problem here is that similar stories can be told about non-Christian entrepreneurs. This is why most BAM advocates maintain that the definition must go beyond the positive social impact. A successful BAM business must demonstrate a positive social and economic impact, *and* draw attention to Jesus, even prompting some people to accept Him as their Lord and Savior. These multifaceted measures of success are often referred to as a "triple bottom line."

It is quite possible that the Guinness Brewing Company had a positive impact both socially and spiritually. Unfortunately we are not told. What we do know is that by the end of his life, Guinness had donated much of his fortune to missionary causes. As laudable as that was, however, such corporate and individual philanthropy is usually ruled out as a defining characteristic of BAM. For example, the document produced by the BAM issue group at the Lausanne conference emphatically says:

> [Philanthropy] is different from business as mission. One might
> call this business <u>for</u> missions, using business ventures to fund
> other kinds of ministry. We recognize that profit from a business
> can be used to support "missions" and that this is good and
> valid. Likewise employees can use some of their salary to give
> to charitable causes. While this should be encouraged, none of
> us would like to be operated on by a surgeon whose only ambi-
> tion is to make money to give to the church! Instead we expect
> he has the right skills and drive to operate with excellence, doing
> his job with full professional integrity. Likewise a business as
> mission-business must produce more than goods and services in
> order to generate new wealth. It seeks to fulfill God's kingdom
> purposes and values through every aspect of its operations. A
> business for mission concept can limit business and business
> people to a role of funding the 'real ministry'. While funding is
> an important function, business as mission is about for-profit
> businesses that have a kingdom focus.[9]

Put another way, the view that Christians should "make as much as
they can and give away as much as they can," while well-intended, runs the
risk of reinforcing the separation between sacred and secular that BAM
seeks to undo.

Nevertheless, we do not believe corporate philanthropy should be cate-
gorically ruled out. Instead, one should ask: "Why was the business created?" and "How is it managed?" If the business was created specifically
for the purpose of advancing the cause of Christ, and managed in a God-
honoring, biblically-sound way, then we maintain it is a BAM business.
Some companies, like Pura Vida Coffee, are created for the principle purpose of generating income for mission.[10] Because its God-honoring management practices line up with its missional purpose, we would say it fits
the definition, even though its contribution is mainly a financial one. On the
other hand, businesses that are created for the purpose of generating income
for missions, but are managed according to worldly ways do not pass the
test. Neither do those that are managed ethically, but are not particularly
concerned about advancing the faith.

Proponents of BAM seek to affirm the calling of entrepreneurs and encourage them to use their God-given creativity in ways that will promote
mission. It would be unfortunate if, in the process of defining BAM, those
same entrepreneurs felt inhibited rather than encouraged. We believe our
two-part test — examining the purpose *and* practices of the company — is a
more useful and flexible approach to identifying a genuine BAM business.

Unique Challenges

The Movement under discussion — which encompasses Tentmaking, Marketplace Ministries, BAM, and, to some extent, Enterprise Development — is being propelled by a renewed understanding that "mission," properly perceived, is something all Christians are called into. Accordingly, the very definition of "missionary" is being challenged as more laypeople take an active interest in fulfilling the Great Commission. As Figure 1 illustrates, the Movement is not merely a western phenomenon, but is emerging spontaneously and simultaneously all over the world. In 2003 there were some 1,200 organizations – for example, 351 fellowship groups and associations, 478 ministries, 98 mission agencies and 52 NGOs – that claimed at least some involvement in this area. This Movement, if encouraged and mobilized effectively, would represent a tremendous injection of human and financial resources for the cause of Christ. However, several barriers stand in the way of this Movement reaching its full potential. These include the still widely-held belief in a sacred-secular divide, cultural differences between the for-profit and nonprofit worlds, inadequate training and support, and a lack of dialogue between the camps themselves and between the camps, the academy and the ecclesiastical Church.

Barrier #1: A Dualistic View of the World that is Still Deeply Entrenched

Few Christians openly support the view that God cares more about the spiritual realm than the physical one. Yet, while this dualistic view of the world — often referred to as the "sacred-secular dichotomy" — is falling out of favor and is now roundly criticized in evangelical circles, evidence of its deep entrenchment and widespread support is easy to find. It shows up, for example, in the tentmaker-missionary heading to the 10/40 Window who must apologetically explain how he will prevent his day job from becoming a distraction from his ministry. It shows up in churches when pastors promote the view that "ministry" is something that is directly linked to a church program, rather than something that laypeople are already doing *outside* of the church building, even at work. It shows up in the hierarchical view many Christians have about vocations — that the work of pastors and missionaries is more highly regarded by God than that of stockbrokers or CEOs. The list could go on.

By encouraging this view, or at least by not *discouraging* it, the Church has inadvertently marginalized its largest constituency. The unfortunate legacy of this is that many lay people now uncritically accept their place in the ministry margins. According to Dallas Willard, the division between sacred and secular has done "incalculable damage to our individual lives and the cause of Christ."[12] If the Movement is to reach its full potential, this dualistic view of the world simply must be abandoned in practice as well as in principle.

Figure 1: The Makeup and Breadth of the Movement

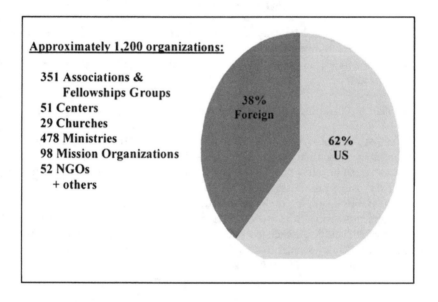

Approximately 1,200 organizations:

351 Associations &
    Fellowships Groups
51 Centers
29 Churches
478 Ministries
98 Mission Organizations
52 NGOs
   + others

38% Foreign

62% US

Barrier #2: Cultural Differences

Without question there are substantial differences between the rules, cultures and expectations of nonprofit and for-profit corporations. Learning to communicate and minister cross-culturally in this sense represents another significant challenge to the Movement. Tom Sudyk, founder of Evangelistic Commerce, poignantly describes the clashing cultures from a business person's perspective:

> A businessperson relocated from the rigor and risk of a business into the culture of the typical church suffers a tremendous shock. Gone is the discipline of the marketplace, which keeps business people constantly accountable for their decisions....Methods of successful business people are suddenly considered harsh, insensitive or, at a minimum, out of place. A new vocabulary must be

mastered, different expectations adopted and varying results tolerated.[13]

Another example is that of an acquaintance of ours who was recently approached about doing business consulting for a well-known mission organization. It was not until well into the discussions and contract negotiations that she realized she was expected to raise her own consulting fee from outside donors. What for one culture is so widely practiced as to be a basic assumption, to another culture can come as a complete shock. Similar shocks undoubtedly occur in people making the transition in the other direction: from traditional ministry to a business environment. Our point here is not that one culture is superior to the other, but rather that the Movement will stymie unless and until these differences are recognized and the clashes minimized.

Barrier #3: Training and Support Challenges

Effectively mobilizing this new generation of missionaries will also require changes in curriculum and new approaches to training and field support. At present, most business people lack any meaningful training in cross-cultural ministry, and most missionaries are inadequately trained in the ways of business. For example, somewhere between 10 and 40 percent of American business professionals return early from extended assignments abroad because of difficulties associated with adjusting to a foreign country.[14] This figure is strikingly similar to the estimates on missionary attrition presented in the excellent book *Too Valuable to Lose*.[15]

A complete discussion of the suggested curriculum changes is beyond the scope of this essay.[16] It is important to point out, however, that the solution is not necessarily a one-size-fits-all curriculum. Business schools should continue to be the preferred place to learn business, and schools of world mission the place to learn missions. Having said that, if the challenges listed above — the dualistic worldview and cultural differences — are to be overcome, it must begin in our universities, colleges and seminaries. Some basic courses in business, cultural anthropology and missiology should be a part of every Christian educational program, whether in business school or seminary.

New thinking must also be brought to bear in the way field support is provided for self-funded missionaries. A complaint we commonly hear is that "our churches don't know what to do with us. We don't fit any of their boxes." Indeed, the source of the problems business-missionaries face on the field is not always related to inadequate training, but rather to a limited and overtaxed network of qualified people who are willing to serve as advisers and mentors. Mission agencies are naturally weak in the area of business strategy and economics, yet have been slow to hire or partner with those with the necessary competencies. This, too, is a formidable challenge that, if unresolved, will undermine the Movement's potential.

Barrier #4: Lack of Dialogue

A fourth challenge is the lack of any meaningful dialogue between the individual camps within the Movement, between the camps and the academy, or between the camps and the ecclesiastical church. For the survival of the Movement, and the long-term effectiveness of its participants, this must change. For example, dialogue between the camps by holding joint conferences is important not only for the sake of improving efficiency, but also because it can serve to expand the vision of the respective participants in each camp. Dialogue between the camps and the academy is important to ensure the Movement's biblical, theological, intellectual and praxeological integrity. Accordingly, there should be a forum in which thoughtful reflection, considered dialogue, probing research and genuine scholarship can take place. And finally, the sustainability of this new Movement is vulnerable to erosion if it does not see itself as part of the larger body of Christ. Dialogue between the camps and the ecclesiastical church is essential to the long-run health of the Movement.

Conclusion

Given the profound changes taking place in the world today — globalization, postmodernism, diasporas and the migration of Christianity to the less-developed world — it would be naïve not to expect an equally profound effect on our understanding of mission and missionaries. The increasing role of business in missions is part of that new understanding. Rather than seeing themselves merely as geese that lay financial eggs, Christian business people are now becoming more directly involved in the mission of the church.

Many observers believe this new understanding, while still in an embryonic stage, represents the beginning of a major new missionary movement. For example, noted missiologist Charles Van Engen says that "the commercial business marketplace may well be the primary mission field of the twenty-first century."[17] Similarly, Ted Yamamori, the current International Director of the Lausanne Committee for World Evangelization, claims that "kingdom business will be a strategy of choice for missions in the twenty-first century."[18] Notice the slight differences in emphasis: Van Engen's is on business people as an overlooked mission *field*, while Yamamori's is in the overlooked potential of business people as *missionaries*. This underscores our point that the Movement is actually broader and more complex than it first appears. It is comprised of different camps, each sharing the same ultimate goal — to see God glorified in and through the marketplace — but each with their own agendas and strategies.

Business as Mission stresses the redemptive potential of business in the poorest and least evangelized parts of the world. Far from being a mere "access strategy" or a source of income for traditional missionaries, BAM promotes a more holistic and more inclusive approach to mission. It directly challenges the traditional view that (a) God calls only a small subset of His people into ministry and missions, (b) such a calling requires specific vocational training, and (c) ministry of any kind is most properly pursued within the framework of a nonprofit organization. It has tremendous potential to mobilize a vast, under-utilized segment of the Church, and for increasing the financial resources available for world mission. However, there are significant challenges that still need to be overcome. For example, each camp is presently working in virtual isolation, hardly aware of the other camps or the similarities and distinctives between their visions. There is little, if any, dialogue taking place between the Movement and the ecclesiastical church, partly because of the inherent challenges related to communicating new ideas cross-culturally. At this stage in the Movement's history here is a critical need for the active and collaborative participation of missiologists, theologians and business scholars who will carry on this dialogue and facilitate the cross-pollination of each camp's ideas, methods and theologies. For the sake of the billions of people who are still suffering and without hope, we must do what we can to encourage and assist this Movement.

Discussion Starters

1. The authors identify four camps within this new movement. What are they? How are they distinguished from each other?
2. Identify five ways a Christian's "secular" job can also be considered "full time ministry."
3. Why do some observers object to Enterprise Development being included as part of the movement under discussion? Explain why you agree or disagree with those objections.
4. Do you think the account of Guinness Brewing Company is an example of business as mission? Why or why not? Would your answer differ if the company was started in a country without a major alcohol problem?
5. Consider the hypothetical case of a missionary team that launches a carpet weaving business in the country of Afar. Suppose that, in addi-

tion to the two American "managers," the company also employs 15 locals, and has established a reputation in the community for fairness, generosity and unwavering integrity. However, in spite of the fact that the Americans draw no salary from the business, the business is not profitable, and requires an annual subsidy of $10,000, which must be raised from American donors. Would you consider this an example of Business as Mission? Why or why not?

6. Do you believe it is easier to make a businessperson out of a missionary, or a missionary out of a businessperson? Please explain your answer.

7. Identify two practical ways your church can do a better job of affirming and equipping those who are ministers in the marketplace.

Notes

1. Mary N. "God so Loves the Creative Access World." Keynote address during the 1993 Intervarsity student missions conference at Urbana, IL.

2. Mike McLoughlin, C. Neal Johnson, Os Hillman, and David W. Miller, eds., *International Faith and Work Directory 2003-2004* (Cumming, GA: Aslan Press, 2003).

3. The dependence on internally-generated revenues and external market forces is one of the most challenging aspects of BAM, and perhaps the hardest thing for many people to accept. There are a host of corollary issues attached to this subject that go beyond the scope of this essay, including questions about accountability, measures of success, and so on.

4. This document is available at
http://www.lausanne.org/lcwe/assets/LOP59_IG30.pdf.

5. Wayne Grudem, *Business for the Glory of God: The Bible's Teaching on the Moral Goodness of Business* (Wheaton, IL: Crossway Books, 2003).

6. R. Paul Stevens, *The Other Six Days: Vocation, Work, and Ministry in Biblical Perspective* (Grand Rapids, MI: Eerdmans Publishing Co., 1999).

7. See, for example, Andrew Kirk, *What is Mission? Theological Explorations* (Minneapolis, MN: Fortress Press, 2000); David Hesselgrave, "Redefining Holism." *Evangelical Missions Quarterly* (1999), pp.278-284; Bryant Myers, *Walk-*

ing with the Poor: Principles and Practices of Tranformational Development (Maryknoll, NY: Orbis Books, 1999); and Steve Rundle and Tom Steffen, *Great Commission Companies: The Emerging Role of Business in Missions* (Downers Grove, IL: InterVarsity Press, 2003).

8. Mark Markiewicz, "Business as Mission: How Two Grocers Changed the Course of a Nation." Presentation made for the Central Asia Business Consultation, 1999, available at http://www.icwm.net/articles _view.asp?articleid=8553&columnid=.

9. http://www.lausanne.org/lcwe/assets/LOP59_IG30.pdf, p.13.

10. See Steve Rundle and Tom Steffen, *Great Commission Companies: The Emerging Role of Business in Missions* (Downers Grove, IL: InterVarsity Press, 2003).

11. McLoughlin, Johnson, Hillman, and Miller, eds., 2003.

12. Dallas Willard, *The Spirit of the Disciplines: Understanding How God Changes Lives* (San Francisco, CA: HarperCollins, 1990), p.214.

13. Thomas Sudyk, "Strategic Considerations in Business as Mission," in Tetsunao Yamamori and Kenneth A. Eldred, eds., *On Kingdom Business: Transforming Mission Through Entrepreneurial Strategies* (Wheaton, IL: Crossway Books, 2003), pp.153-167.

14. J. S. Black and H.B. Gregersen, "The Right Way to Manage Expats," *Harvard Business Review*, (March/April, 1999), pp.52-62; J.S. Black and M. Mendenhall, "Cross Cultural Training Effectiveness: A Review and a Theoretical Framework for Future Research." *Academy of Management Review*, 15, no. 1 (1990), pp.113-136.

15. William Taylor, ed., *Too Valuable to Lose: Exploring the Causes and Cures of Missionary Attrition* (Pasadena, CA: William Carey Library, 1997).

16. Those interested in this topic are encouraged to read C. Neal Johnson, "Toward a Marketplace Missiology." *Missiology: An International Review*, 31, no. 1 (2003), pp.87-97; Steve Rundle, "Preparing the Next Generation of Kingdom Entrepreneurs." in Tetsunao Yamamori and Kenneth A. Eldred, eds. *On Kingdom Business: Transforming Mission Through Entrepreneurial Strategies* (Wheaton, IL: Crossway Books, 2003), pp.225-244; and Joseph Kilpatrick, "The Role of Business in Missions: A Collegiate Perspective on Micro-enterprise Projects and Business Training." Presentation made for the Southeast Regional Meeting of the Evangelical Theological Society, Louisville, KY, March 19, 2005.

17. Charles Van Engen, Personal conversation between C. Neal Johnson and the Professor of Biblical Theology of Mission, School of World Mission. Pasadena, CA, January 12, 2002.

18. Tetsunao Yamamori, "Preface." in Tetsunao Yamamori and Kenneth A. Eldred, eds., *On Kingdom Business: Transforming Mission Through Entrepreneurial Strategies* (Wheaton, IL: Crossway Books, 2003), pp.7-10.

2

Missional Geometry: Plotting the Coordinates of Business as Mission

Dwight Baker

Books, web sites, and conferences—not to mention the theme of the Evangelical Missiological Society for the year 2005—offer abundant evidence that the topic of business as mission has a currency today that was not apparent forty, thirty, or even much over ten years ago. Not that harnessing business with mission is particularly novel; it is not. Linking commercial and industrial enterprises with missionary endeavor in order to provide a financial base for mission has a long history and has taken many forms. Taking on a business role so as to obtain entrée for missional proclamation also has historical depth; the Waldensians in fourteenth-century Italy are reported by an inquisitor to have traveled about as peddlers preaching and teaching wherever they could gain a hearing.[1] Current attention to, in the words of Steve Rundle and Patrick Lai, "creating businesses for the express purpose of advancing the gospel in the economically and spiritually most impoverished parts of the world"[2] updates and refurbishes a venerable model to match the allure and pace of globalization.

Over the years the relationships between business and mission have been multifarious, but the diversity of these relationships has received insufficient attention. Even a glance, however, hints at the dynamic variety of their interrelations. The New England Company for Propagation of the Gospel in New England and the Parts Adjacent in America, chartered in

1649, for example, is Protestantism's earliest and longest enduring mission society.[3] Money raised by subscription was invested by the Company, primarily in landed estates. Income from these properties supplied the funds year by year that supported the Company's agents working as missionaries to Native Americans in New England.[4] Among the missionaries of the New England Company were John Eliot, several generations of the Mayhew family, John Sergeant, and, for a few years, Jonathan Edwards, Sergeant's successor at Stockbridge in western Massachusetts. Publication of Eliot's translation of the Bible in Algonquin was the Company's largest single undertaking. This is *business funding mission*.

But there is another possibility: *business subverting mission*. In 1710, by the terms of the will of Christopher Codrington, the Society for the Propagation of the Gospel in Foreign Parts (SPG; founded in Britain in 1701) found itself the owner of two sugar plantations in Barbados. The will stipulated that "the trustees were to ensure the maintenance on the plantations of three hundred slaves, who were to enjoy the benefit of medical attention and religious instruction. This slave population was to provide the labour for the two plantations."[5] For the next century and a quarter the SPG derived part of its income from slave labor and found itself in the anomalous position of being an apologete for the institution of slavery, carefully explaining, for example, why Christian conversion did not confer emancipation.

In 1898 a recently arrived missionary in Alaska by the name of P. H. Anderson acquired a gold mining claim, Number Nine Above, on Anvil Creek near Nome, Alaska. The claim paid off handsomely. Around $500,000 worth of gold was extracted, not an insignificant sum in 1900. In going prospecting, Anderson merely followed the lead of the senior missionary at Cheenik on Golovin Bay where he was stationed as a schoolteacher. But questions soon arose. Was Anderson, appointed as a missionary by the Swedish Evangelical Mission Covenant of America, an agent of the Covenant, and did the mine and profits from it for that reason belong to the Covenant denomination? Had Anderson acquired the mine, in whole or in part, as tacit trustee for certain Eskimos? for the mission? for the denomination? Did he simply voice, in the first flush of potential wealth, exalted expressions of doing well by each of the above and later, when real riches came within reach, cool in his ardor for doing good?

These and other questions embroiled the Evangelical Covenant Church in controversy, mudslinging, and unseemly behavior. Lawsuits related to the case stretched out over two decades and twice reached the U.S. Supreme Court, with final disposition not arriving until 1920. The attention of the denomination, its institutions, its conferences, and its congregations, was turned aside. Missionaries left the field; energies were diverted; leaders were disaffected; reputations were besmirched. The gold fever that swirled around and beyond Anderson and Number Nine Above, writes Karl Olsson, broke the back of promising mission work begun by the Covenant Church in Alaska.[6]

The Basel Mission provides an admirable contrast as it engaged in both *mission founding auxiliary businesses* and *mission founding ancillary businesses*. The Mission's intention was that the businesses themselves be missional instruments. "The commercial efforts were...part and parcel of the real mission work, not merely an appendage to it. They provided a graphic illustration in daily affairs of the power of the gospel at work in the hearts of Europeans and Africans who were concerned about demonstrating 'faith active in love' not only in church services but also, where it may matter even more, in the market place and on the plantation. The lay missionaries built a solid reputation for dependable Christian character, becoming a model for many Africans."[7] The same held true for the Basel Mission's factories in India.[8]

Sometimes business seeks to dictate missional goals and strategies. In 1900 Robert Arthington, an eccentric recluse and mission devotee, died, leaving a considerable estate. Arthington stands out for both the size of his estate and the stipulations in his will. Shrewd investments in railroads in Britain and the United States had enabled him to multiply the £200,000 he inherited from his father fivefold. During his life he gave generously to mission outreach and even for a while ran his own mission society. At his death he bequeathed almost £1,000,000 to mission; two mission agencies, the London Missionary Society (LMS) and the Baptist Missionary Society (BMS), were to receive nine tenths of these moneys "with the understanding, although not with the express condition, that they be applied to the opening-up of work in as yet untrodden mission fields."[9] At this time the total annual revenue of the BMS was £95,575 and of the LMS £148,930. Depending on how one apportions start-up costs to ongoing maintenance costs for a work underway, Arthington's stipulations entail as much as a fourfold ramp-up of activity, personnel, and continuing revenue as well as a redirection of the two societies' efforts. The will was so poorly drafted that five years were spent in court seeking guidance on the money's use. By then the principal had grown even larger, to £1,273,000.[10] Arthington was only partly successful in his bid to take over the reins of power and reset the course for the two mission societies, but he stands as a premier example of *business dictating mission* through the power of the purse.

There are lessons to be learned from the struggles of our spiritual forebears. To engage in business so as to raise money to support missionary projects, conceived of as a separate activity, is not the same thing as to create a Great Commission company in which business and mission are blended into a single business/ministry plan.[11] Still, today's new endeavors would be foolish not to seek profit from ancient experience. At the least, acquaintance with earlier ventures serves to deflate unwarranted self-congratulation induced by misapprehension of being embarked on a wholly novel course. To facilitate wider discussion, it is helpful to situate business *as* mission within the wider field of business *and* mission.[12] Historical topography serves to bring recurring motifs into focus. Though the business models may differ, together they provide markers that are instructive for the conduct of any business operated for missional purposes.

Background

Though neither *business for mission* nor *business as mission* is of recent vintage, the topics barely surface in standard histories, theologies, and surveys of mission. This lacuna may be due to the inherently greater labor involved in documenting organizational issues and daily practice, which is the terrain where business dwells, than is true for mission theology, mission statistics, and institutional relationships—all of which come to hand with ready-made documentation in the form of texts, tables, yearly reports, proposals, and monographs, including secondary volumes which go some distance toward winnowing and integrating the flood of documents available. Recovery of the history of business linked to mission has affinities with social history, involving perusal of letters, logs, and diaries; company memos and ephemeral business plans; as well as orders, requisitions, and financial statements.[13]

In histories of mission, the absence of entries for "business," "commerce," and "industry" is striking. That is not to say that such volumes never touch on the topics of business or commerce—their complete omission would hardly be possible in treatises obliged to mention David Livingstone, to look no further—but business as a mission strategy is accorded only passing notice.[14] It is never the main track upon which the narration runs; the writers' attention is elsewhere. The words "business," "commerce," and "industry" do not occur in the index to Stephen Neill's *History of Christian Missions*. The word "commerce" does occur in the index to Kenneth Scott Latourette's two-volume *History of Christianity*,[15] but only in reference to four out of the work's 1,552 pages, and those references are not to mission activity.

Attention in recent general surveys is equally sparse. In the most recent edition of *Perspectives on the World Christian Movement*, edited by Ralph Winter and Steven Hawthorne, one can cite James Gustafson's "Pigs, Ponds and the Gospel" as well as Ruth Siemens's "Tentmakers Needed for World Evangelization," but not much more—twelve and a half pages out of 782.[16] The topic is not on the radar screen of the report that came from the World Evangelical Fellowship Mission Commission's 1999 Iguassu Missiological Consultation anymore than it was for J. Herbert Kane's *Global View of Christian Missions: From Pentecost to the Present* twenty-eight years earlier.[17] The slim volume by journalist Stan Guthrie, *Missions in the Third Millennium*, does have a chapter on tentmakers (six pages), about half of which is devoted to problems missionaries encounter by using tentmaking as a key for access to restricted countries.[18]

Looking further, kingdom professionals wanting to wed mission and business will find be disappointed by Martin Higginbottom's "Industrial Evangelism" in *Let the Earth Hear His Voice*, a compilation of the papers presented at the 1974 International Congress on World Evangelization held in Lausanne, Switzerland.[19] Higginbottom's concern is to gain the cooperation of British (and other) factory owners and managers for allowing evangelistic preaching services to be held on company premises. Evangelicals at the1974 International Congress on World Evangelization assumed the overwhelming priority of oral proclamation in set times and contexts as the way to be faithful to Gospel imperatives. They were struggling to encompass a return to concern for biblical social action and were not looking to business as a strategy for missional outreach. Six years later when Edward Dayton and David Fraser—in a volume of over 500 pages specifically dealing with strategies and methods for world evangelism—faced the question of what to do if there is no mission agency working in the area to which one feels led, their answer is not to start a business but to launch a new mission agency or to carry a well-developed proposal to an existing agency.[20]

Two more recent volumes are *Transforming Mission: Paradigm Shifts in Theology of Mission*, by David Bosch, and *Constants in Context: A Theology of Mission for Today*, by Stephen Bevans and Roger Schroeder.[21] Whereas *Let the Earth Hear His Voice* gave much attention to methods and strategies for mission, these latter two volumes deal, in historical fashion, with theology of mission. Although they are concerned with modes and conceptions of mission, and business as a focal means for carrying out mission does not appear to be within their horizon of concern.

Becoming Engaged

Despite this apparent neglect of business as mission, the past two decades have provided an increasing flow of how-to and why-to articles and books for persons wanting to become cross-cultural entrepreneurs for God,. We find J. Christy Wilson's *Today's Tentmakers: Self-Support—An Alternative Model for Worldwide Witness* (1979) and Tetsunao Yamamori's *God's New Envoys: A Bold Strategy for Penetrating "Closed Countries"* (1987) and *Penetrating Missions' Final Frontiers: A New Strategy for Unreached Peoples* (1993). More recent titles include *Working Your Way to the Nations: A Guide to Effective Tentmaking*, (1996; orig. 1993), edited by Jonathan Lewis, and *Walking with the Poor: Principles and Practices of Transformational Development* (1999), by Bryant Myers.[22] This last volume is not restricted to setting up businesses cross-culturally, but it is filled with content that ought to be in the heads and hearts of those who do. David Befus, in *Kingdom Business: The Ministry of Promoting Economic Activity* (2001), gives practical advice for launching church-based and church-related economic enterprises, ranging from small-scale microfinance outreach to large-scale business ventures. He shows special concern that such projects stay true to their intended spiritual as well as economic ministry.[23] Today Web sites supply dynamic, real-time resources, contacts, leads, discussion forums, archives of articles, conference listings, class prospectuses, and much more.[24]

The year 2003 saw the appearance of two significant books—*Great Commission Companies: The Emerging Role of Business in Missions*, by Steve Rundle and Tom Steffen, and *On Kingdom Business: Transforming Missions Through Entrepreneurial Strategies*, edited by Tetsunao Yamamori and Kenneth A. Eldred. *Great Commission Companies*, in its first half, provides a rationale for business as mission and assesses risks and pitfalls to be met along the way. Through the use of five case studies, the second half of the book points up the diversity of forms and divergent trajectories Great Commission companies can take. *On Kingdom Business* gathers the papers and reports presented at the Consultation for Holistic Entrepreneurs held at Regent University in October 2002.[25] A strength of *Great Commission Companies* is that the volume's two-person authorial team offers sustained reflection coming from a single, informed viewpoint. *On Kingdom Business*'s strength comes through the multiplicity of voices and vantage points it draws together.

Relationships of Business to Mission

Viewed logically, at least the following progression of interrelationships between business and mission can be discerned.

- business opposed to mission
- business subverting mission
- business capitalizing on mission
- business relying on mission
- business enabling mission
- business inherent in mission
- business funding mission
- business dictating mission
- business auxiliary to mission
- business ancillary to mission
- business as mission

- mission opponent of business
- mission buffer against business
- mission generator of business
- mission ally of business
- mission as template for business
- mission as exemplar for business

- mission indebted to business
- mission supplicating business
- mission founding auxiliary businesses
- mission founding ancillary businesses
- mission via strategic businesses

Let us look at each of these relationships briefly in turn.

Business Opposed to Mission

In view here is outright, adamant opposition—in the name of business and profits—to Christian proclamation with a view to conversion. Bosch reminds us that under Christendom where territorial expansion and colonization occurred, mission moved forward under the aegis and patronage of the king. It was not questioned but that where the king's power and authority reached, his religion would extend also (Latin, *cuius regio, eius religio*; literally: whose the region, his the religion). This was as true of the Protestant powers as of the Roman Catholic empires.[26] Hence, one finds clauses in the charters of the English colonies in the Americas providing for conversion of the inhabitants of the newly acquired lands. It is when extension of empire was entrusted to commercial trading companies as proxies that resistance to mission activity arose in pronounced form. The English East India Company stands as the prime example of outright opposition to missionary activity, famously occasioning the need for William Carey to sneak himself and his family into India and, until he removed to the Danish enclave at Serampore, to show that he was carrying his weight commercially by managing an indigo factory at Mudnabatti.

That commerce, which should aid and support mission outreach, has instead obstructed, opposed, undercut, and overturned the efforts of missionaries is the unrelenting burden of an extended sermon preached in 1839 at Trinity Church in New Haven, Connecticut. In this sermon John Stone indicts commerce for corrupting and enslaving populaces and for distorting and resisting the reception of the Gospel. If only, he appeals, commerce would at least cease from actively hindering the Gospel, missional success would be almost certain. "Missions have often succeeded in spite of all the vices and corruption of a most degraded condition; and, what is more, in spite of all the adverse influence which a destroying commerce has exerted in opposition to their movements. And if those who direct commerce, would leave Christianity unobstructed, to do her own proper work, if they would place truth, justice and mercy, at the basis of their system, these missions would generally succeed."[27]

Business Subverting Mission

Business simply by being what it is can be seductive and has demonstrable power to draw missionaries away from their missional commitments. Whether initially conceived by penurious missionaries—such as the original London Missionary Society appointees who received no financial support from the society[28]—as a means for obtaining a minimal livelihood for their families, or thought of as offering access to great wealth and, therefore, holding out the potential for doing great good, business wrongly indulged in can lead to modes of behavior that are exploitative of the very people to whom one is supposed to be Christ's minister. As noted earlier, the lure of gold exercised just such a power over Evangelical Mission Covenant missionaries (and others) in Alaska at the end of the nineteenth century. Greed for Alaskan gold "did the work of the [Evangelical Covenant Church] incalculable harm," not only in its Alaskan mission where "the back of the Alaska mission was broken," but in the wider denomination as well.[29]

Long before P. H. Anderson mined for gold in Alaska, from 1710 to 1834, the SPG derived income from the labor of slaves it owned on the island of Barbados.[30] In the South Pacific, trade links that grew up around London Missionary Society stations led, according to Tom Hiney, to the first accusations "in the British press that the Protestant missionary movement was pursuing commercial interests."[31]

Business Capitalizing on Mission

At the end of the nineteenth century and beginning of the twentieth, businesspersons and mission apologists of a certain stripe were eager to point out the service missionaries rendered as forerunners, pathbreakers, and intermediaries for commerce.[32] Missionaries were pulled into the orbit of business, whether they wanted to be or not, just as they were pulled into the orbit of colonialism, whether they wished it or not. Missionaries were lauded for the invaluable work they did in rendering native populaces acquiescent to colonial overlordship and in creating openness for commercial trading companies.[33] Missionaries were useful as interpreters, as cultural guides for business travelers, and as intermediaries able to identify significant powerholders and able to facilitate negotiations with them.

Business Relying on Mission

Even though missionaries might try to stay clear of commercial entanglements or even to oppose the forces of commerce outright, by their presence they acted as agents of acculturation upon which commercial interests could rely. The contact national, tribal, and island populaces had with missionaries attuned them to Westerners' objectives and ways of acting. A pool of cultural brokers arose. Employment by missionaries and training in mission schools acclimated nationals to Western languages and equipped them to serve in domestic employ and as clerks and functionaries in commercial enterprises.

Business Enabling Mission

By the eighteenth century and even more the nineteenth, the outflow of European exploration and commercial shipping had quickened. A steady stream of ships transversed the globe, and later, railroads crisscrossed continents, transporting goods and persons. Missionaries traveled along and lived off the growing network of transportation and services. The nineteenth-century mission enterprise as a whole could not have taken the form it did without this network of transportation and support services, a form that was markedly different from the incremental pushing out of a network of monasteries characteristic of mission outreach in an earlier era.

Business Inherent in Mission

Mission has a business component inherent to it. As soon as mission is carried out in a fashion that stretches further than the reach of single individuals or extends beyond the span of solitary lives, it necessarily takes on a business hue. Mission agencies and institutions have systems of management and governance, properties owned or rented, utilities and upkeep on those properties, policies and procedures for acquiring finances and personnel and for the disbursement or investment of funds, as well as for the assignment, evaluation, care, and retention or dismissal of personnel. If persons and goods are to be transported to a field, logistics are involved. Contracts will be entered into. If contact with field personnel is to be maintained, elaborate systems of communication will be called into play. The skills displayed by office staff—competent handling of correspondence and records; bookkeeping; maintaining a telephone log; courtesy, promptness, dependability, and efficiency in processing the endless demands of constituency and personnel in the field—will look pretty much the same as those valued by any commercial enterprise.

The *Mission Handbook, 2004–2006: U.S. and Canadian Protestant Ministries Overseas* lists 70 nondenominational and denominational mission agencies that reported income of $10,000,000 or more for the year 2001. At $358,703,000 World Vision ranked highest in income. Aggregate income for the 690 U.S. agencies in the directory totaled $3,752,306,193.[34] Those figures are not vast, but they do presage the investment of considerable time and money in carrying out ordinary business processes and procedures.

Business Funding Mission

Throughout the centuries some Protestant mission work has been underwritten by income from "captive" businesses established expressly for that purpose by the mission societies themselves. The Moravians and the Basel Mission come immediately to mind as societies that established commercial enterprises, sometimes in conjunction with their mission projects, sometime separate from them, but with the intention that the profits generated would support mission personnel and activities. To assure wholehearted agreement with that policy, staff appointments were made internally, either from mission personnel or from the mission constituency.[35] Profits from the businesses supplied funds for mission outreach.

These businesses differed in a significant way from Great Commission companies, such as are mentioned by Rundle and Steffen, that are started by entrepreneurs with the intention of creating profits which can be put at the disposal of various mission agencies.[36] For the former, being essentially wholly owned subsidiaries, the question was whether they would make a profit, not where that profit would go. Their profits were critical as sources of funding for their parent societies. The latter are not contractually or organizationally bound to supply any one mission society; they may donate or withhold their contributions at will. Their funding may rise to significant levels and be important for some organizations, but no organization would do well to depend wholly on them. Their owners' interests might as easily go another direction next year.

The New England Company is an example of a society that operated a business whose profits served to fund its missionary projects. The U.S. Center for World Mission supplies a comparable example from our own day. Money contributed to it was used to purchase the grounds and adjacent rental housing owned by Pasadena Nazarene College. Income derived from renting out campus office space and adjacent housing in turn supports the ongoing projects and activities of the USCWM.

Business Dictating Mission

Money talks. Immense wealth often speaks loudly and in preemptory tones. While he was still living, Robert Arthington set up his own mission agency funded out of his personal fortune. When he became dissatisfied with it, he shut it down. At his death in 1900 his bequest of nearly £1,000,000, primarily to two mission agencies, is a striking example of vast personal wealth being put forward in an attempt to reshape the character and direction of mission practice. Through the sheer massiveness of his contribution, Arthington's intent to set mission outreach on a new course was, in part, achieved.[37]

Business Auxiliary to Mission

Business, in the sense of businesses, also plays an auxiliary, instrumental role that is integral to mission. How do you do certain things that are important for missionary purposes? You set up a business. William Carey and his colleagues started a printing plant to publish Bibles and tracts, and they became newspaper publishers so as to promote the growth of a reading public for their Bibles and tracts. Other missions have set up elementary schools, high schools, Bible institutes, colleges, universities, and seminaries as well as clinics, orphanages, rest homes, guest houses, and hospitals— each with its own inherent business component—as means through which to give expression to their missional thrust.

Business Ancillary to Mission

Other businesses have been seen, not as inherently missional in themselves in the way that printing Bibles might be viewed, but as serviceable instruments for the accomplishment of missional purposes extraneous to the business. Thus, the Basel Mission's decision to launch tile and textile factories in India was made to foster missional ends—the factories served as means for long-term contact, as venues for the demonstration and inculcation by precept and example of a Christian outlook and Christian virtues, and as means of providing employment for national believers and augmenting the economic base of the national Christian community.[38] Creation of the businesses was intentional, but selection of those particular lines of business was adventitious. The businesses that were entered into held promise of profitability and long-term durability. But in other circumstances, the businesses chosen could easily have been quite different.

Business as Mission

In addition to embodying the three characteristics just mentioned—vehicle for long-term contact on a "natural" footing and in a "natural" context, venue for both showing and explaining Christian beliefs and values, and means of providing employment for believers (and others)—business as mission or kingdom entrepreneurship is intended, as I understand it, to go at least one step further. This segment of Great Commission companies is intended to provide entry into otherwise "closed" or restricted countries and supplies reasons for their governments to tolerate Christian witness.[39] As businesses, these enterprises are simply seeking to seize an apparent opportunity. In the light of market possibilities, financing, governmental permissions, technical and educational competency of the contemplated workforce, raw materials, transport, present or potential competition, and other factors, they appear to hold promise of being viable, of providing long-term residence for the businessperson/missionary, and of offering ongoing benefit for those among whom the business will be situated. The extra feature they provide is that they are a means of access and contact. The particular line of business selected has missional accompaniments, but another line of business might serve the purpose as well or better. No particular business is intrinsically the single right one, though many businesses can be ruled out as inherently incompatible with the kingdom values for which the business is intended to be a vehicle.

Relationships of Mission to Business

Perspectives differ when viewed from opposite sides of the street. Neither mission nor business is a passive vessel, waiting to be filled or used. Each has its own dynamics and its own proper interests. Therefore, relationships between the two, though reciprocal, may have a different cast when seen from the vantage point of mission. The lines of contact, attraction, and opposition between the two do not remain static, but will fluctuate, subject to ongoing negotiation and realignment.

If Tertullian was not sure that Jerusalem had much to do with Athens, how fares the traffic between Jerusalem and London or Jerusalem and New York City? Again, we will look at each relationship briefly in turn.

Mission as Opponent of Business

This is mission in the mold of Bartolomé Las Casas. It is marked by the shrill voice of outrage and consists of flat-out opposition to and denunciation—to perpetrators and to the world at large—of brutality, rape, theft, expropriation, mangling, starving, slaughter, cheating, infection, degradation, enslavement, preying upon, and obliviousness toward the needs of those too weak or uninformed or insufficiently organized or under equipped to defend themselves. The missionary movement can be proud to point to those among its number who, like David Livingstone, spoke out forcefully against land grabs in South Africa and trafficking in human slaves in Central Africa; those who denounced "black birding" (forced labor) in the South Seas and who had earlier earned the wrath of the whalers because, by preaching the Gospel, they had fortified the islanders against the sailors' depredations and wanton licentiousness; and those like Alice and John Harris who exposed the brutality of King Leopold's Congo.[40] If John Stone found commerce to be an opponent thwarting mission effectiveness, missionaries were not slack in opposing commercial exploitation of native peoples through sale of liquor and theft of lands (except, of course, for atypical renegade missionaries who joined in the theft of native lands, gold, and other wealth[41]).

Mission as Buffer Against Business

Missionaries have often acted as advocates in behalf of their host tribal peoples before governments and large commercial enterprises.[42] Beyond acting as ombudsmen, many missionaries have consciously acted as directed change agents, seeking to prepare the people they served so that they could be better equipped to deal with traders and peoples politically dominant over them. Having seen the devastation wrought during the past several centuries among tribal peoples who were unequipped to cope with new forms of social organization, new legal systems, new commercial forces, and new diseases—and knowing that the question was not whether contact would be made or whether change would come, but on what terms change would be encountered—missionaries have sought to equip tribal peoples with skills they could use to navigate the swirling rapids of cultural conflict on terms more advantageous to themselves. Don Richardson, for example, states that missionaries in Irian Jaya sought "to teach them the value of money, so that unscrupulous traders cannot easily cheat them. And better yet, set some of them up in business so that commerce in their areas will not fall entirely into the hands of outsiders."[43]

Mission as Generator of Business

Missionaries themselves, by going where they did and providing the services that they did, such as medical services, opened up new markets. Missionaries tend to be early adopters of new technology, whether of photography a century and a half ago or computers and satellite phones today.[44] In the 1800s the appurtenances with which missionaries surrounded themselves aroused new appetites wherever they went. Whether trekking or established on stations, missionaries were living advertisements for Western goods. At this level the contribution of mission was indirect, but noticeable enough to be recognized by many as being good for commerce. James Dennis, turn-of-the-century sociologist of mission and compiler of missionary statistics, claimed that the rise and fall of commercial activity in a region, e.g., Korea, could be correlated with the strength of the missionary presence there.[45] He cites the estimate of Henry Venn of the CMS in 1857 that "when a missionary had been abroad twenty years he was worth ten thousand pounds a year to British commerce."[46] In straight commercial terms, money given to missions paid off handsomely; some pegged the return at ten to one,[47] some much higher. That anticipation underlay the suggestion sometimes floated that, in its own self-interest, commerce would do well to support missions financially.

Mission as Ally of Business

Mission was an inadvertent ally to business simply by employing nationals as aides, by training them to be teachers in mission schools, and even by employing them to work as cooks and domestic help. The types of training offered and the level of skill imparted varied; much more significant was the cultural knowledge such persons obtained through these contacts. The fact of having gained some familiarity with Western expectations; having become accustomed to some degree with European ways of framing the workday and work week, terms of employment, and handling of salaries; and having acquired some level of competence in a European language put such persons—or their offspring—at an advantage as prospective employees when opportunity or need arose. In this way, by inadvertence, mission contributed to and enlarged the pool of potential employees for Western enterprises. Mission contributed to business also through early missionary attrition. Disaffected and disaffiliated missionaries were a windfall to commercial companies, coming as they did with superior equipage, having learned a language, having already undergone some degree of cultural adjustment, and being able to present themselves on the spot with transport already accomplished and previously paid for by the mission.[48]

Beyond these indirect contributions in support of business, mission societies over many years and in numerous locations set up schools, industrial missions, and apprenticeship programs with the express purpose of educating nationals and equipping them with marketable skills. The products of these schools and programs became a growing pool available to commercial enterprises.

Mission as Template for Business

Even in the late twentieth century, "in some broken-backed nations, those marked out by poverty of resources, technological breakdown, political instability, or economic disaster," writes Andrew Walls, "the missionary bodies, often working in concert (Missions Incorporated, as one may say), now have the most flexible, powerful, and efficient organization in the country. They can fly people around the country and in and out of it; they can bring in machinery and service ailing plants; they have radio telephones that work; they can arrange currency, get foreign exchange, and send an international message quickly. They sometimes do things that the government itself cannot do."[49] One thinks immediately of the mission stations encountered by Alex Shoumatoff in Zaire twenty years ago—"The mission's store was better stocked than any of those in town"[50]—and by Helen Winternitz and Timothy Phelps.[51] These three are not the only trekkers to find in mission vehicles a good way to get around.

But mission provided a template on a more fundamental level even than that of providing models of can-do-it-iveness, of having access to adequate funding, of providing essential services, and of doing so with commendable honesty, integrity, and selflessness. Mission organizations in the nineteenth century (and religious organizations such as the spreading denominations in the United States) provided prototypes and templates that businesses seeking to develop large-scale corporate marketing and management structures could emulate.[52] The American Bible Society provided path-breaking technological innovation for book printing and distribution.[53] When junk mail arrives in our mailbox, we can reflect on the role of nineteenth-century evangelicals and their abolitionist mail campaigns in helping to perfect the technique of mass mailing.[54]

Mission as Exemplar for Business

John Stone, after describing at length the opposition thrown up by commerce to mission, does not merely call for the reform of commerce. He thinks he descries the approach of a day when a "converted," "sanctified commerce" "will go forth over the world—the great, high-minister of His mercies to mankind!"[55] Striking not quite so high a note, Arthur Porritt states that "Christian missionary work, as [British colonial administrator] Sir Harry Johnston says, has been in recent times the right antidote to the wrong form of Imperialism." Johnston himself declared missionary work to be "the extension of the best kind of British Empire," yielding commercial returns, but yielding much more than monetary returns narrowly conceived.[56] Something of this higher standard is caught by anthropologist Paul Bohannan's comment written forty years ago: "The great debt that Africa owes to missionaries is that in a situation in which the forces of trade, colonial government, and the missions themselves were creating cultural havoc, it was only the missions that began to rebuild, and gave [the Africans] a chance to rebuild. Whatever any individual Westerner may think of the missionary edifice, every African knows that it is to missionaries that they owe the beginning of the African educational system."[57] Mission embodies a challenge for business to rise to a higher standard of integrity and concern for the well-being of others.

Mission Indebted to Business

Though Arthur Porritt overstates the case for Christian missionaries as having paved the way and opened the doors for commerce, there is an element of truth in the claim. But the converse also holds; mission during the high tide of the William Carey era in mission was indebted to commerce. Christian missions would not have taken the form they did, spread so widely as they did, advanced so quickly as they did, or gone to the locales they did if it had not been for the wide-flung network of commerce. Merchants underwrote the ventures of mission, served mission societies as their treasurers, profited betimes from trade related to them, provided the ships that transported missionaries, and, to repeat the point, gave much money to underwrite mission subscriptions.

What Tom Hiney says of mission and colonialism can, with slight adjustment of the wording, be applied to mission and commerce as well: "The relationship between missionaries and colonialism was never . . . straightforward. That they were contemporaneous forces and at times mutually useful does not mean they were predominantly co-operative; very often they were ranged against one another, particularly over slavery."[58] But each did help to shape the configuration of the other, and they were intertwined. The example Hiney offers shows the three forces of mission, colonialism, and commerce inextricably interwoven: "It would be true to say, . . . that the missionary movement could never have happened without colonialism. Bennet [who at his own expense spent eight years, 1821–1829, on an 80,000-mile tour of inspection of the mission stations and activities of the London Missionary Society] is a good example of this. He went to his death an anti-slavery campaigner, but he would not have been so effective a philanthropist had he not inherited his uncle's fortune, which was made from an improvement in the sugar-refining process, that is to say from an industry dependent on West Indian sugar plantations worked by African slaves."[59]

Mission Supplicating Business

The end of the nineteenth and beginning of the twentieth centuries saw mission agencies in the United States eagerly looking to the business world for models and for resources. This was the period when mission agencies and denominational mission boards, agog at the growing achievements of the corporate business world, sought to emulate it in turn, seeking to recast their organizations along "scientific" lines and to apply scientific principles of management, especially of fund-raising. John Mott was far from alone in seeking to loosen the purse strings of the moneyed class for the benefit of mission, though he was surely the most successful.[60] The quest for the next Robert Arthington or D. Willis James (whose $1,000,000 donation in 1919 was the largest to that date given by a living person as a single gift to a foreign mission board[61]) could become unseemly. Cornelius Patton wrote in *The Business of Missions*, "Plan at the earliest moment, as God prospers you, to make an *investment* in the foreign work of your denomination, to become *A CAPITALIST FOR CHRIST*. Such investments are not made through Church envelopes, nor do they come in response to general appeals.... There is an element of ownership, of personal initiative in the lump sum that goes into such an investment, which can never obtain in respect to what goes on the plate with the gifts of the throng."[62] This same spirit a century later leads to "investment" in New Era schemes and, in the name of being businesslike and giving rigor to mission, leads to "managerial missiology."

Mission Founding Auxiliary Businesses

Mission is often carried out through auxiliary businesses that are or are seen as being more or less indispensable for accomplishing missional tasks. As already indicated, radio stations, TV broadcasting studios, campgrounds, boarding schools, hostels, publishing houses, printing plants, bookstores, orphanages, hospitals, and community development projects are only some of the types of businesses created as direct expressions of the missionary imperative.

Mission Founding Ancillary Businesses

Historically, many mission organizations have established businesses so as to generate funds to support their missional endeavors, that is, such businesses were not considered to be directly instruments of mission outreach. Alternatively, they have managed the investment of donated funds for the same purpose.

More directly in view in this heading, though, is a mission's decision to establish a business in order to create a setting in which extended and non-contrived contact between missionaries and disciples or potential disciples can take place. This is intended as a context for transmission of the faith by example as well as through overt instruction. Historically, the Basel Mission stands out for deliberately establishing businesses that were themselves to be missional in this sense. Businesses were essential to the missionary method in view, but were ancillary in the sense that another form or line of business could have been chosen.

Tentmaking is a form of mission practice that is practically defined by the establishment of ancillary businesses. The businesses, however, have too frequently been seen more as a ticket into some country than as being themselves the locus and exemplar of mission. The practice of filing business papers that become fictional through lack of any meaningful effort to earn a living or produce a profit through the "business" has unfortunately tarnished the label of tentmaker. Also, the "business," if functional, was seen more as a place of employment for the expatriate than as a way to augment employment opportunities for nationals. In Yamamori's words, tentmakers became job takers, at best displacing national workers (when they operated as true businesses), rather than job makers, creating new jobs for local residents.[63]

Many ancillary businesses, in another sense of the term, have grown up around mission. They are seen as being useful to mission personnel and to mission organizations, but are not thought to be directly instrumental in accomplishing missional purposes in the same sense as the category of auxiliary businesses referred to above. Sometimes classified as mission support agencies, these businesses cater to needs of mission personnel by printing prayer cards, providing Web services, leasing cars to missionaries on favorable terms, handling specialized insurance needs, operating boarding schools, or supplying texts for home schooling of missionary children, plus many other services.[64]

Mission Via Strategic Businesses

Business as mission, in my understanding of current discussion, consists of entrepreneurial activity conceived of and carried out in such a way that a single entity fulfills a dual role. One role is financial and economic, leading to income, profits, increased economic opportunities for locals, and a sound basis for expatriates to obtain residency permits. The other role is spiritual and missional, leading to salvation, spiritual growth, and facilitation of formation of fellowships of followers of Jesus Christ in otherwise politically closed or restricted settings. All of the above are important. Individual projects may have any number of subemphases—they may be initiated to gain entry to one people group or another or for the owner/manager to be able to live in a certain political subregion; they may be designed to build on a particular strength of the management team or to instill or capitalize on a particular skill of the surrounding populace; they may strive to exploit a particular market niche or to benefit a particular set of producers—but they must fulfill at least the demands outlined. Business as mission seeks to cultivate and build upon perceived business opportunities in such a way as to also fulfill missional objectives.

Directionality:
Sowing Broadcast vs. Cultivating Intensively

In seeking to locate *business as mission* within the larger field of *business and mission*, it can be helpful to compare and contrast the outward-focused tendency of auxiliary businesses established by mission agencies with the inward orientation of *business as mission*.

In *mission businesses* (businesses auxiliary to mission):

> The employees of the mission business are *not* the point.

Mission businesses are turned outward. What is done *here* (in the mission studio, shop, or plant) is for the sake of influencing or transforming someone *out there*.

Mission businesses frequently strive for large-scale impact and seek to generate many points of contact (radio, printing, film, TV). The potential audience is measured in the thousands, hundreds of thousands, and potentially millions.

The product and the message converge or are identical. The relation of the product to the message is intrinsic.[65]

Ideally, the audience reached (reader, hearer, viewer) becomes both consumer of the product and potential convert of the product's message.

Points of contact frequently are remote, being both long-distance and impersonal.

The message is informational and, in principle, textual (e.g., if a spoken word, it can be converted to a text).

The ideal tends toward minimal time investment per individual contacted and seeks to maximize the number of persons contacted.

Mission businesses sow broadcast and practice extensive cultivation.

In *business as mission* the lines of implication and proportionality run in the opposite direction.

The employees *are* the point.

Business as mission is turned inward. What is done in the plant, shop, or office is done, not for the sake of influencing or hoping to transform people out there, but so as to influence and transform the people *here* who comprise the work force.

Business as mission may have grand ambitions for business growth, but the contactor-contactee ratio stays low. The prime missional ambition is inherently small-scale, based on person-to-person points of contact. The focal "audience" is measured in the tens and hundreds instead of the thousands or millions.

The product and the message diverge and are minimally related, if at all. The relation of the product to the message is extrinsic.[66]

The "audience" is distinct from the consumer of the product. Consumers exist to buy products so that the business can continue to exist and so that contact with the "employee/audience" can therefore be maintained. Consumers have little and potentially no relation or exposure to the business's "spiritual" message.

Points of contact are direct interaction and immediate, even intimate, conversation.

The message is personal and modeled in life.

The ideal tends toward maximum duration and intensity of contact time per employee, which necessarily limits the number of meaningful contacts that can be sustained per staff person.

Business as mission plants in prepared seedbeds and practices intensive cultivation.

A Picture of the Whole

Mission is embedded in a world saturated by business. Just as truly, mission—being rooted in the character of God and in God's intent, present and active from eternity past, to make God's love and grace known worldwide—everywhere and at all times confronts business with corrective and redemptive words and deeds.[67] Mission impinges upon business; mission is impinged upon by business and necessarily so. They contact, influence, and have effects upon each other. Some of the ways mission draws upon and utilizes business are given in schematic form in the chart on the following page. For convenience, mission is situated in the center. The chart flows from bottom to top. That which conduces toward missionary formation, selection, and appointment appears at the bottom; businesses that shore up missionary existence and that assist in the routine activities of daily life are placed to each side; and businesses through which missionaries operate in order to accomplish the tasks and purposes of mission are at the top.

Business Aspects of Mission

Printing/publishing establishments
Radio/television stations and networks
Film production/showing/distribution
Libraries
Web sites/Web archives of books and articles
Bookstores/Web stores
Houses of worship
Lecture halls
Mass evangelistic campaigns/rallies
Saturation evangelism
Day schools, boarding schools
Bible institutes, seminaries, colleges, universities
Medical clinics/hospitals
Agriculture/silviculture programs
Industrial missions
Community development organizations
Business/commerce creation

Mechanisms of engagement
using systems of
    • communication
    • formation
    • ministration

Post-approval support services
(enabling missionary to get to field
and perform assigned field tasks)

Telephone/e-mail/postal services
Travel/shipping/logistics
Outfitting companies
Vehicle dealers
Insurance
Housing/mission compound
Medical services
Schools/boarding schools
Accounting/bookkeeping
Performance review

Mission/Missionary
on the field
poised at interface
of missional outreach

Post-approval adjunct services
(assisting connections to
constituency and facilitating the
missionary's personal office and
time/work management)

Computer services
Telephone/e-mail/ postal services
Photography
Prayer letter/newsletter services
Web page services
Support receiving/finance
  management services
"Home" church trips/visits

Mechanisms leading up to
appointment using institutions of
    • evaluation
    • formation
    • introduction/induction

Application/review/approval process
Psychological evaluation
Hospitals/clinics/physical evaluations
Financial review/credit approval
Jungle camps/internships
Seminaries/universities/colleges/Bible institutes
Short-term mission programs/trips
Mission conferences
Candidate secretary itineration
Advertising/referral services
Churches/Sunday schools/camps

Opportunistic and parasitical
enterprises
  Holy hardware
  Pseudo–special rates/services
  Come-ons

Discussion Starters

1. Mission and business often have not been comfortable partners. In what ways do the goals, methods, and intentions of business and mission differ?
2. In the conduct of business as mission, when legitimate business considerations and crucial missional concerns seem to diverge, which has priority?
3. Business without profit is a self-contradiction and cannot be sustained. Christian mission without charity is oxymoronic and ought not to be supported. In what ways can these two axioms be reconciled? In what ways are they wholly incompatible?

Notes

1. See Giorgio Tourn, *You Are My Witnesses: The Waldensians Across 800 Years* (Torino, Italy: Claudiana, 1989), pp. 39–40. I am indebted to Dwight Acomb for this reference.

2. Steven L. Rundle and Patrick Lai, "Appendix D: A Guide to Further Reading," in *On Kingdom Business: Transforming Missions Through Entrepreneurial Strategies*, ed. Tetsunao Yamamori and Kenneth A. Eldred (Wheaton, Ill.: Crossway Books, 2003), p. 325.

3. Society for Propagation of the Gospel in New England, *The New England Company of 1649 and John Eliot* (Boston: Society for Propagation of the Gospel in New England, 1920); William Kellaway, *The New England Company, 1649–1776: Missionary Society to the American Indians* (London: Longmans, 1961).

4. "The total contributions for these ten years |1649–59| were £15,367:01:04, and of personal gifts £1241:19:01. The rents meantime rose steadily to £800:19:11 in 1657, dropping to £272:16:09 in 1660, when tenants, like everyone else, waited to see what would happen to those who had prospered during the Puritan regime.

"During this same decade, £4673:10:09 was expended for the benefit of the New Englanders; £11,957:15:04 was invested in landed property in England; and the charges for salaries and other sundries incidental to the business of the Corporation were £1468:03:02." (George Parker Winship, "Introduction," in *New England Company of 1649 and John Eliot*, p. xxxvi).

According to Economic History Services, £12,000 from 1655 would be worth £1,422,821.26 in 2002 pounds, using the retail price index. See www.eh.net/hmit/ppowerbp/. The current valuation of the New England Company and its yearly activity can be found at www.charitiesdirect.com/charity4/ch016374.htm.

5. Noel Titus, "Concurrence Without Compliance: SPG and the Barbadian Plantations, 1710–1834," in Daniel O'Connor et al, *Three Centuries of Mission: The United Society for the Propagation of the Gospel, 1701–2000* (New York: Continuum, 2000), p. 249.

6. Karl Olsson, *By One Spirit* (Chicago: Covenant Press, 1962), pp. 373–78. For a full account, see Leland Carlson, *An Alaskan Gold Mine: The Story of No. 9 Above* (Evanston. Ill.: Northwestern Univ. Press, 1951). The money being contested was significant, though its current value can be computed several different ways. The value in 2003 dollars (see www.eh.net/hmit/compare/) of $500,000 in 1900 would be:

$10,894,257.43	using the Consumer Price Index
$9,266,666.67	using the GDP deflator
$53,723,021.43	using the unskilled wage
$77,007,167.64	using the GDP per capita
$294,001,606.00	using the relative share of GDP

7. William Danker, *Profit for the Lord: Economic Activities in Moravian Missions and the Basel Mission Trading Company* (Grand Rapids: Eerdmans, 1971), p. 99.

8. Danker, *Profit for the Lord*, p. 85: the Indians "deplored the sale of the mission plantations which they considered 'the glory of the mission.'"

9. Samuel Southall, "An Uncommon Life," *Friends Quarterly Examiner: A Religious, Social, and Miscellaneous Review, Conducted by Members of the Society of Friends* 35 (1901): 286. I thank Jonathan Bonk for this reference.

10. See www.eh.net/hmit/ukcompare/. In 2002, £1,000,000 from 1900 would be worth:

£66,164,501.55	using the retail price index
£80,879,884.00	using the GDP deflator
£346,638,219.22	using average earnings
£385,964,066.84	using per capita GDP
£555,261,195.61	using the GDP

11. The phrase "Great Commission Companies" is taken from Steve Rundle and Tom Steffen, *Great Commission Companies: The Emerging Role of Business in Missions* (Downers Grove, Ill.: InterVarsity Press, 2003).

12. The topic of business and mission falls within the wider field of study of the business aspects of religious organizations and religious aspects of business organizations. See the work of Peter Dobkin Hall, e.g., "Religion and the Organizational Revolution in the United States," in *Sacred Companies: Organizational Aspects of Religion and Religious Aspects of Organizations*, ed. N. J. Demerath III, Peter Dobkin Hall, Terry Schmitt, and Rhys H. Williams (New York: Oxford Univ. Press, 1998), pp. 99–115; "Religion and the Origin of Voluntary Associations in the United States," Yale University, Program on Non-Profit Organizations, Paper No. 213, 1994; "Inventing the Nonprofit Sector," in *Inventing the Nonprofit Sector and Other Essays on Philanthropy, Voluntarism, and Nonprofit Organizations* (Baltimore: Johns Hopkins Univ. Press, 1992); and "Moving Targets: Evangelicalism and the Transformation of American Economic Life, 1870–1920," in *More Money,*

More Ministry: Money and Evangelicals in Recent North American History, ed. Larry Eskridge and Mark A. Noll (Grand Rapids: Eerdmans, 2000), pp. 159–67.

13. For an excellent example, see Peter J. Wosh, *Spreading the Word: The Bible Business in Nineteenth-Century America* (Ithaca, N.Y.: Cornell Univ. Press, 1994).

14. For example, Stephen Neill, *A History of Christian Missions*, 2nd ed., rev. Owen Chadwick (New York: Penguin Books, 1986; orig. 1964), pp. 66–67, mentions Boniface's establishment of monasteries as "pioneer houses . . . for the most part placed in remote and uncultured regions. In order to live, the monks had to carry out the ideal of St Benedict by cultivating the land with their own hands, as well as carrying out the regular *opus dei*, the ceaseless round of prayer and praise," and in doing so they came into intimate contact with the peasant populace, whom they converted. On page 327 he notes that "*Nyasaland* was divided between the UMCA and the Scots, the two great Presbyterian Churches of Scotland coming in with a wonderful array of enterprises—evangelistic, medical, educational, industrial, and agricultural, certainly among the best organized mission projects in the world (Blantyre 1877, Livingstonia 1881)."

15. Kenneth Scott Latourette, *A History of Christianity*, 2 vols. (New York: HarperSanFrancisco, 1975; orig. 1953).

16. James W. Gustafson, "Pigs, Ponds and the Gospel," in *Perspectives on the World Christian Movement: A Reader*, 3rd ed., ed. Ralph D. Winter and Steven C. Hawthorne (Pasadena, Calif.: William Carey Library, 1999), pp. 677–80; Ruth Siemens, "Tentmakers Needed for World Evangelization," in ibid., pp. 733–41.

17. William D. Taylor, ed., *Global Missiology for the 21st Century: The Iguassu Dialogue* (Grand Rapids: Baker Academic, 2000); J. Herbert Kane, *A Global View of Christian Missions: From Pentecost to the Present* (Grand Rapids: Baker, 1971). The WEA Missions Commission formally renamed itself Mission Commission in 2004.

18. Stan Guthrie, *Missions in the Third Millennium: 21 Key Trends for the 21st Century* (Waynesboro, Ga.: Paternoster Press, 2000).

19. International Congress on World Evangelization, Lausanne, Switzerland, *Let the Earth Hear His Voice: Official Reference Volume, Papers and Responses*, ed. J. D. Douglas (Minneapolis: World Wide Publications, 1975).

20. Edward R. Dayton and David A. Fraser, *Planning Strategies for World Evangelization* (Grand Rapids: Eerdmans, 1980), pp. 235–36.

21. David J. Bosch, *Transforming Mission: Paradigm Shifts in Theology of Mission* (Maryknoll, N.Y.: Orbis Books, 1991), and Stephen B. Bevans and Roger P. Schroeder, *Constants in Context: A Theology of Mission for Today* (Maryknoll, N.Y.: Orbis Books, 2004).

22. J. Christy Wilson, *Today's Tentmakers: Self-Support—An Alternative Model for Worldwide Witness* (Wheaton, Ill.: Tyndale House, 1979); Tetsunao Yamamori, *God's New Envoys: A Bold New Strategy for Penetrating "Closed Countries"* (Portland, Ore.: Multnomah, 1987); Tetsunao Yamamori, *Penetrating Missions' Final Frontiers: A New Strategy for Unreached Peoples* (Downers Grove, Ill.: InterVarsity Press, 1993); Jonathan Lewis, ed., *Working Your Way to the Nations: A Guide to Effective Tentmaking*, 2nd ed. (Downers Grove, Ill.: InterVarsity

Press, 1997; orig. 1993); Bryant L. Myers, *Walking with the Poor: Principles and Practices of Transformational Development* (Maryknoll, N.Y.: Orbis Books, 1999).

23. David R. Befus, *Kingdom Business: The Ministry of Promoting Economic Activity* (Miami: Latin American Mission, 2001).

24. See, for example, the Web sites of Scruples (www.scruples.org/ and www.scruples.net/). An extensive annotated bibliography, up through 1999, on business and mission can be found at http://www.scruples.org/bizetmiz/web/articles/bmbiblio.htm. Tetsunao Yamamori and Kenneth A. Eldred, *On Kingdom Business*, p. 339, and Rundle and Steffen, *Great Commission Companies*, pp. 198–99, each list a dozen pertinent Web sites.

25. Consultation for Holistic Entrepreneurs: The Integration of "Kingdom Business" with Missions to Unreached Peoples in the 21st Century, October 3–5, 2002, Regent University Graduate School of Business, Virginia Beach, Virginia, U.S.A. See http://www.gospelcom.net/lcwe/newsletter/0107b.htm and http://www.regent.edu/news/holisticentrepr.html.

26. For the relation of mission to colonialism, see Bosch's discussion, "Mission and Colonialism," in *Transforming Mission*, pp. 302–13.

"Since the sixteenth century, if one said 'mission', one in a sense also said 'colonialism'. Modern missions originated in the context of modern Western colonialism. . . .

"During the fifteenth to the seventeenth century both Roman Catholic and Protestants were, admittedly in very different ways, still dedicated to the theocratic ideal of the unity of church and state. No Catholic or Protestant ruler of the period could imagine that, in acquiring overseas possessions, he was advancing only his *political* hegemony: it was taken for granted that the conquered nations would also have to submit to the Western ruler's *religion*. The king missionized as he colonized" (p. 303).

On the shift from trading to imperialist impulses in colonialism and the consequent shift in attitude toward missionaries—in the earlier phase, when trading was the point, "missionaries were not welcomed"; later during the imperial phase, when the point of empire became to rule populaces, "missionaries were henceforth allowed to operate more or less freely"—(see pp. 306–7).

27. John S. Stone, *The Bearings of Modern Commerce on the Progress of Modern Missions: The Annual Sermon, Before the Bishops, Clergy, and Laity, Constituting the Board of Missions of the Protestant Episcopal Church in the United States, Delivered in Trinity Church, New Haven, on Wednesday, June 19, 1839* (New York: William Osborn, 1839), p. 21. In the latter part of his sermon Stone gives voice to an amazing eschatological vision of a redeemed and renewed commerce assisting in carrying the Gospel to the peoples of the world. Unfortunately, it falls out along the lines too frequently encountered of "you have taken their land and their gold, at least make restitution by giving them your Gospel and your Bible."

28. Tom Hiney, *On the Missionary Trail: A Journey Through Polynesia, Asia, and Africa with the London Missionary Society* (New York: Atlantic Monthly Press), p. 335.

29. See Leland Carlson, *An Alaskan Gold Mine,* and Karl Olsson, *By One Spirit,* pp. 373–78, 414–32; quotations from pp. 378, 426.

30. See Titus, "Concurrence Without Compliance," in Daniel O'Connor et al, *Three Centuries of Mission,* pp. 249–61.

31. Hiney, *Missionary Trail,* p. 340n16.

32. See, for example, James S. Dennis, *Commerce and Missions* (New York: Laymen's Missionary Movement, n.d.); S. M. Zwemer, *What Business Has a Business Man with Foreign Missions?* (New York: Board of Foreign Missions, R[eformed] C[hurch in] A[merica], 1901); Arthur Porritt, *What Business Has a Business Man with Foreign Missions?* (London: London Missionary Society, n.d.).

33. Dennis, *Commerce and Missions.*

34. A. Scott Moreau, "Putting the Survey in Perspective," in *Mission Handbook, 2004–2006: U.S. and Canadian Protestant Ministries Overseas,* ed. Dotsey Welliver and Minnette Northcutt (Wheaton, Ill.: EMIS, 2004), pp. 28–30, 11.

35. Danker, *Profit for the Lord.*

36. Rundle and Steffen, *Great Commission Companies,* chap. 8.

37. Brian Stanley, "The Legacy of Robert Arthington," *International Bulletin of Missionary Research* 22, no. 4 (October 1998).

38. On Basel Mission activities in India, see Danker, *Profit for the Lord,* pp. 83–92.

39. Rundle and Lai, "Appendix D: A Guide to Further Reading," in Yamamori and Eldred, eds., *On Kingdom Business,* p. 325; Tetsunao Yamamori, "Preface," in ibid., p. 9.

40. Bartolomé de las Casas, 1474–1566, went to New Spain with the conquistadors and was initially their willing accomplice. He became the documenter of atrocities and injustices committed against Native Americans and the native people's outstanding defender at the Spanish court. The Yale University's electronic catalogue carries 135 titles by and about Las Casas. For Livingstone, see the recent volume by Andrew Ross, *David Livingstone: Mission and Empire* (New York: Hambledon and London, 2002). On "blackbirding" see Darrell L. Whiteman, "Human Rights and Missionary Response: The Case of the South Pacific Labor Trade," *Missiology: An International Review* 24, no. 2 (April 1996): 247–56. On the wrath of whalers falling on missionaries "because the native women did not visit the ship as formerly," see "Commerce and Missions," in *The Encyclopedia of Missions: Descriptive, Historical, Biographical, Statistical,* ed. Edwin Munsell Bliss (New York: Funk & Wagnalls, 1981), p. 309, and Hiney, *Missionary Trail,* p. 74. On the work of Alice Seely Harris and her husband John Harris in exposing the atrocities in King Leopold's Congo, see Jack Thompson, "Light on the Dark Continent: The Photography of Alice Seely Harris and the Congo Atrocities of the Early Twentieth Century," *International Bulletin of Missionary Research* 26, no. 4 (October 2002): 146–49.

41. Consider, for instance, Samuel Marsden. Sent by the CMS to Australia as senior chaplain, he was party to a scheme "to purchase the entire South Island of New Zealand from a number of Maori chiefs." That scheme came to the attention of the governor, who blocked it. Other of Marsden's business dealings occasioned

protest during his lifetime. But "in 1845, seven years after Marsden's death, it was revealed that he and the other Anglican chaplains operating in Australia for the CMS had together amassed a total of 387,000 acres of privately owned property" (Hiney, *On the Missionary Trail*, pp. 342–43nn 7, 10). But see also Hiney's observation, p. 238: "That characters such as Samuel Marsden in Sydney may have exploited the homestead marriage of Evangelism and commerce to forge personal fortunes should not blind hindsight to the less controversial fact that for the great majority of missions farming was a form of sustenance and survival, not of profit. All money made was put back into the mission. Men like Micaiah Hill died as poor as they had arrived, and generally poorer." For Marsden, see Hiney, *Missionary Trail*, pp. 143–52.

42. See Thomas L. Headland, "Missionaries and Social Justice: Are They Part of the Problem or Part of the Solution?" *Missiology: An International Review* 24, no. 2 (April 1996): 167–78, and indeed this whole issue of *Missiology*, subtitled "Missionaries, Anthropologists, and Human Rights," for which Headland provides the lead article. A recent example is the work of Laura Meitzner Yoder in Oecusse Enclave, East Timor. See Laura S. Meitzner Yoder, "Custom, Codification, Collaboration: Integrating the Legacies of Land and Forest Authorities in Oecusse Enclave, East Timor" (Ph.D. diss., Yale University, 2005).

43. See Don Richardson, "Do Missionaries Destroy Cultures?" in Winter and Hawthorne, *Perspectives*, pp. 460–68; quotation from p. 465.

44. The October 2002 issue of the *International Bulletin of Missionary Research* is devoted to the theme "Rediscovering Missionary Photography." The Internet Missionary Photography Archive, based at the University of Southern California, offers online access to missionary photographs at www.usc.edu/isd/archives/arc/digarchives/mission/.

45. Dennis, *Commerce and Missions*, p. 25: "Trade returns there, as we have noted in so many instances, have increased in a kind of rhythmic accord with mission progress." See also Zwemer, *What Business Has a Business Man with Foreign Missions?* and, with the same title, Arthur Porritt, *What Business Has a Business Man with Foreign Missions?*

46. Dennis, *Commerce and Missions*, p. 21. The sum of £10,000 in 1857 would be equivalent in 2002 to:

£566,379.83	using the retail price index
£840,473.81	using the GDP deflator
£5,236,926.97	using average earnings
£6,401,515.98	using per capita GDP
£13,446,431.20	using the GDP

From www.eh.net/hmit/ukcompare/. Even at the lowest figure, the value indicated by Venn's statement, if it had any real meaning at all, was large.

47. Dennis, *Commerce and Missions*, p. 6.

48. Hiney, *Missionary Trail*, p. 345n9: "This tendency was being highlighted by those missionaries (as had happened in Singapore and Java) who resigned their stations to accept more comfortable garrison livings in India. This was an infu-

riating trend for the society, reducing the LMS to the role of clerical appointors for the East India Company, and—since each missionary to leave or die had to be replaced from London—also incurred continuous expenses for the Board."

49. Andrew Walls, "The American Dimension in the Missionary Movement," in *Earthen Vessels: American Evangelicals and Foreign Mission, 1880–1980*, ed. Joel A. Carpenter and Wilbert R. Shenk (Grand Rapids: Eerdmans, 1990), pp. 22–23.

50. Alex Shoumatoff, *In Southern Light: Trekking Through Zaire and the Amazon* (London: Corgi Books, 1988, 1986), p. 117.

51. Helen Winternitz, *East Along the Equator: A Journey Up the Congo and Into Zaire* (New York: Atlantic Monthly Press, 1987), pp. 140–42, 159–60.

52. See references in note 12.

53. See Wosh, *Spreading the Word.*

54. David Paul Nord, "The Evangelical Origins of Mass Media in America, 1815–1835," *Journalism Monographs*, 84 (May 1984): 1–30.

55. John S. Stone, *Bearings of Modern Commerce*, pp. 26–27.

56. Arthur Porritt, *What Business Has a Business Man with Foreign Missions?* pp. 10–11.

57. Paul Bohannan, *Africa and Africans*, rev. ed. (Garden City, N.Y.: Natural History Press, 1971, orig. 1964), p. 187. See the comments of Nelson Mandela, quoted in Hiney, *Missionary Trail*, pp. 332–35.

58. Hiney, *Missionary Trail*, p. 329.

59. Hiney, *Missionary Trail*, pp. 329–30.

60. See C. Howard Hopkins, *John R. Mott, 1865–1955: A Biography* (Grand Rapids: Eerdmans, 1979).

61. Cornelius H. Patton, *The Business of Missions* (New York: Macmillan, 1924), p. 266.

62. Patton, *Business of Missions*, p. 263.

63. Yamamori, "Preface," in Yamamori and Eldred, *On Kingdom Business*, p. 8.

64. For a helpful typology of mission organizations, see Ralph D. Winter, "The Six Spheres of Mission Overseas," *Mission Frontiers* 20 (March–April): 16–24, 40–45.

65. For example, a sermon broadcast by radio, a documentary film depicting styles of worship, and a printed text of Scripture or Bible commentary are all products that might be seen as carrying elements of the Christian message, quite apart from the life or sanctity of the preacher, actor, or printer.

66. The message is conveyed by the businessperson's life and professional conduct rather than being inherent in the product. The product may be nothing more than an adventitious artifact, produced according to opportunity and circumstance.

67. See Dwight P. Baker, "The Scope of Mission," *The Covenant Quarterly*, February 2003, pp. 3–12.

3

God's Kingdom Purpose for Business: Business as Integral Mission

Norm Ewert

Thomas Friedman earlier this year in a *New York Times* Op Ed piece said that the US is currently funding both sides of the war on terrorism: first, the military campaign against terrorism in the Middle East, and secondly, through our purchases of oil.

In a similar vein, evangelicals in essence support both Christian missions and Muslim missions. Reza F. Safa, author of "Inside Islam" claims that many of the mosques built in the US in the last 20 years have received funding from the Wahabis in Saudi Arabia, and that 60-90 percent of US converts to Islam are black, 80 percent of whom grew up in the church.[1] Given the distribution of remaining global oil reserves the next 50 years will see the most massive redistribution of wealth from what may be called the Christian world to the Muslim world that the global economy has ever seen. The Wahabis in Saudi Arabia do not sit around worrying where the billions for their next Muslim evangelism program will come from. They will be even less anxious over time as the global demand for energy continues to rise. Christians are currently helping to support the wrong kind of missions.

A growing literature surveys the numerous and creative ways in which Christians are more intentionally incorporating business activity into the global witness and mission of the church. The history and current practice of promoting the Kingdom through business is rich and diverse including tentmaking, service ministries, market-place ministry, business funding missions, microfinance, small and medium enterprise development, venture capital, or other ways.[2]

This chapter affirms these efforts but it also calls for a broader and more holistic transformational view of business. God's Kingdom Purpose for business is to express the love of Christ in all of business by demonstrating and promoting stewardship, justice, servanthood, respect for human dignity, community and shalom in and through business operations. In essence it is to make the love of Christ concrete in all of life in all ends of the earth through business. In short, Christians need to develop and commit to an integrated mission in which business serves the goals of holistic Christian witness. An evangelical vision of business integrally holds together business and economic life *with* the demonstration of moral witness as an expression of the love of Christ.

Integrating Business and Moral Witness

If God's vision of shalom, stewardship and justice should, indeed, inform all business practice in order to holistically spread the gospel through word and deed, what might that look like? How does a business demonstrating the love of Christ differ from secular business?

Any business, secular or otherwise, must be profitable in order to survive. One objective of any viable business is obviously financial sustainability. Secular society has over the years, however, gradually been changing its expectations of business. There is much in the secular views of business that Christians can embrace, but we must do more.

The traditional business paradigm assumed that the primary responsibility of business was to maximize wealth for shareholders. This perspective may be illustrated in the model above where business is accountable primarily to shareholders and is accountable for maximum financial performance alone.[3] Profits are necessary for a business to survive. If a business is not sustainable, it is not doing a whole lot of good for anyone. Michael Naughton calls financial sustainability "foundational" for any business.[4]

Secular society has been asking more from businesses than just maximizing profits. Kenneth Mason, former president of Quaker Oats put it this way: "Making a profit is no more the purpose of a corporation than getting enough to eat is the purpose of life. Getting enough to eat is a requirement of life; life's purpose, one would hope, is somewhat broader and more challenging. Likewise with business and profit."[5]

Early corporate social responsibility thinking emphasized accountability to a broader range of stakeholders, including employees in terms of working conditions; customers in terms of product quality, reliability, and service; communities in terms of philanthropy, and society in terms of pollution. The domain of business accountability also increased to include among other things: integrity, product quality, respect, service, fairness and pollution. Many corporations also became involved with philanthropy.

More recently a growing number of corporations and agencies are expanding the scope of business accountability to include society at large.[6] It is also expanding the domain of accountability to include human rights, civil society, environmental sustainability, and conflict mitigation, among other things. The World Council on Business and Sustainable Development, for example, says that business cannot survive in a society that fails.[7] The UN through its Global Compact initiative and the Prince of Wales International Business Leaders Forum have both encouraged business to broaden its range of accountability.[8]

Kingdom-purposed businesses must be profitable and run professionally using the best management practices. Kingdom businesses must also embrace the best principles of corporate social responsibility. Indeed, many of the new secular expectations regarding business behavior reflect values that we as Christians will certainly recognize. But financial sustainability alone is not adequate for a Kingdom-purposed business. Adopting the best principles of corporate social responsibility is necessary, but also not adequate for a Kingdom-purposed business.

Implications for Business as Integral Mission

What then are the implications of doing *Business as Integral Mission?* Winston Churchill once said: "Some people regard private enterprise as a predatory tiger to be shot. Others look on it as a cow they can milk. Not enough people see it as a healthy horse, pulling a sturdy wagon."[9] True, but the horses need to be working together as a team pulling *everyone* along in the wagon and going in the right direction

The modified diagram illustrates a broader scope and domain of accountability for Business as Integrated Mission (BAIM). BAIM includes accountability to key stakeholders and to society at large as do secular paradigms, but it also extends to the church worldwide. Further, the domain of BAIM accountability includes financial performance, legal responsibilities as well as legitimate claims as do secular paradigms, but it also includes accountability for stewardship, justice, peace, dignity and community.

Values and Principles

The following values and principles are necessary for BAIM. One primary
principle of BAIM is stewardship. Stewardship is much more than an exercise in fractions. It is a way of life dedicated to furthering the Kingdom and
pleasing God. It is managing all of the resources, time, and energy God has
entrusted to us to produce goods and services to meet the needs of all. The
chief purpose of creation is to glorify God.

Jeremiah encourages Israelites to do two things: (1) become involved
in the local economy even though temporarily in exile, and (2) work for
peace and prosperity:

> This is what the Lord Almighty, the God of Israel, says to all
> those I carried into exile from Jerusalem to Babylon: 'Build
> houses and settle down; plant gardens and eat what they pro-
> duce. Marry and have sons and daughters; find wives for your
> sons and give your daughters in marriage, so that they too may
> have sons and daughters. Increase in number there; do not de-
> crease. Also seek the peace and prosperity of the city to which I
> have carried you into exile.' (29:4-7, NIV)

What does it mean to use God's creation in ways that ensure that it will
continue to glorify Him in the future? Stewardship requires that we responsibly use resources to produce goods and services to meet current human
needs, but to do so in ways that do not compromise the ability of future
generations to also meet their needs. Business is the institution that has the
greatest impact on how we as a society steward the resources God entrusted
to us. There are many opportunities for Christians in business to demonstrate stewardship. For example, a Christian homebuilder in Chicago builds
houses that use much less energy than typical houses but at little additional
cost. He tries to design and construct his homes to minimize the ecological
footprint as a matter of Christian stewardship.

The World Bank suggests that, "The wars of the next century will be
about water."[10] Are there ways in which business can redesign products to
reduce the amount of water used in laundry facilities and sanitation systems
for example? Are there crop varieties that can be developed which require
less water? Are there transportation systems that require significantly less
energy and which emit fewer effluents into the environment? Are there recycling possibilities that reduce the demand for resources? Given the materialism and individualism so rampant today, evangelicals have a tremendous opportunity to give witness to our faith in how we live, how we produce, how we steward all of the resources God has entrusted to us.

A second primary principle of BAIM is justice. Many passages reflect
the importance of justice. James warns the rich oppressors that even if they
can get by with paying low wages, their deeds will not go unnoticed:

> Now listen, you rich people, weep and wail because of the misery that is coming upon you. Your wealth has rotted, and moths have eaten your clothes. Your gold and silver are corroded. Their corrosion will testify against you and eat your flesh like fire. You have hoarded wealth in the last days. Look! The wages you failed to pay the workmen who mowed your fields are crying out against you. The cries of the harvesters have reached the ears of the Lord Almighty. You have lived on earth in luxury and self- indulgence. You have fattened yourselves in the day of slaughter. (Jas 5:1-5)

Ezekiel emphasizes responsibilities to the needs of the poor. "Now this was the sin of your sister Sodom: She and her daughters were arrogant, overfed and unconcerned; they did not help the poor and needy. They were haughty and did detestable things before me. Therefore I did away with them as you have seen" (16: 49 – 50). The book of Acts records stories of sharing believers. Just as the neglect of the Hellenistic widows was a negative testimony in Paul's time, neglect of the 1.1 billion people living in marginal countries is a negative testimony today:

> Now listen, you rich people, weep and wail because of the misery that is coming upon you. Your wealth has rotted, and moths have eaten your clothes. Your gold and silver are corroded. Their corrosion will testify against you and eat your flesh like fire. You have hoarded wealth in the last days. Look! The wages you failed to pay the workmen who mowed your fields are crying out against you. The cries of the harvesters have reached the ears of the Lord Almighty. You have lived on earth in luxury and self- indulgence. You have fattened yourselves in the day of slaughter. (Jas 5:1-5)

In his biblical expositions at the CLADE I conference René Padilla developed a broader concept of restorative justice:

> But what is justice? In the Bible, and especially in the Old Testament, it is not merely a justice of distribution; nor is it a justice of retribution; it is rather a justice of restitution, a justice that includes the two former, but goes much further in that it seeks to restore or return that which has been taken away from 'the oppressed', 'the hungry,' 'the exiled,' 'the orphans,' 'the widows,' from all the victims of the abuse of power and the injustice of a society stained by sin (Ps 146:6-9; Jer 22:3; Pr 31:8-9).[11]

Recent research on the relationship between economic welfare and health suggests that distributive or restorative justice may have a more significant impact on society than we realize. Costa Rica, Greece, Italy and 20 more countries have longer life expectancies than that of the US but all have lower average incomes. Numerous studies in socioeconomic epidemiology have found that life expectancy tends to increase as income increases, but only up to an average income of around $10,000. After that further increases in do very little if anything to extend life expectancy.[12]

After a country reaches an average income of around $10,000, life expectancy is more directly related to the distribution of income rather than the level of income. Specifically, these studies have discovered that for two countries with similar average income levels, life expectancy is likely to be higher in the country with the more egalitarian distribution of income all other things equal. The primary pathway between income inequality and lower life expectancy is the loss of community.

Economic growth needs to be more socially inclusive. Rather than waiting for poverty to disappear at the end of a hot pursuit of national economic growth, economic growth should be targeted at eliminating poverty. If the distribution of income becomes more unequal (i.e., the gap between the rich and the poor widens), virtually every income bracket will experience lower life expectancy. A person's health is, therefore, influenced not only by their personal income, as has long been thought, but also by the degree of income inequality in society. These findings suggest that for a high income country such as the United States making the distribution of income more equal will do more to increase life expectancy than increasing the average personal income level. A consistent pro-life worldview would require one to be deeply concerned about the growing inequality in the distribution of income.

How can business promote justice? Business is the institution that has the most significant impact on justice issues. Michael Naughton suggests that business is the distributor of justice, more so than governments, even more than non-government organizations.[13] When a firm changes wage rates someone gains and someone loses, in relative terms if not in absolute terms. When a firm changes prices charged for goods and services someone gains and someone loses. When a firm decides ownership structures, someone gains and someone loses.

Businesses are constantly making decisions regarding product pricing, wage rates, hiring procedures, procuring inputs, ownership of assets. Each of these management decisions can have significant implications for justice. It is essentially impossible to avoid making ethical judgments when making wage, price and other financial decisions. It is in making these decisions that businesses have the opportunity to promote greater justice. It is in making these decisions that businesses are "distributors of justice." For example, the owner of a textile business in Colombia sold her company to her former employees, empowering them. Fair trade programs attempt to provide better living conditions for economically disadvantaged. One weaving business in south Asia specifically promotes justice in several ways, first by providing jobs for people in a region where the unemployment rate is high and where wages are low. By reducing financial spreads between producer and final markets by working with an alternative trade organization the firm is able to raise worker income from less than $1/day to as much as $6-10/day. Further, the firm helps empower local producers by enabling them to acquire income-earning assets.

There are many opportunities to promote justice in the course of doing business such as determining wages and salaries. Should the maintenance engineer on the shop floor receive less than an office worker? What should be the salary range within a business? Should there be a limit to executive compensation? Are necessities priced to take advantage of higher demand? What does restorative justice look like when establishing product and service prices?

Business has as much or more potential to promote justice and empower people economically and socially than any other institution. Evangelicals in business should be promoting justice in whatever way they can in their business operations. The local church will be empowered when its people are empowered.

A third principle of BAIM is shalom. Nicholas Walterstorf writes that: "Ashalom incorporates right, harmonious relationships to *God* and delight in his service...shalom incorporates right harmonious relationships to other *human beings* and delight in human community...shalom incorporates right, harmonious relationships to *nature* and delight in our physical surroundings...We are workers in God's cause, his peace-workers. The *missio Dei* is our mission."[14] Peace is more than the absence of war.

The incidence and nature of conflict and violence globally have changed significantly since the end of WWII. A growing share of more recent conflicts are intra- rather than inter-national (25 of 27 conflicts transpiring in 1999 were internal) civil wars have become longer, more frequent (there were 39 conflicts during the 1990's in which more than 1000 persons died) and have involved close to 25 percent of all countries in the world from WWII to the mid-90's. Conflicts killed over 4 million people between the fall of the Berlin wall and the end of 2000.[15]

Conventional wisdom identifies several root causes of conflict.[16] Conservatives tend to attribute civil war to ethnic and religious tensions while people on the left tend to attribute conflict to income inequalities or the effects of colonialism. People in the middle tend to view conflict as a result of a lack of democracy and participation in the decision-making process.

Major research fails to support any of these theories. According to work by Paul Collier and others at the World Bank the incidence of conflict depends on characteristics of specific countries. For a number of reasons including the high opportunity cost of conflict, the probability of conflict in developed countries is very low. The risk of civil war in middle-income countries comprising roughly 4 billion people worldwide is about four times higher than the minimal risk of conflict in developed countries.[17] However, about 1.1 billion people live in marginal countries that face a risk of civil war about 15 times higher than the risk in developed countries.

Most of the global growth in civil war is increasingly concentrated in countries that have failed to realize economic development where incomes are stagnant or declining, and where their economies continue to be dependent on primary commodities. The research found that "the key root cause of conflict is the failure of economic development."[18] These findings suggest that global economic growth will do little to promote a more peaceful world as long as the marginal countries are not included. Economic growth must be more socially and globally inclusive. Marginal countries will continue to face increasing risks of conflicts until they participate in development. Specifically their income levels must be increased, their rates of economic growth must be improved, and their dependence on primary commodities must be reduced.

The number of conflicts can be reduced by diversifying the local economy, particularly by reducing dependence on primary products and natural resources. Since prices of primary products tend to fluctuate more than other prices incomes in countries heavily dependent on primary products are not as stable as in more diversified economies. The risk of conflicts is particularly high when commodity prices are low.

How can business promote peace? In their recent book, Andreas Wenger and Daniel Mockli argue that "corporations must become comprehensively involved in economic peace-building."[19] They are not referring to the privatization of security efforts. Rather, if, as the research suggests, the primary causes of conflict globally are low income levels, low rates of economic growth and heavy dependence on primary product exports, a necessary strategy for promoting peace is to foster socially inclusive economic growth in marginal countries. This economic growth can only come from a dynamic business community that embraces conflict prevention. A growing number of efforts are exploring how business can become more involved in promoting peace.[20]

A former oil executive responded to the fact that the remaining oil reserves are found in environments that are increasingly challenging environmentally, economically and even politically. He therefore decided to establish a commercial business that has as its mission to help firms operating in insecure regions address underlying causes of conflict rather than merely the effects of conflict. In his words:

> Our purpose is to help clients phase out their practice of relying solely on security to protect themselves from the effects of conflict, to finding ways in which they can create safer environments by reducing the causes of violence. This means making the reduction of violence integral to our business, versus relying

on the current practice of insulating ourselves from its symp-
toms.[21]

The weaving business in south Asia also promotes peace and community by having workers from different ethnic and religious backgrounds
work together in a common purpose. Christians and Muslims working side-
by-side have developed a better understanding of each other, building trust
and appreciation for each other's perspective. A business can be structured
in ways that promote greater understanding and yet be financially sustainable.

On a more global level, Thomas Friedman in the *New York Times* has
repeatedly said that a necessary precondition for obtaining sustainable
peace in the Middle East is for the US to wean itself from oil. That requires
a major paradigm shift in lifestyle, transportation, production and distribution. A challenge here is for Christians in business to develop businesses
that use less energy, or that supply products that use less energy, or to develop alternative forms of energy altogether.

A fourth principle of BAIM is to promote dignity and community.
There challenges are tremendous. A UN report contends that 24,000 people
die worldwide each day due to poverty-related factors. There are some two
billion people worldwide living on $2/day or less. Some 1.2 billion people
will be added to the labor force in the next 20 years, 90 percent of them in
the developing world. We need to create some 120,000 jobs/day just to
keep up with the rate of growth in population, say nothing about finding
jobs for the millions who are unemployed or under-employed.

There are some two billion peasants deriving their primary livelihoods
in agriculture worldwide. Technology and globalization have drastically
reduced the number of people in agriculture in developed countries. The
same forces of technology and global markets that have reduced the demand for farmers in developed countries will be challenging the way of life
for the two billion peasants in developing countries—and doing so within
the next 10 years. These forces are likely to continue to push millions more
into the major cities in the developing world creating huge demands on
their infrastructures, educational and health facilities, say nothing of the
jobs required. We are likely to have a major global job creation crisis on our
hands.

Thomas Friedman, in *Flat Earth*, suggests that globalization is raising
income levels around the world and in essence leveling the global economic
playing field.[22] Richard Florida suggests that while the earth may appear to
be becoming flatter, in reality the world is becoming "spiky," with higher
income spikes in a growing number of cities. But he says there are larger
gaps between the lows in the valleys and the highs in the spikes.[23] The challenge is to move toward a more socially inclusive society and economy.

What does this look like? Alternative Trade Organizations provide market outlets for disadvantaged artisans around the world. Ten Thousand Villages helps an artisan in Uganda sell baskets so she can pay university fees for child. Craft items purchased by others affirms their culture, empowers them not only economically but socially as well. The Chicago area homebuilder mentioned before not only builds houses that leave a much smaller ecological footprint, he also designs new housing developments in ways which promote community. A Christian mission in Surinam promoted dignity among a small people group by developing a financially sustainable radio ministry in the local language.

Prahalad and Hammond, in *The Fortune at the Bottom of the Pyramid*,[24] says that the primary driver to promote economic growth and dignity at the bottom of the pyramid is going to be small and medium size business development. He identifies and illustrates many ways in which larger firms can connect with and empower smaller firms.

Finally BAIM must be consistent with good development principles.[25] The development profession has made many mistakes in doing development, but it has learned much during that time. BAIM practices in low-income countries particularly need to incorporate the best development principles. A major study at Cornell University identified the following tenets as the foundation of effective development practice:

a. The participation of people in their own development
b. Local ownership of the decision-making process
c. Commitment of local resources to the community development process
d. Role of outside agents as facilitators of change
e. Belief in people's capacity to effect change
f. The value of people's indigenous knowledge
g. The need to transform limiting structures that impede local initiatives
h. The primacy of "process" over "projects."[26]

Jeffrey Sachs, the lead author of the *United Nations Millennium Development Goals* stresses the challenges of doing development work. He says that the:

> ...development community lacks the requisite ethical and professional standards....(and) does not take on its work with the sense of responsibility that the tasks require. Providing economic advice to others requires a profound commitment to search for the right answers, not to settle for superficial approaches. It requires a commitment to be thoroughly steeped in the history, ethnography, politics and economics of any place where the professional adviser is working.[27]

This admonition applies to all business professionals working in cross-culture contexts. Christians doing business as integral mission need to be equipped with an entire tool kit which includes an understanding of best business practice, and an understanding of how business can contribute to biblical principles of stewardship, justice, shalom, dignity and community. They must also be equipped with a good understanding of best community development practice.

Potential Dangers Within the BAM Movement

There are several potential dangers within the business as mission (BAM) movement. One is that it is a new venue through which to export American individualism, American values, consumerism, and American business ideology. A specific danger is that the BAM movement ends up preaching an individualistic gospel, that Christians do business and live out their morality as a matter simply between an individual and God alone. As Mark Husbands says, "We need to move beyond the individualistic and atomistic ethics of a solitary self. Business is a fundamentally social reality; and so too is mission, witness and ethics. We desperately need an account of the relationship between business and the witness of the church that holds together social and moral responsibility with the biblical mandates of stewardship, justice, mercy and love."[28]

A related danger is that the BAM movement essentially serves as a fig leaf for doing any business an entrepreneur desires. A Great Commission company invited Christian investors to establish businesses in the former Soviet Union that theoretically would support the local church. In reality the plan was not ecologically sound, did not empower the local church in a sustainable way, and in the end provided huge financial returns to the outside investor with little lasting impact on the local community. This business venture could easily do more harm to the local church over time than good. Evangelicals in the twentieth century have been suspicious of Christians who advocate social justice without a clear commitment to evangelism and mission. In the 21st century we should be equally suspicious of Christians who affirm a vision of business as simply the generation of capital for missions.

A third danger is that the business community will violate principles of good community development. To date there has been no significant reference in the business as mission conversation acknowledging an understanding of and an appreciation for the importance of good development principles. This is a recipe for trouble.

Summary

In summary where does this take us? How can business more effectively promote the Kingdom? This chapter has suggested that God's Kingdom Purpose for business is to make the love of Christ concrete in all of life in all ends of the earth through business. It is to express the love of Christ in all of business by demonstrating stewardship, justice, servanthood, respect for human dignity, promoting community and shalom in and through business operations. These biblical values should be incorporated into the DNA of every enterprise and should help inform every decision a business makes. The horses should be working together, pulling everyone along in the wagon and heading in the right direction.

The natural disaster created by Katrina creates an opportunity for the Christian business community to implement the principles identified above. It would be exciting to see greater efforts by Christians to help in the reconstruction process by building houses that are more ecologically friendly, creating jobs for local citizens, by designing re-developments that promote community, and rebuild businesses in ways which empower the residents.

Some businesses are already incorporating these values and principles into their core business activities, and are doing so in financially sustainable ways. These values and principles apply to Christians operating businesses whether in developed countries, low-income countries, the 10-40 Window, or wherever.

The evangelical community has a tremendous opportunity to take seriously its understanding of stewardship, justice, shalom, dignity and community and intentionally promote them through business. Business is the institution most underutilized by the evangelical community to holistically enhance the Kingdom. This is not business in missions, or business for missions, but rather Business as Integral Mission.

Discussion Starters

1. Is there a fundamental incompatibility between doing BAIM, and financial sustainability? Or, do values pay?

2. This chapter merely scratches the surface of potential opportunities in which BAIM can promote Kingdom work. What additional illustrations, or potential opportunities do folks see in doing business holistically?

3. What do folks see as the primary blocks preventing the evangelical community from embracing a more holistic view of doing business?

4. Should evangelical financing of the Muslim mission work be of concern? Why or why not?

Notes

1. Reza F. Safa, author of "Inside Islam" contends that the dominant religion among African Americans in inner city US could well be Islam within 20 years. Much of this mission work is funded by oil revenues from Saudi Arabia. http://www.worldnetdaily.com/news/article.asp?ARTICLE_ID=27327

2. See, for example, Ken Eldred, *God is At Work,* (Regal Books), 2005; David Befus, *Where There Are No Jobs,* (LAM), 2005; Steve Rundle and Tom Steffen, *Great Commission Companies*, (InterVarsity Press), 2003.

3. Model adapted from Lynn Sharpe, *Value Shift*, (McGraw Hill), 2003.

4. Helen J. Alford, Michael J. Naughton, *Management as if Faith Mattered: Christian Social Principles in the Modern Organization* (University of Notre Dame Press), 2001.

5. Quoted in *Business Week,* August 13, 1979, p.14.

6. See, for example, World Council of Business and Sustainable Development, *Doing Business With the Poor, A Field Guide*, available online at: www.wbcsd.org; C.K. Prahalad and Allen Hammond, *"Fortune at the Bottom of the Pyramid,"* 2005, pp.;99-112; Jane Nelson, *The Business of Peace*; *Human Rights are Everybody's Business* (Amnesty international), 2002

7. See World Bank, http://www.ifg.org/bgsummary.html

8. See: http://www.unglobalcompact.org/ and http://www.iblf.org/

9. Quoted in Business for Development: Business: Solutions in Support of the Millennium Development Goals, 2005, p.22. Available at: http://www.wbcsd.org/web/publications/biz4dev.pdf

10. Maude Barlow, International Forum on Globalization, quotes the World Bank in Blue Gold. The Global Water Crisis and the Commodification of the World's Water Supply online at http://www.ifg.org/analysis/reports/bgsummary.htm

11. Washington Padilla, Hacia una Transformacion Integral (Buenos Aires: Fraternidad teologicca Latinoamericana, 1989), p.10.

12. See Richard Wilkinson, *The Impact of Inequality* (New Press), 2005; Wilkinson, Kawachi, and Kennedy, *The Society and Health Reader: Income Inequality and Health* (New Press), 1999.

13. Alford & Naughton, *Management as if Faith Mattered*, 2001.

14. Nicholas Walterstorf, *Until Justice and Peace Embrace*, (Williams B. Eerdmans), 1983, p. 72.

15. See Macartan Humphreys, AEconomics and Violent Conflict, Harvard Center for International Development, August, 2002, available online at: http://www.preventconflict.org/, "Economic Causes of Civil Conflict and Their Implications for Policy," June 15, 2000, Washington, D.C. Available online at: http://www.worldbank.org/html/extdr/extme/pr061500.htm

16. Paul Collier, et. Al., *Breaking the Conflict Trap, Civil War and Development Policy*, (World Bank), 2003, 99.53+.

17. However, this risk was five times higher some 30 years ago.

18. Collier, Breaking the Conflict Trap, pp.53+.

19. Andreas Wenger and Daniel Mockli, *Conflict Prevention: The Untapped Potential of the Business Sector* (Riener, Boulder, CO), 2003, p. 8.

20. See also Jane Nelson, *The Business of Peace; Investing in Stability: Conflict Risk, Environmental Challenges and the Bottom-Line*, UNEP Finance Initiative, paper presented at the symposium AEnvironment for Peace: The Role of the Business Sector in Germany, Oct 2003.

21. See Rod McAlister at Business and Conflict website: www.businessand conflict.com

22. Thomas Friedman, *Flat Earth* (Farrar, Straus and Giroux, NY), 2005.

23. Richard Florida, "The World is Spiky," *Atlantic Monthly*, October, 2005, pp.48-51.

24. Prahalad and Hammond, 2005, pp.99-112.

25. See for example, Robert Chambers, *Ideas for Development* (Earthscan, London), 2005; David Korten, *Getting to the 21st Century*, (Earthscan, London) 1990; Richard A. Yoder, Calvin W. Redekop, & Vernon Jantzi, *Development to a Different Drummer* (Good Press), 2004.

26. The major findings are presented in Master's theses by Delores and Thomas Yaccino (1992) at the Wheaton College Graduate School, Wheaton, Illinois, and used in further research at Cornell University.

27. Jeffrey Sachs, *The End of Poverty*, (New York: Penguin Press), 2005, p.80.

28. Mark Husbands, Bible and Theology Professor, Wheaton College. Personal conversation.

4

Tentmaking Uncovered

Patrick Lai

This chapter is a brief summary of the data compiled from my research, *Problems and Solutions for Enhancing the Effectiveness of Tentmakers Doing Church Planting in the 10/40 Window*. The central question of the research was the "effectiveness of tentmakers working in restricted access nations in doing evangelism, discipleship and church planting." By discovering the areas in which workers in the 10/40 Window are effective, discernable traits and patterns of productive tentmakers are revealed.

To clarify, productivity or effectiveness is defined in terms of evangelism (men and women won to Christ), discipleship (teaching/training new believers) and church planting (believers gathered into worshipping bodies). The survey sample was taken from 450 workers serving within the 10/40 Window. The 10/40 Window was chosen because that is where the greatest need for evangelism, discipleship and church planting exists. It is also the area where a tentmaking strategy is believed to be most needed and effective, as many countries are closed to regular missionary work. A worker includes all types of missionaries, including tentmakers, who are laboring for the sake of Jesus Christ.[1]

Revelations and Recommendations

Despite some limitations, this is the most extensive and thorough survey ever done on tentmaking. Factors in the background, education, training, motivation, life, ministry and work of those serving in the 10/40 Window have been identified and related to their effectiveness in serving Jesus Christ. Many myths about tentmaking may be dispelled by this research. The findings of this survey may be utilized immediately (with appropriate caution) to help recruit, train and send workers.

The survey is broken down into four major sections: "Pre-field Experiences," "Motivation for Overseas Service," "Present Ministry: Life and Work on the Field," and "Personal Background." "Pre-field Experiences" has four sub-sections, while "Present Ministry" has thirteen sub-sections. The conclusions written here follow the outline of the survey.

This chapter is too brief to explain the binomial equation developed to construct and test the hypothesis and the resulting distribution curve. The weighting values for questions focused on evaluating the workers effectiveness solely in evangelism, discipleship, and church planting. I recognize there are other important areas that contribute to the life and ministry of a worker, but for this research that was the focus. The effectiveness scores for each worker have been separated into two main categories, "positive effectiveness" and "negative effectiveness." Questions or factors that increase the worker's effectiveness are considered good, or positive. Questions or factors, which if not done, hinder a worker from being effective are considered bad or negative. Each area of positive and negative effectiveness was broken down by rank into four categories/factors: "excellent," "superior," "good" and "fair." There were also questions that were in the middle of the bell curve which showed no effect on the worker's effectiveness. "Excellent positive effectiveness" is the highest possible score, meaning the question is very important to the effectiveness of the workers. "Excellent negative effectiveness" indicates that the question, if answered in this way, has the worst effectiveness on the worker's productivity.

To help the reader match these conclusions to the questions in the survey, where a question, or part of a question, is copied into this paper, I have *italicized* the words from the survey question. Thus, italics are not used for emphasis. Quotations will be used for emphasis. It is also helpful to know that within each section or sub-section, those factors that are stronger indicators of effectiveness are discussed first. The earlier a point is discussed within a section or sub-section, the higher its value in determining the effectiveness of the worker. This is not a complete review of the research but a summary of pertinent highlights.

The questions and conclusions of the first two main sections of the survey should be helpful to senders, trainers and recruiters of workers. These two sections are entitled "Your Pre-field Experiences" and "Your Motivation for Overseas Service." The questions from "Your Pre-field Experiences" reveal factors that effective workers practiced before going to the field; thus, these practices should be encouraged among those who would follow in their footsteps. The questions from "Your Motivation for Overseas Service" reveal some motives effective workers have for living and working overseas. Understanding the pre-field experiences and the motivations that God has used to lead effective/productive workers overseas should help church and mission leaders in training and evaluating new candidates, so as to better equip them for serving the Lord overseas.

Pre-Field Experiences

Church and Spiritual Life

In considering the worker's pre-field church and spiritual life, two factors stand out. The first "good" factor concerns the worker's *daily devotional life*. Workers who did not have a daily devotional life prior to moving overseas are clearly less effective than those who did. Thus, in recruiting and preparing workers to serve overseas, it is important to examine each potential candidate's devotional life. If a candidate does not have a good daily devotional life, I would want to know why and offer to give them some suggestions in how to upgrade their devotional life. I'd also suggest they reapply to the mission when their devotional life is good and consistent.

The second "good" factor concerns *workers who were personally discipled by someone more mature in the Lord* before going overseas. Workers who were discipled by others are more effective. Thus, I would want to ask potential candidates, "Who discipled you?" "How were you discipled?"

In this sub-section there are eight other questions that showed no impact, good or bad, on the effectiveness of a worker. However, it should be noted that over 80 percent of those surveyed *attended church regularly;* set *aside special times to study the Word, pray, and meditate*; were *commissioned/sent out as a missionary or tentmaker by a home church; regularly experienced the power of answered prayer*; and *regularly read Christian books or magazines.*

Preparation & Training

A large percentage of workers had training in either missions or Bible school/seminary. A solid majority (78 percent) had training in missiology. A majority of the workers had both Bible and missiological training. The workers prepared themselves in traditional ways by attending Bible school/seminary (65 percent), missiological training courses (78 percent), short-term trips (80 percent), and language training (55 percent). Nearly 30 percent completed all four. This is thorough preparation and training, indicating that the message of getting training before going overseas is getting across.

In this section one "superior" point stood out from the others. The most effective way workers can prepare to serve overseas is to *invest one or more years ministering with international students*. This question should be asked of all potential candidates, "Are you, or have you ministered to international students? – Explain." The research reveals that ministering with international students before going overseas is the best way to prepare. Candidates who desire to enhance their probability of being effective on the field should minister with international students before moving overseas. Conversely, the survey reveals that workers who do not spend time ministering to internationals before going overseas will actually decrease their chances of being effective. The question in the survey was phrased as *ministering to international "students."* However, I believe working with internationals or immigrants in the community would be equally beneficial. The point here is to tell potential workers to get out and minister to internationals in their community or school.

In addition to working with international students, there are three other points on the "good" level that decreased a potential worker's effectiveness. One, workers who did not have *missiological or cross-cultural training* are more likely to be ineffective. Having cross-cultural training does not guarantee success, but not having it increases the worker's chances of being ineffective. This tells us that workers should be strongly encouraged to get at least a few weeks of cross-cultural training before moving overseas.

The second point related to a worker's *marriage*. Workers whose marriages were not good *(spiritually, emotionally and sexually)* before going overseas have a good probability of being ineffective. Again, having a good marriage does not mean the worker will succeed, but not having a good marriage before setting out greatly increases the worker's chances of being unproductive on the field. When interviewing candidates, their marriages need to be thoroughly evaluated, and major issues need to be resolved before sending them abroad.

Third, a curious revelation is that workers who *told others that they would be a tentmaker*; are less effective. Workers who said nothing about being a tentmaker are not more effective, but there is a mild indication that those who intended to be tentmakers are less effective. This points to a trend that workers/tentmakers who are focused on work (their entry strategy job) appear to be less effective.

One "good" score, is that workers who have some *training in how to learn a language* are more effective than those who do not. Sending organizations need to emphasize taking time to receive training in missiological/cross-cultural ministry and language learning.

Though short-term trips do not enhance or hurt a worker's effectiveness, 80 percentage of all the workers went on short-term trips before moving overseas. Nearly 30 percent of these workers had their short-term experience in the country they are presently living in. Clearly short-term trips do
impact the worker's decision to serve overseas, but have no impact on their
success once on the field.

Those workers who attended Bible college or seminary do not prove to
be any more effective than those who did not. That does not mean going to
a Bible college or seminary is bad; it only means that such experiences neither help nor hinder the worker's effectiveness in their ministry of evangelism, discipling, and church planting. Admittedly, this research did not explore the personal and spiritual value individual workers may gain from
such training and how that training may impact the worker while living
overseas. However, the traditional way of preparing workers for the field is
to have them go to a Bible college or seminary. If organizations wish to
send candidates to Bible college or seminary to equip them in their spiritual
life, or to serve in churches or among Christians overseas, this training may
be valid. But for those candidates intending to minister to non-Christians in
the 10/40 Window, attending a Bible college or seminary does not enhance
the worker's effectiveness.

Nearly 88 percent of the workers were committed to joining a team before going overseas. This is encouraging because it shows people understand the value of teams; however, being committed to a team before going
overseas has no bearing on a worker's effectiveness.

The data was gathered from around the world with 93 percent of those
surveyed being from the West and 73 percent from North America. Nearly,
100 percent of workers spoke English well enough to pray and teach in it
before going overseas; however, the ability to speak English has no bearing
on the worker's effectiveness.

Work Place

This sub-section turned up only two factors of interest, and both of them
rated "good" and are negative. First, those *who worked in a secular job at
home, similar to the type of work they are doing now overseas* are less effective. Second, *workers who had training for getting a business started
overseas* before going overseas are also less effective. Both of these points
may seem unexpected, but my experience would agree that such workers
are so committed to their jobs that they are all work and no ministry. As is
confirmed in other areas of this research, workers who place a high emphasis on their secular job often do not do much evangelistic ministry either
inside or outside of the workplace.

Workers who were *self-employed*, or *set up their own business*, or *had
a leadership position in their job* scored higher than others, but not high

enough to make conclusive statements about the effectiveness of having these experiences before going overseas. Over 77 percent of the workers are currently working in jobs overseas that are different from what they did back home. The amount of time they worked at their jobs before going overseas has no impact on their effectiveness.

Witnessing

Because the plumb-line for effectiveness in this study is evangelism, discipleship and church planting, it is not surprising to find seven questions in this section on "Witnessing," which have a bearing on the effectiveness of the worker. Three "superior" factors tell us that before going overseas very effective workers *regularly did personal or campus evangelism or house-to-house visitation*; *led one or more evangelistic Bible studies with non-Christians*; and *described their involvement with the majority of new believers they helped to bring to Christ as a "close friendship."* These points should be a part of any organization's evaluation of perspective candidates. Obviously, those who are better witnesses at home are more likely to be better witnesses overseas. The survey tabulations reveal that on the average the workers led one to five people to the Lord before going overseas. The general trend for this section indicates that more workers are interested and/or experienced in doing discipleship than evangelism.

Still important, positive, and on the "good" level, those workers *who led more than 20 people to Christ* before going overseas have a good chance of being effective overseas. It is clear that the more people a worker led to Christ before going overseas, the higher the probability of their being effective.

Finally, there are three other indicators of effectiveness on the "fair" level, which have lower values than the four already stated. *Workers who before going overseas evangelized people other than their own culture or race* scored better than those who did not. This reminds us of the value of ministering with internationals before going overseas. The other two indicators relate to discipleship. Workers scored well who said that *over half of those who they had discipled before going overseas are doing well and are active in a church or ministry.* Workers *who discipled more than 20 people before going overseas* also enhanced their probability of being effective. As with witnessing, the more people the workers discipled, the higher their probability of being effective. Again, recruiters/senders should take note and ask candidates specific questions about the people they are witnessing to and discipling. Candidates should be asked to give at least one of the people they have discipled as a reference. Workers who have not done much evangelism or discipleship before going overseas should set aside a period of time to get trained and apply that training before being sent out.

Candidates should have the experience of being a witness and being personally discipled.

Other questions in this sub-section yielded no results about effectiveness. Though doing evangelism clearly enhanced the worker's effectiveness, doing *evangelism through a church*, taking *evangelism courses*, being *told they have the gift of evangelism* or focusing *on co-workers or neighbors* have no impact on effectiveness.

Motivation for Overseas Service

In seeking to understand the worker's motivation for overseas service, there are over thirty indicators placed in the survey. Only three of these showed a slight blip on the radar screen of effectiveness.

For those who saw themselves as tentmakers, none of their motivations for tentmaking positively impacted their effectiveness. The two most common answers given are *the country does not provide missionary visas* (90 percent) and *being a tentmaker is a more credible/natural way to witness than being a regular missionary* (72 percent). Though most of the listed motivations bore no impact on the worker's effectiveness, two motivations had a negative influence; both are on the "good" level. Tentmakers scored poorly who chose to go into tentmaking because *they enjoyed their job back home and wanted to use it to glorify God overseas;* similarly, *tentmakers who wanted to use their secular education and training for God* scored poorly. Again, workers who predetermine the job/training they wish use to glorify God overseas are not effective. It may sound good to glorify God with your job or your education, but is the emphasis on you or God? Is it God's idea, or man's? Other reasons for being a tentmaker had neither good nor bad effects on the worker; only these two negative reasons stood out. Thus, workers who choose to enter into tentmaking because of *a calling;* or *it's the only way into the unreached people group*; or from a *desire to identify as something other than a Christian worker*; or because they *believe tentmaking is more credible* should be effective overseas.

As a tentmaker, I will throw the first stone and advocate that aspiring tentmakers take a closer look at their motivation for serving overseas, at least if they wish to prove effective in outreach. We need to be aware that tentmakers may become so focused on their entry job, they will not be effective in ministry. Our motivation needs to be God-centered, not self-centered. As a T-3 tentmaker,[2] I would like to take issue with this, but as a missiologists, I wish to accurately report what the findings have uncovered. Though the research did not cover this issue, having interviewed over seventy tentmakers for this research and the books I am writing on tentmaking, I sense that workers who are focused on their job are not balanced in doing ministry. Tentmakers need training in balancing their job and ministry.

A "fair" indicator of positive effectiveness is that those who *read books on missions/missionaries* are slightly effective.

The most frequently attended missions conference is "Urbana," and the most attended missions training course is "Perspectives." These would be good places for recruiters to go to fish for recruits. Recruiters/senders should be asking candidates, "What is your motivation for doing tentmaking?" "Are you reading books about missions and missionaries?"

There are three questions in the survey relating to "God's calling." Having a calling from God to work/serve overseas did not generate any impact on a worker's effectiveness. The most common answers given as influencing the worker's motivation to serve overseas are *a desire to be a witness* and *talking with missionaries*. However, neither of these points registered on the effectiveness scale. Yet, as a step toward moving people overseas, we need to get them reading and talking with field workers.

Present Ministry: Life and Work on the Field

"How do I live and work on the field in order to be productive?" This is a commonly asked question by people considering service among the unreached. This section of the survey was written to answer that question and others like it. The final two sections of the survey are entitled "Present Ministry: Life and Work on the Field" and "Personal Background Information." These questions and conclusions should be helpful to field personnel and especially field leaders. This information should help leaders understand the issues workers are facing on the field. By understanding what works and what does not work in the areas of evangelism, discipleship and church planting, leaders should be able to enhance the effectiveness of their people.

Social and Personal Life

There are fifteen questions in this sub-section which had a bearing on the worker's effectiveness. The questions are discussed in order of their weightiness.

The first point scored "excellent," but was actually a gauge of ineffectiveness. Workers who said, *it is hard for me to socialize with nationals* have an "excellent" probability of being ineffective. On the other side of the coin, workers who said that *most of my closest friends are nationals,* and workers who *have nationals in their home (not counting servants) 3 times a week or more* are "superior" in their good effectiveness. Over 70 percent of the workers maintain a higher standard of living than most nationals. Yet, workers who have a *higher standard of living compared to their national co-workers* also score "superior" in positive effectiveness. Though my personal experience says that living among the people is greatly appreciated by the nationals, living above or at the level of the people has no negative implications on the worker's evangelism, discipleship and church planting. Workers, who have *free time, and spend that time with their family or alone*, are "superior" toward ineffectiveness. The implication is the more time we invest with the locals, the more effective we will be.

On the "good" level, it is affirmed that time spent with non-believers is key to seeing them come to Jesus. Workers who *have taken a vacation with national friends* enhance their good effectiveness, while those who do not are shown to be less effective. Clearly, workers who have close national friends enable them to see their lives up close and be attracted to what they see. What we eat and how we dress is important but not as important as how we relate to people. The importance of being with locals, or "logging hours," is repeated again in the understanding that workers who *visit in nationals' homes 3 times a week or more* are of "good" effectiveness. Workers who *eat the national or local food more than their own cultural food* show a positive effectiveness. This affirms that workers who are comfortable with the people and the culture are apt to be more effective.

On the "good" level, but negative, workers *who abstain from foods the nationals abstain from* are "superior" in ineffectiveness. On the negative side, workers *who worry they will get sick from the unclean foods and the unhealthy environment*s are less effective. Obviously, it is important to feel at home in the culture, wherever you are. Workers *who usually dress like their national friends or co-workers* also turn out to be less effective. Abstaining from foods and dressing like the nationals prove to be unhelpful. Perhaps contextualization is not as important a factor in reaching the unreached as we thought. As stated in the "Pre-field" factors, workers who report their *marriage is not good (spiritually, emotionally and sexually)* are less effective. Obviously, moving to the field does not improve a couple's marriage problems. It is essential to teach our workers the value of a good marriage and that evangelism begins at home.

A large number of workers (65 percent) *eat local food the way the locals do* and *abstain from foods locals abstain from* and *dress the way locals dress*. However, this research reveals that none of these factors make a difference in winning the people to Jesus. The primary lesson to be learned is that the time a worker spends with the people and the worker's personal comfort with the culture are much more important than strategy or contextualization. It is interesting to note that fears/concerns about a worker's children or children's education do not have a negative bearing on the worker's effectiveness. It is encouraging that 84 percent of all workers feel they were *adequately prepared for living cross-culturally*, and though adequate preparation may be helpful for their longevity in the country, it had no bearing on their effectiveness.

There was not enough variance in scores related to the worker's standard of living to make any definite conclusions, apart from stating that the worker's standard of living compared to nationals does not have an impact on effectiveness. Thus, whether the worker's houses are culturally styled like a local's home, styled after their home culture, or a mixture of both it had no affect on effectiveness. The way a worker lives in relationship to other expatriates did not impact effectiveness either. Workers may go home because they cannot get along with a team member, but it does not affect their outreach. Rich and poor workers are the same when compared to one another; neither the rich or poor worker is more effective than the other. Well over 75 percent of the workers *live in homes that are decorated with a mixture of items from the local culture and their own culture.*

Spiritual Life

Workers often struggle to maintain their spiritual, mental and physical well being while on the field. The strongest spiritual factor relating to effectiveness is that those who practice *fasting as an important spiritual discipline* score "excellent" in good effectiveness. Only 43 percent of the workers fast. I do not remember ever having even one lesson in seminary or in my missiological training on fasting. Could fasting be more important than Bible study? More important than prayer? Yes, and yes, at least when it comes to effectiveness in evangelism, discipleship and church planting.

There are four more indicators that render a very slight "fair" score on the worker's effectiveness; three are positive and one negative. Workers who *consistently set aside special times to study God's Word, pray and meditate*, and workers who *regularly read Christian books or magazines or listen to message tapes* are slightly more effective. Both issues point to the need to be feeding our spirits regularly. While Bible study and prayer do have a positive impact on the worker's ministry, fasting scored much higher. Also, workers who, a*part from meal time prayers pray together regularly with their spouse* show a slightly higher positive effectiveness. On the down side, workers *who on the average invest 45 minutes or less a day in Bible devotions or quiet time, or biblical reflection, study or prayer* are ineffective. Workers who invest more than forty-five minutes in the Word and prayer each day are not necessarily more effective, but workers who spend less than forty-five minutes in the Word and prayer daily are to a small degree, less effective than other workers.

The good news is that 85 percent of all workers *have a daily devotional*, but interestingly, having a daily time in the Word and prayer has no influence on effectiveness. Another encouraging figure is that 87 percent of the workers are *experiencing the power of prayer*, though this also does not show any affect on outreach. Leaders should take note that 39 percent of the workers expressed a need for more spiritual support from co-workers and leaders.

Home or Sending Church Relationship

Sending churches are very much involved in the lives of their workers. Exactly 90 percent of the workers were commissioned by their home church, and 92 percent are in regular contact with their home church. Nonetheless, the home church is not making much of a contribution to the effectiveness of the workers.

There are no strong effectiveness indicators in this section. Only a few questions scored in the "fair" range. The data shows that *workers who send out prayer letters and have over 151 people committed to praying for them* and workers *who receive communication from their sending church on a quarterly basis* are to a small degree, positive in effectiveness. Churches that communicate with their workers quarterly will enhance their workers effectiveness.

Though it did not impact their effectiveness, workers appreciated being held accountable by their home churches. Over 65 percent said they are *satisfied with the spiritual and emotional support of their sending church*, but that means 45 percent are not satisfied. Moreover, 30 percent of the workers send prayer letters home on a monthly basis; 28 percent do so bi-monthly; and 35 percent write quarterly.

Identity and Visa

There are four questions in this sub-section of the survey that have a solid bearing on effectiveness. Workers who *have a tourist visa or social visit visa* are found to be ineffective on the "superior" level. A bit lower value, on the "good" level, and on the positive side, workers who are *a missionary sent out by a missions organization AND recognized as a missionary/Christian worker by the people they minister and live with* have good effectiveness. This reveals that those who are perceived as missionaries both at home and overseas are likely to be effective. This may be expected as such workers do not have to deal with a job, security issues, dual identity, work income, and other issues which set tentmakers apart from regular missionaries. Workers who are *perceived as a missionary by friends at home, but something other than a missionary or Christian worker by my friends overseas* are slightly less effective. Workers who *have a resident visa* or *employment pass* or *work visa* are positively effective on the "fair" level.

None of these findings are surprising as the T-1, T-2, and T-3 tentmakers may be seen as the opposite of the missionary. Missionaries have only one job to fulfill, while tentmakers have at least two jobs. Missionaries work for one boss, and whether they succeed or not in their job, they still get paid. Tentmakers have dual roles and work for at least two bosses – the mission and the business. Though many tentmakers evangelize through their job, discipleship and church planting often take place in another context, outside of work. Tentmakers cannot fail at their job, lest they be fired or the business goes broke. Thus, the issues tentmakers face are more complex and logically lead to their being less effective than regular missionaries in doing ministry.

Missionaries living on a *missionary visa* are no more effective than others. It is clear that the visa the workers hold is not as important as how the workers are perceived by the locals. Those who have a tentmaking job are also affected by their secular activities, which will in turn influence their effectiveness. Non-Residential Missionaries (NRMs) or Strategic Coordinators (SCs) are neither effective nor ineffective. In their defense, this is to be expected as their main job is to facilitate others and not do evangelism, discipleship or church planting.

Field or Overseas Church Relationship

On the highest level of good effectiveness, "excellent", the workers who are *regularly involved with a national congregation or house church that uses the local language* are very effective. This could be because the workers have already planted the church they are meeting in. On the "good" level are two negative points on effectiveness; workers who *regularly attend an expatriate/foreigner church or fellowship that speaks their native language* and workers who *regularly attend an expatriate/foreigner English speaking church/fellowship* are less effective. Clearly, workers who regularly attend an expatriate and/or English speaking church have a higher probability of being less effective. Whenever possible, workers should worship in the language of the people.

One other question in this section concerned workers who *are in active fellowship with other tentmakers or missionaries in the area.* Being in fellowship with other tentmakers had no bearing, good or bad, on the worker's effectiveness. Whereas about half of the workers attend English-speaking churches, 89 percent are in fellowship with other tentmakers.

Witnessing and Ministry Overseas

This sub-section contains many indicators of both good and negative effectiveness; it also includes the eighteen "defining questions." These defining questions are omitted from my comments, as they were the basis for defining an effective worker. Certainly, the workers who planted a church would score very high on the church planting questions.

The highest scoring question in the "excellent" range that is not a "defining question" involves workers who *have experienced a demonic confrontation.* It is logical that those who have encountered demons are likely to be more effective, due to the fact that one step in some people's conversion is the casting out of demons. Workers who are active in evangelism are going to deal with spiritual warfare issues. There are two questions that scored very high in effectiveness but in negative ways. Workers *who find it hard to initiate conversations about their faith* are "excellent" at being ineffective, along with workers *who share their faith only when obvious situations arise. I don't force opportunities to evangelize.*

Continuing this theme of "reluctant workers," on the "superior" level, several questions validated the ineffectiveness of workers who did not proactively seek to share their faith. Workers who *prefer not to verbally share their faith, but rather let their life be a witness* and *workers who usually try to build relationships with people before sharing their faith* proved to be highly ineffective. These questions tell us that workers who stress building relationships before sharing their faith are likely to be less effective. This may be due to the small number of relationships one person can be involved in at one time; little sowing yields little reaping. This is a plug for trainers to stress confrontational evangelism, proclamation, and other evangelistic strategies in their training. Location also proved to be a detriment to many worker's productivity. Workers who felt that *where I live, it is unwise or improper for me to share my faith verbally* were highly ineffective. It cannot be determined if it is truly "unwise" to share in the area the worker lives, or if that is just the worker's perception. Workers who *said it is illegal to witness openly in the country where I live* and who are *working with a people group that does not have even one indigenous church among their people in the country they are ministering in,* also scored high in ineffectiveness. This is logical in that workers serving in more highly restricted access nations will have a lower effectiveness, due to the greater number of barriers that need to be overcome to share the Gospel. On the opposite side of the spectrum, workers who *actively seek opportunities to verbally share their faith with everyone* are "superior" in positive effectiveness. Being bold in taking opportunities to share one's faith has proven to be effective. Workers who *take risks* are more effective.

Workers who said *there are no hindrances to the local Christians evangelizing all people* are a bit more positively effective. This seems logical, for if workers serve in areas where there are no hindrances to local Christians evangelizing all people, then sowing the Gospel would be easier, or at least less risky. The involvement of the *local churches in reaching the unreached people group* has no bearing on the worker's effectiveness. The fact that local *Christians may actively witness to the unreached people* does not impact a worker's effectiveness. These points indicate that though the worker's effectiveness may be helped by the openness of the country to the Gospel, the activities of the local church have no impact on a worker's effectiveness. Whatever people group or segment of society the workers are focusing on makes no difference, good or bad, on their effectiveness.

Workers usually meet people via language learning and through established friends.

Adopted Country/People Group

In this sub-section of the survey there were only two questions which impacted the worker's effectiveness, and then only very slightly, on the "fair" level. Workers who serve in countries *where the government has arrested or deported people for witnessing/converting people* are a bit more effective. Persecution does hamper our effectiveness. In addition, workers serving in areas where the *official religion of my area is tribal-animistic* are slightly more effective.

Serving in *countries that allow religious freedom to distribute literature*; *that grant missionary visas*; and have *religious freedom to live freely and witness* has no impact on the worker's effectiveness. *Nationals who are given the religious freedom to witness* to anyone, and having *freedom for converts to openly practice Christianity* does not alter the worker's effectiveness. The percentage of believing Christians within the worker's city and within the people group a worker is reaching also has no influence on the worker's effectiveness.

Language

Experienced workers will not be surprised to learn that language fluency rated among the highest factors in the effectiveness of the workers. Two language questions are placed among the highest scores on the "excellent" level of positive effectiveness.

Workers who said they are *fluent in the local language* scored among the highest in the whole survey. Conversely, workers who said *I am learning the language but I have not been here long enough to be fluent* had among the lowest scores in the survey. Though these workers have not been overseas very long, it again stresses the importance for good language.

In line with this point, workers who said they *minister to the people in their heart language* scored "superior," while those who said they *minister to the people in English or their native language* are very ineffective. Workers who *read the newspaper in the local language 2 or more times a week* also prove to have very good effectiveness.

Less important and in the positive "good" range are workers who replied that *they have written letters or articles in the local language*. This is another indicator that fluency is a key to seeing fruit in evangelism and church planting.

The scoring consistently reveals that the more fluent the workers are, the more effective they will be. Though fluency will increase the potential of the worker's effectiveness, speaking through a translator has no effect, on a worker's ministry. Also, the number of languages the local people speak has no impact on the worker's effectiveness.

Security

There are just two questions in this sub-section that impact the effectiveness of workers. Both are on the "good" level, only slightly influencing effectiveness, and both are negative. Workers who *have had to lie to ensure the success of a business deal* are less effective. Obviously, our character will affect not only our walk with God but our relationships with humans, as well. This may also indicate that these workers place a higher value on doing business than on other aspects of their life and work. Workers who said their *home church has never jeopardized their security* are a bit less effective. Turning that around means that workers who have had their home church jeopardize their security are more likely to be effective. That causes one to think, until we remember that this survey has been distributed among workers in the 10/40 Window where security concerns are important. Thus, this is logical on two counts. One, workers who are aggressive in evangelism will be at a higher risk than those who are not, and workers who are aggressive in evangelism are more effective. Two, in comparison with related questions, we find that workers who often take risks have a high degree of effectiveness. If this is true, taking risks is important for effectiveness and explains why those who have not had their home church jeopardize their security are slightly less effective.

The church's understanding of the worker's security needs bears no impact on the worker's effectiveness. Workers who *worry about security and the safety of one's family* or *have stress caused by having to leave the field* reveal that such worries do not alter their effectiveness. Yes, it may impact other areas of their lives, even their longevity in the country, but it does not influence their outreach. As many questions in this sub-section had no affect on the worker's effectiveness, it is safe to assume that security issues have little impact on effectiveness. The fact that 84 percent of the workers feel their church understands their needs for security and 88 percent are satisfied with the care and help their mission has shown them during times of sickness and stress bodes well for both the churches and the missions agencies.

Accountability

There are six accountability questions which impact effectiveness. By far the most important positive factor, scoring "excellent," is that workers who *have a clear strategy for planting a church* are very effective, while workers who do not have a clear church planting strategy are ineffective.

On the "superior" level, we discover that workers who *have someone hold them accountable in ministry... monthly* have a good probability of being effective, compared with others who are held accountable less frequently. On a negative note, workers who said *they feel they are not accomplishing their original goals because...I had no goals in the beginning* and *because of family needs* scored high in ineffectiveness. Again, the value of setting goals is clear. Workers who are accomplishing their goals are a bit more effective, but workers who had no goals in the beginning are likely to be ineffective. Missions agencies need to help workers set goals at the beginning of their terms of service and evaluate those goals regularly. Workers who have emotionally needy families are also likely to be less effective. This is a warning to avoid what Phil Parshall calls, "raising families overseas," meaning workers may spend so much time with their families that it becomes detrimental to their ministry. The most popular answer indicates that many workers are held accountable by *team colleagues/members*, yet being held accountable by a fellow team member shows a slightly negative influence on the worker's effectiveness. Workers who hold one another accountable are less effective. Predictably, the worst answer is *no one*, telling us that not having any accountability will certainly hinder the worker's effectiveness.

Mission leaders should take note that nearly 50 percent of the workers wish they had more accountability in their lives. Eleven areas are listed in which workers would like more accountability; "character" and "relationship with God" are the top two.

Team

It is encouraging that 93 percent of all workers are on a team. Like language, the questions on team life drew some of the highest positive effectiveness scores outside of the "Witnessing" sub-section. Workers scored "excellent" who said they are *currently leading a team*. Workers were also "excellent" who *recruited others to join the team they are on* and who *recruited people to join other teams or other ministries*. Clearly, workers who recruit others to ministry have a very good probability of being effective.

On the negative "superior" level, workers who are on teams *where most or all team members work for the same company/school/project/organization* are less effective. Could this be because of a greater emphasis on the business? Thus, putting your eggs all in one basket may not be a good strategy. Workers are effective who serve on teams where *the team members are from more than one home country*.

On the positive, "good" level, those who are on teams where the *number of adults in the country who are considered to be on the team is 11-15*, are most effective. Interestingly, teams with sixteen or more workers are less effective than teams with ten or less team members. The data indicates the ideal team size is eleven or twelve members. A team becomes more effective as it increases from three to twelve, plateauing at fifteen, after which the effectiveness of the team decreases.

Workers whose *team meets... weekly or twice a month* are "fair," slightly more effective. The least effective are those teams that *meet once a month or rarely. Workers serving with a team where the nationalities of the team members are a mix of nationals and locals* are a tad more effective, so one expatriate working with a national team should be effective.

Being *a part of a team with similar goals* has no bearing on a worker's effectiveness; this is also true of a team where *all the team members are from the same missions agency. Agreeing to a team covenant* may help team life, but it has little impact on a worker's effectiveness. Finally, whether or not a *team pays the salaries of local Christian co-workers* has no bearing on the worker's effectiveness.

Work/Job Overseas

As the object of this study is to determine the factors that enhance the effectiveness/productivity of workers/tentmakers in the 10/40 Window, this section has great relevance for tentmakers. A positive "excellent" factor is that workers who say that *most of their co-workers are from the people group they are targeting* are very highly effective. For workers already overseas, this is a good question to determine a worker's effectiveness. Again, as we saw earlier, the more time workers spend with the people they are trying to reach, the more effective they will be. There are also two "excellent" negative indicators. Workers who answered that *most of their co-workers are expatriates or foreigners* are very highly ineffective. If a worker's place of employment/office does not have a least a few local employees from the focus people group, something should be done to increase their presence. Even hiring unskilled people and training them as secretaries or clerical staff would be an improvement. Another negative point is workers *who spend less than 1 hour a day working with their target people* are very likely to be ineffective. This reinforces the earlier point of bringing those you are trying to reach into your work place, so you may spend more time with them.

Workers who *have received an official commendation or award for their work performance* have good effectiveness. This reflects that doing good work in the office will carry over into the worker's witness/ministry and is a good reflection of the Lord to others. In addition, workers who *invest 3 or more hours a week of their free time in reading secular work related books/magazines etc.* are effective. This is in agreement with the point that those who read Christian books and magazines are also more effective. The key idea here may be that those who are continually learning new things are more effective. Those workers *who spend 1-2 hours a day work-*

ing with Christians are slightly more effective. The need to have employees who are of the people group that the worker is reaching supports this. In my interviews with tentmakers, more and more are discovering the power of "community" in the workplace. By this I mean, where there is more than one believer interacting with a non-believer, the impact of the Gospel on the non-believer may be exponentially increased. Workers who *on the average, work 1-2 hours each day in their secular job* are to a small degree, more effective. This favors the T-3 model, implying that those who can control their working hours and invest time building relationships both inside and outside of the office are more effective. Closely related to this, on the negative side, workers who see their *project as a cover to stay in the country and do little non-ministry work* have "good" ineffectiveness. Having a real job in a real workplace that allows flexible working hours seems to be the ideal tentmaking entry strategy. This works well for those who begin their own small businesses or NGO's so they can be their own bosses and have control of their time. Continuing with the theme of time, workers who do not *feel they have a proper balance of time between their project/job and ministry* are less effective. Workers who do not *feel their job performance is productive and a good witness* are ineffective. Those who work *for a company/project or boss who has told them not to witness to others* are less effective. Before accepting a position, workers need to read the fine print.

Workers whose local friends recognize them as something other than a *missionary* score in the "fair" range of ineffectiveness. Being a full-time missionary shows a small advantage over being a tentmaker. However, if a worker cannot be a missionary, being a "real" tentmaker has a great advantage over "faking it."

The workers whose *projects/businesses employ zero expatriates/foreigners and team members,* are a bit more effective. Again, comparing to other parts of this research, the best projects/businesses employ a mix of national believers and non-believers with a minimum of foreigners.

Having the *freedom to share his/her faith at work or with neighbors* does not impact a worker's effectiveness. Those who are tentmakers will find that work is not a hindrance to ministry; however being a fulltime missionary is advantageous to a small degree. When possible, being a missionary certainly has fewer hassles. Good workers find ministry opportunities both at work and at other places. *Using a business plan to start a project/business* does not impact a worker's effectiveness in ministry. Nonetheless I would strongly suggest new start-ups write one as it will affect the success of the business. *Workers serving on teams who operate their own project/business* are no more effective than those who do not. *Working closely with the government* has an impact on security but no bearing on the worker's effectiveness in doing ministry.

Money/Salary

There are only three questions in this sub-section which impact effectiveness and all in a minor way. Nearly 78 percent of the workers indicate they have sufficient income. The majority of workers' total income is between US$1,400 and US$2,800/month. Workers who say *my family's personal monthly salary from all sources, is under US$700/month* are less effective than workers who earn more. The majority of workers (61 percent) are fully supported by churches and friends. Exactly 68 percent receive no income from their tentmaking job. However, as 42 percent of the workers surveyed get their visas via NGO's, missions organizations or are T-5 tentmakers (fakers), that means only 21 percent of those who have tentmaking jobs, are not earning some income from their work. The source of the worker's personal monthly salary, whether the money comes from churches, individuals or their secular job, in no way alters the worker's effectiveness. The data concludes that more money does not increase the probability of the worker's positive effectiveness; however, *earning less than US$700/month* will enhance the probability of a worker's negative effectiveness.

The Lord's words, "It is more blessed to give than to receive" (Acts 20:35) certainly hold true. Workers who say *the approximate percent of their personal monthly income that they give or tithe to various ministries is more than 11 percent* are a tad more effective than those who give 10 percent or less. It is safe to say that a worker's effectiveness is enhanced when they give more.

Personal Background

This section contains data about individual workers. While it reveals a few surprises, most of the findings are common sense.

On the positive "excellent" level, workers who *have lived in their present country or among their target people group for more than 5 years* were found to be very highly effective. The reverse also proved true; *workers who have been overseas less than 2 years* are very ineffective. Clearly, the longer workers are overseas, the better their chances of being effective. Workers who said what they *seemed to enjoy most is starting new projects* also score "excellent." To a much lesser degree, those who said what they *seemed to enjoy most is managing projects* are "fairly" effective. Workers scored "good" on the negative side who said what *they seemed to enjoy most is one–on–one contacts with people* and *doing projects or technical work under the supervision of others.*

Workers who see themselves *as adventuresome, an entrepreneur, a risk taker,* score "superior" in positive effectiveness. Workers who see themselves as *taking calculated risks* or as *doing things that are "safe,"* or *prefer to do things where others lead and support them or the team* show no effect, good or bad. Workers who are of the *opinion that the ultimate objective of missions is the transformation of society to a godly life-style* are "superior" in good effectiveness. On the negative side, those who are of the *opinion that the ultimate objective of missions is winning people to Christ*, to a "fair" degree, are a tad less effective than others. Workers who are of the opinion that *the ultimate objective of missions is planting of reproducing churches*, or *the training of reproducing disciples* did not measure on any scale of effectiveness. Workers who are *married with children* show that those who have three children are to a "fair" degree, more effective than those who have more or less children. Singles, widows and divorcees are neither effective nor ineffective.

The most effective level of education for workers is a *masters degree* (35 percent). Exactly 6 percent of the workers have doctorate degrees and 45 percent have bachelor or university degrees. Only 3 percent of all workers *did not attend a college/university*. Workers have a positive "good" effectiveness when their *visa is currently provided by a small foreign business*, but none of the other entry strategies resulted in workers being marked effective or ineffective.

In studying the effectiveness scores closely, I attempted to prioritize the visa assignments that have a stronger relationship to positive effectiveness. This might not be the worker's actual job or identity, but it is the worker's government approved visa that permits the worker to legally reside in the country. The visas that are most likely to be effective in the 10/40 Window, in order of priority are as follows:

1. business/finance/administrative/marketing
2. medical/health care
3. missionary
4. school teacher
5. tie = computers & engineering/technical & science
6. tie = TESOL/TEFL & NGO/social services
7. student
8. tourist

Note, when "missionary" is compared with all "jobs," it is a slightly more effective entry strategy; however, when compared to the breakdown of these eleven jobs, it ranks third.

Workers who *have zero years of full-time Christian work experience before going overseas* enhance their probability of being ineffective. Beyond one year, the number of years spent serving in fulltime Christian work before going overseas has no bearing on effectiveness. Time is an important factor in effectiveness; the longer workers are overseas, the more effective they become.

Men and women are equally effective. Age is not an issue, whether it be the age of the worker, the age of becoming a Christian, or the age of moving overseas. Whether a worker's children are living with him/her or not, does not change the worker's effectiveness. The positions a worker served in the church before going overseas does not alter effectiveness. Finally the organization the missionary/tentmaker is associated with has no impact on effectiveness.

Summary

1 Corinthians 8:1-3 says, "We know that we all possess knowledge. Knowledge puffs up, but love builds up. The man who thinks he knows something does not yet know as he ought to know. But the man who loves God is known by God." I confess that during the past five years of writing, researching, speaking, and interviewing, my mind and heart have been "puffed up" at times. Yet in the end, I wish to proclaim that I recognize that the man who thinks he knows something does not yet know as he ought to know. True wisdom and true knowledge are found in loving God and obeying Him. This entire research has been done as a gift that I hope reflects my love for Jesus, a gift that by His empowerment may expedite the desire He has placed in my heart; that some day I may join with a great multitude that no one can count – people from every nation, tribe, people and language, standing before the throne and in front of the Lamb, crying out in a loud voice: "Salvation belongs to our God, who sits on the throne, and to the Lamb." Amen.

Discussion Starters

1. Which parts of the survey stand out to you? Why?

2. From your choices above, what are possible implications for spiritual development? Career development? Missiological development? Cross-cultural competency development?

Notes

1. Patrick Lai, *Tentmaking: Business as Missions*. Waynesboro, GA: Authentic Media, 2005.
2. Following is a tentmaker taxonomy I developed in which all tentmakers can identify themselves: T-1: no specific ministry call; primary motivation for being overseas is employment, not witness; T-2: specific ministry call; have plan for evangelism/discipleship and possibly church planting goals; ministry is their job and their job is their ministry; T-3: partially or fully financially supported by a church "at home;" similar to T-2, but work part-time or operate their own business; sees their job as a vehicle to enter the country first, a way for reaching out to people second, and a means of financial support last; T-4: fully supported as a missionary from "back home" and raise support like regular missionaries; not recognized as "religious professionals" by the people group; examples include missionary dentist, doctor, social worker, or even a student; T-5: regular missionary, not a tentmaker; working in areas that do not grant "missionary" visa; work for shell companies; have identity other than being a missionary; enter countries under a "cover."

5

Economic Development and Holistic Mission

David Befus

I do not ask for a house of steel,
Or even one built of stone;
But for the exultation to feel
The tug of muscle and bone.

Not for wealth or men at my command,
Nor peace when I am through –
I only ask work for these hands,
Work for these hands to do.[1]

The Missionary Legacy of Holistic Outreach: Health and Education

Salvation is the regeneration of the soul *and* transformation of the whole person to glorify God with the totality of their being. Missions have been at the forefront of demonstrating this phenomenon: "Separating gospel-as-word, gospel-as-deed and gospel-as-sign has serious consequences. In cultures in which words have lost their meaning, as is often the case in the West, deeds are necessary to verify what the words mean."[2]

The call to holism in Christian outreach has long been part of international missions, and demonstrated by significant investment in health and educational programs. As early as 1773 there were missionary physicians deployed with William Carey in India.[3] Another major part of that mission outreach was educational, resulting in the founding by William Carey of the Serampore College in 1818.[4] Mission hospitals and mission schools were characteristic of the holistic outreach of international missions in Africa, Asia, and Latin America in the 19th and 20th centuries.

The *Centro Evangelico*, a church in the low-income neighborhood of Blas de Leso, Cartagena, Colombia, is growing by leaps and bounds. Many have come to the church through its elementary school programs in the slum villages, where the church has taken the initiative for creating schools for the poor. Others come because of the health clinics and nutritional programs the church operates. But it is the Saturday training sessions in basic business skills that draw the largest crowds. Programs are designed to help create income opportunities for the poor, with new enterprise promotion of various types, and most targeted at women. The two morning services filled to overflowing! The multiple venues for evangelism and discipleship are attributed, to a large extent, to the programs of outreach in economic development.

U.S. Christians often hear reports of missionary doctors and teachers, but business and economics can also be tools for Christian ministry. Jesus taught us to pray: "give us this day our daily bread." There were no social welfare programs available when he taught this, and in the 21st century the world's poor majority want a job, not a handout. In environments like Northern Colombia, where thousands are displaced by civil war and unemployment is over 50 percent, the instructions of the Apostle Paul "to make it your ambition to lead a quiet life, to mind your own business and to work with your own hands, just as we told you, so that your daily life may with the respect of outsiders and that you will not be dependent on anybody" (1 Th 4:11-12) are seldom cited. Should any preacher dare to use this as a sermon text, "How do we do this?" would be the sure response. This chapter presents just that: an outline of how to promote productive economic activity so that people can earn their daily bread.

Economic Development: Adding a "New" Ministry Tool

Productive economic activity is a means to enhance and support Christian ministry. This phenomenon of "Kingdom business,"[5] though relatively unknown, has seen successful implementation in the church since the Apostle Paul first discussed his own work habits in his letters to young churches. He was quite clear that people should work to make a living, and returns to this theme in the second letter to the same church of Thessalonica, where he says, "if a man will not work, he shall not eat" (2 Th 3:10). But this is not always so easy to put in practice (either working or eating!) in a world where poverty and unemployment are commonplace.

Models are needed that combine economic development with a clear focus on holistic Christian outreach. They need to be integrated with church ministry and a clear emphasis on Christian witness. It is the love of money, not money itself that "is a root of all kinds of evil" (I Ti 6:10). God created economic activity, and gives us the ability to use this tool for good. God, the provider, reminds us to: "to remember the Lord your God, for it is he who gives you the ability to produce wealth..." (Dt 8:18, NIV). It is not the Internet, not neo-liberal economic models, not globalization or free markets, but our God who provides for us through productive work.

The potential of international economic outreach as a ministry tool goes beyond the blessing it brings as it incarnates the gospel. It can provide a socially understandable foundation for social interaction with those who do not know Jesus. It can empower and mobilize an entire new population, the marketplace people, to get involved in missions. Economic projects can address the critical resource constraints facing international ministry projects, creating innovative new structures for financial support.

God worked for six days in making the world we live in, and created man in His image to work. The encouragement to work is presented throughout the Scriptures, and the expectation that those who follow God's path for their lives will "work with your hands." Jesus teaches us to pray "give us this day our daily bread," and work (not alms) is the foundation for the realization of that prayer.

Historical Review: Missionary Economic Projects

The concepts presented in this chapter are not new. The history of the church is full of examples of the importance of productive economic activity:

*   Apostle Paul worked as a leather artisan to provide for his support. We find in his 1 Thessalonians "we worked night and day not to be a burden on you" (2:9) and in many other references (2 Th 3:7-9; 1 Co 9:6,18; Ac 20:34-35) that Paul wanted to fund his ministry through economic enterprise as an example for others. The reference in Acts 18 to "making tents" with Aquila and Priscilla is in reference to leather working, as mobile housing units were made from leather in those days, as they still are in some places in the Middle East today. Perhaps references to the armor of God in Ephesians 6 also come from Paul's leatherwork, as much of this armor was based on leather. For example, the shield can quench the fiery darts (vs. 16) because it was coated with leather that was soaked in water.

- Religious orders such as the Franciscans , Jesuits, and Benedictines[6] utilized productive economic activity to finance their programs, and gave a very important place to the concept of work. "I worked with my hands, and moreover wanted to work, and I desired that all the other Brothers be occupied with honorable work. And those who could do not work must learn it, not for the desire of remuneration, but to give a good example and not be lazy."[7]

- Some early Protestant denominations utilized productive economic activity to support ministry and as their foundation for international mission outreach. The spiritual unity of the Moravian Brethren in Europe was evidenced by communal economic enterprises in Europe: salt processing, clothing production, and even a brewery.[8] When the Moravians sent people to minister to the Indians in North America in 1741, their assumption was that the entire program be supported by economic activities: textiles, pottery, a tannery, and again, a brewery.[9] Though John Wesley disagreed with them on matters of doctrine, he praised their economic program: "you are not slothful in Business, but labour to eat your own Bread;, and wisely manage the Mammon of Unrighteousness, that ye may have to give to others also, to feed the Hungry, and cover the Naked with a Garment."[10]

- William Carey, the famous missionary pioneer mentioned previously as a promoter of health and education mission programs, was also a shoemaker. He taught that to be a missionary, it was necessary that a person have a work skill that would enable the person to sustain his or her needs in the chosen missionary environment. Even as he promoted health and educational projects, he also developed the concept of savings banks for India, helped establish the print industry, and even introduced the steam engine.[11]

Given the importance of work, the church should acknowledge the role of business people who are gifted entrepreneurs and administrators of productive economic activity. As was cited by one of the speakers at the Latin America CLADE IV meetings, there is a tendency in Christian society to "demonize the businessman, and the economic sector." The article generated by that meeting and published as chapter 7 of *"Palabra, Espiritu, y Mision,"* says that "in the church we need to create a space for the businessman, where making money is not an offense for those "called to the ministry."[12] Rather, those with gifts in business should be a blessing. "These hands of mine have supplied my own needs and the needs of my companions" (Ac 20:34), Paul says at the end of his ministry. We need more hands like that.

Five Types or Models of Economic Outreach[13]

The most common example of mission related economic activity, and one that is also seen in the church projects in Northern Colombia, is the **service business.** This model has the capability for generating revenue to cover its costs. These generally start out as ministry projects begun in response to a specific need for promoting health (clinics, hospitals, etc.), education (schools, literature distribution, etc.) or other ministry outreach such as camp programs and radio stations. Services may initially be offered for free, but a fee for service is often introduced to guarantee that the service is being valued[14] and to help to pay for costs. Over time, as donated support deteriorates, the cost of services is generally increased, and in many cases a two-tier fee structure allows ministries to charge commercial rates to clients who are able to pay, thus allowing the ministry to subsidize services to poorer target groups.

Another type of economic enterprise that has evolved in relation to overseas ministry is the **endowment enterprise**, commercial activity that is developed solely for the financial support of local ministry. The concept of "endowment" is well known in Western Christian institutions and is a contemporary cornerstone of the financing of most Christian colleges and seminaries. Overseas institutions also struggle with the need to create a long-range foundation for financial sustainability, facing fewer opportunities for local self-support due to a poorer national population, and also confronting donor fatigue. In this context many overseas ministries have created innovative businesses organized solely to generate funds for ministry, managed as completely separate units.

Sidebar 3.1

Ministry Service Businesses: The development of self-sustaining enterprises such as Christian clinics, dental offices, schools, and bookstores, where the ministry charges a fee for services. Some of these projects, like the Clinica Biblica (hospital) in Costa Rica, have grown to have multi-million dollar budgets. The Colegio Latino-americano in Cartagena, Colombia (elementary and high school) has over 800 students. Both of these projects were initiated by missionaries, developed national leadership, and have been run for several decades by national boards recruited from local church leadership.

Another example of the enterprise approach to funding ministry is Scripture Union of Lima, Peru. It supports its inner city program for street children with:

- A fleet of 20 taxis in Lima
- An additional 65 motorcycle taxis in Iquitos
- A riverboat ferry
- A bakery
- A carpentry shop
- A shoe factory
- A silk-screen T-shirt business
- A water purification plant
  Handicraft exports

Sidebar 3.2

Ministry Endowment Enterprises: A local foundation for long-term support of Christian ministry in the field. For example, the Granja Roblealto, an agricultural farm that produces chickens, pigs in Costa Rica, employs more the 90 people, but was created to support the children's ministries. It channels thousands of dollars of direct financial support to local Christian day care centers and other children's ministries. Entrepreneur donors, desiring to generate alternative support, were instrumental in this project.

The combined revenue from these enterprises totals almost $400,000 per year, a major portion of their ministry costs.[15] The employment created often involves the graduates of the street children program, who see work as the basis for support, rather than donations.

Related to the "endowment" approach is the use of the **"tentmaking" enterprise** to support ministry for the mobilization of missionaries from Latin America to the rest of the world. The local church in Latin America is generally not able to fund the full cost of expatriate ministry overseas. Innovative international business concepts are being developed to allow Latin American missionaries not only to generate a substantial portion of their costs from business activity, but also to secure visa permits. These "tentmaking" operations require business concepts that exhibit a comparative advantage in technology or markets that result in a viable and profitable enterprise, and are not just a "platform" to get into a country. An added benefit of this enterprise activity is that is creates a social context to meet and minister to local people that is often more understandable than "full time Christian worker" funded through donations.

The tentmaking enterprise approach is far more complicated than funding ministry from funds donated from abroad, but has become increasingly attractive in Latin America because donated funds are so difficult to access. In churches where the pastorate is bi-vocational because the local church cannot provide fulltime support, the concept of supporting fulltime workers overseas with donated funds becomes remote. The enterprise approach to international ministry is often the only realistic means to become a missionary.

Sidebar 3.3

Tentmaking Enterprises: Provide legal entry, financial support, and a ministry context for expatriates. A Mexican family is able to minister in a Muslim country because they set up a retail store, which provides the major part of their monthly income, as well a context for ministry. Another group in Mexico is sending out people with training in specialized ceramics, and in the restaurant business. In all of these cases the initial business concepts, loan funding for the projects, technology, product, supplies, and overseas connections involved expatriate missionary consultants.

The church in the developing world is increasingly confronted by the poverty that surrounds it, as economic globalization has resulted in declining levels of income for the poor majority. Responding to this situation, many ministry programs have added job creation to the traditional missionary outreach of health and education. The **business incubator** development approach is being used in these contexts to increase income levels and generate employment for church members, and as an evangelistic tool targeted at specific populations. The business incubator promotes viable business projects to create employment or generate income.

The incubator approach is applied in contexts where the population being served does not have a defined business concept, and the business idea comes from others who have experience and knowledge of the marketplace. Another increasingly popular approach to helping poor people in developing countries is **micro credit** programs. These programs require the development of sustainable revolving loan credit programs for people who have business experience and the capacity to manage a loan.

Sidebar 3.4

Business Incubators: The creation of new businesses for target populations in need of income or employment, but not having a background or experience in productive economic activity. The business idea is generated by the ministry. Training, production, sales, and all assets are controlled by the ministry until participants have learned to manage the business on their own. The Colombia church teaches women how to be hairdressers, and then set up a beauty shop. Ex-drug addicts in Mexico are taught how to make simple tortilla presses, using scrap wood. Through business activity, these young men learn to support themselves and stay off the street. As they are able, the production activity is transferred to their homes, the equipment provided is paid back, and the payback is used for new enterprises. (An entrepreneurial missionary started this.)

The reason that many mission organizations are interested in developing these projects, rather than relying on existing specialist agencies that do such work, is that the poor populations served by the church are generally not eligible for assistance from any other source. Furthermore, many existing Christian organizations that offer programs in the area of micro credit shun integration with church programs overseas, for fear that any direct involvement with church programs might adversely affect their rates return. At the same time, the interest rates that these agencies offer are often considered too high.

Church-based models have been created to do micro credit on a small scale that also allow for close ties between economic programs and ministry outreach. The success of these models is seen not only in rates of return and sustainability of the projects, but also in the economic benefits to those in the church, and outreach with those who do not know the gospel. Involvement in helping a person with their business allows for direct contact on an intensive level, and many opportunities for witness.

Though the type of productive economic activity varies in each of these five programs, there are some common economic training issues. These include at least the following: how to identify a viable business idea, where to obtain funding, definition of ownership, management oversight, and marketing (perhaps the most important).

> **Sidebar 3.5**
>
> **Micro Credit Programs:** Revolving loan programs for people who have a business idea, and usually some experience, and who, with additional capital, can generate funds to pay back the loan with interest. Generally requires an administrative unit capable of organizing basic paperwork, evaluating loan proposals, disbursing loans, providing training, collecting loans, and financial reporting. The OPDS program in Barranquilla, Colombia, is an LAM affiliate ministry with assignment of one LAM missionary family. It operates a small loans program averaging $350/family to allow poor people to begin to fully support their families, and many of these are displaced people from the civil war in Colombia. The economic programs are integrated with church outreach of the AIEC denomination.

A great challenge, once the concept of economic activity is accepted as a tool for ministry, is to avoid a trivialization of business activity, as if it were a simple matter. The organization of business enterprise as a ministry requires competitive technologies, prior definition of distribution of profits, and connections with ministry or church institutions. A critical point is to define and monitor the relationship between the enterprise activity and ministry outreach and local church.

Social Enterprise/Social Entrepreneurship in the Academic Arena

"A state is first of all an organization that provides public goods for its members, the citizens."[16] But the services provided by the public sector for citizens have collapsed in many countries of the world today, even while they are more necessary than ever. Government leaders in developed and developing countries are calling for approaches that address the terrible "weapon of mass destruction" called poverty, and economic development offers principles and specific cases where economic enterprise sustains social programs, generates income, and creates jobs for the poor.

Christians should be at the forefront of confronting the problem of an economic segment described by secular experts as "the bottom of the pyramid, where 4 billion people reside, whose per capita income is less than $1,500 per year."[17] Ironically, this is a challenge from a business professor famous for strategic planning. When the prestigious University of Michigan inaugurated a new president in March, 2003, it was this professor of business administration taking a prophetic stand: "If Michigan is to realize its potential as a global university, it must aspire to new and larger goals, including serving the poor."[18] Many professionals troubled by current world economic trends echo this challenge. "Although major strides were made after 1960 in lowering rates of poverty and improving life expectancy, education and health standards, the tragedy of the 1980s and 1990s was that progress was halted and even reversed for many countries as economic stagnation eroded the gains of the past decades."[19]

Over the past five years a "social enterprise" network has developed in the U.S. business community, with a conscious focus on using business as a tool to help the poor. The book *Compassionate Capitalism* was published in 2004, and "is dedicated to corporate leaders who strive to use the resources of their companies to make the world a better place..."[20] Social entrepreneurship is now promoted as a career track in some prestigious MBA schools, promoted in business magazines, and generating an entirely new area of business research.[21] Prahalad's book, *The Fortune at the Bottom of the Pyramid* (2005) is subtitled *Enabling Dignity and Choice Through Markets*. This bestseller in the business community is about using business to help the poor![22]

The Bible is overwhelming in promoting care for the poor; Jesus came to "lift up the humble, and to fill the hungry good things" (Lk 1:53). There are more poor people today than at any time in history and in many cases they are getting poorer. For example, economists have noted, "Africa, south of the Sahara, accounted for only about 1 percent of total world trade in the 1990s."[23] It is not even part of the world economy, but is a place for where the ministry of economic development is needed. As missions integrate economic ministry with their outreach, they become part of a movement of social entrepreneurship that exhibits the concept of "doing good" described in the letter to Titus: "Our people must learn to devote themselves to doing what is good, in order that they may provide for daily necessities and not live unproductive lives" (3:14, NIV).

Proposal for Missionary Enterprise/Missionary Entrepreneurship

The context of a business project presents wonderful opportunities for Christian witness. Beyond Sunday or evening participation in church, one can see how a person relates to their family, to their employees, how they use their time, and their money. The Bible is rich in lessons drawn from the world of business, and it is very easy to integrate administrative training with faith lessons.

The economic development program of the Centro Evangelistico Church started after unsuccessful attempts to get help from other Christian organizations. Many tried to promote programs related to economic development with Christian non-profit organizations that specialize in this area, but found that their prospective "clients" did not qualify for loans or assistance. It may be that the potential beneficiaries are not in the right geographic area or do not have sufficient experience or collateral. The phenomenon of "mission creep" seems to take place very quickly in business projects, where integration with the church and focus on the poor can quickly disappear. For whatever reason, outsourcing such programs is often not an alternative, and missions need to develop the capacity to implement such programs themselves.

"Mission creep," the loss of the initial vision and purpose for the program, can impact all forms of economic development activity. The focus on helping the needy gradually moves to a wealthier target group, or the emphasis on Christian witness becomes diluted as the economic activity takes on central importance. Instead of becoming a means to help others, these projects can become an end in themselves. Nowhere is this more apparent than in the history of micro finance where the livelihood of the service delivery mechanism, the entity providing the loans, has often become more important than the livelihood of the clients: "achieving financial sustainability but having little outreach to poor clients."[24]

This is why missionary participation is so important. Expatriate staff can be recruited for these types of programs, resulting in the creation of a new type of missionary-consultant able to provide these elements of training and assistance, while keeping the focus on Christian witness. These promoters of Kingdom businesses need to assess the viability of economic projects, and promote governance and a staffing structure that is self-reliant. They can also be responsible for on-going training and relating the business to ministry objectives. They use business as their social context for ministry.

There is currently a great interest in the potential of economic development and job creation programs with Christian missions. Like programs in health and education, the economic development tools are great resources for ministry outreach, ever more relevant in a world where poverty and unemployment are rampant. The growth of economic enterprise that serves mission also means that there are tremendous needs for a new type of expatriate professional worker: the missionary businessperson.

Discussion Starters

1. "Give us this day our daily bread." Think back to the parables of Jesus. How many can you remember that were about the workplace? What did Jesus do before he started his public ministry?

2. How are the people in your church from the business world viewed in terms of ministry? Do they see their productivity and innovation in the marketplace as a part of God's work in this world?

3. Are there overseas ministry projects that you support that could perhaps develop "endowment support" through business endeavors? Would this provide a new way to get business people involved in overseas ministry?

4. The short letter to Titus refers seven times to "doing good" as evidence of Christian commitment. What do people in your neighborhood think of as a sign of Christian commitment?

Notes

1. Raymond Kresenky, "Prayer of the Unemployed," *1000 Quotable Poems,* (New York: Willet, Clark and Company, 1937), 191.

2. Bryant Myers, *Working with the Poor,* (Monrovia, CA: World Vision, 1999), xvi.

3. Ruth Tucker, *From Jerusalem to Irian Jaya: Biographical History of Christian Missions,* (Grand Rapids, MI: Zondervan, 1983), 337.

4. A. Scott Moreau, "Educational Mission Work," *Evangelical Dictionary of World Missions,* (Grand Rapids, MI: Baker Books, 2000), 304.

5. *Faith in Action Study Bible,* "Kingdom Business," World Vision/Zondervan, 1525.

6. "The Benedictine monk Bernardo Vincelli helped the order make a handsome profit with his famous Renaissance elixir, now known as Benedictine. The liqueur, bottled profitably for the church for many years, still bears the initials D.O.M., for *Deo optimo maximo* ("Praise God, most good most great")." From Ochs, B. Van, "Ten Challenges that Make Staying Home Look Attractive," *Evangelical Missions Quarterly* (Vol. 41, No. 2, April 2005), p.160.

7. Francis of Assisi, "Foundations of the Order," in *St. Francis of Assisi,* (New York: Image Book, 1911), 74.

8. William J. Danker, "Some Economic Attitudes and Activities in the Life and Mission of the Brethren in Europe," *Profit for the Lord,* (Grand Rapids, MI: Eerdmans, 1971), 20.

9. Ibid., 25.

10. From the Letters of the Reverend John Wesley, quoted in Danker, *Profit for the Lord,* p, 24.

11. Vishal and Ruth Mangalwadi, *The Legacy of William Carey: A Model for Transformation of a Culture,* (Wheaton, IL: Crossway, 1999), 18.

12. "Testimonio Cristiano en el Ambito Empresarial," *Palabra, Espiritu y Mision,* [documents of CLADE IV] (Buenos Aires: Kairos Ediciones, 2001), 98.

13. All cases can be visited, and more information on each case can be obtained from the Latin America Mission, 305-884-8400, or e-mail dbefus@lam.org.

14. "Si no nos cuesta, hacemos fiesta." (If it doesn't cost us anything, let's have a party.) This common refrain in Latin America is indicative of the "2 Thessalonians 3" problem of serving others, that many people just come along for a handout. What is given away for free is often not valued, and over time expected as a right or an entitlement.

15. Pablo Lavdo, "Insuring the Life of a Ministry," *Latin America Evangelist* (July/October 2004) [Miami: Latin America Mission] 17.

16. Mancur Olson, *The Logic of Collective Action,* (Harvard University Press, 1965), 15.

17. C. K. Prahalad, *The Fortune at the Bottom of the Pyramid* (New Jersey: Wharton School Publishing, 2005), 4.

18. *Dividend,* "C.K. Prahalad Challenges Michigan to Expand World View" (Ann Arbor), Fall, 2003, 38.

19. Merille Grindle, "Ready or Not: The Developing World and Globalization," *Governance in a Globalizing World,* (Washington D.C.:Brookings Institution Press, 2000), 186.

20. Marc Benioff and Karen Southwick, *Compassionate Capitalism: How Corporations Can Make Doing Good an Integral Part of Doing Well,* (New Jersey: Career Press, 2004), 4.

21. David Bornstien, *How To Change the World: Social Entrepreneurs and the Power of New Ideas*, (U.K. Oxford University Press, 2004).

22. C. K. Prahalad, *The Fortune at the Bottom of the Pyramid* (Wharton School Publishing, 2005).

23. Robert Gilpin, *Global Political Economy,* (New Jersey: Princeton University Press, 2001), 6.

24. Thomans Fisher and M. S. Sriram, Beyond Micro-Credit: Putting Development Back Into Micro-Finance, (Oxford, U.K., 2002), 20.

Part 2

Missiological Foundations

6

The Biblical Basis for the Integration of Business and Missions

Mark L. Russell

Before one can conclusively determine whether the integration of the business world and missions is an effective global shift, we have to decide if business is really a worthwhile endeavor. Does business bring glory to God? When we think of missions or doing things that glorify God, business is probably one thing that never comes to mind for the majority of Christians. Primarily we tend think about church planting, evangelism, discipleship or some other type of worthy service-oriented ministry.[1] When the topic of business is raised, generally it is accepted as a necessary means to another end. For example, most evangelicals would accept business as worthwhile because it generates revenue that can then be funneled to paying church staff, building churches, sending out missionaries and supporting evangelistic endeavors. Others would point out that working in the business world also gives Christians an opportunity to share their faith on a personal basis with co-workers and to provide a witness through their integrity in the workplace. In regards to missions, most would point out the importance of business in enabling evangelical missionaries to creatively access unreached people groups residing in countries ruled by oppressive governments who do not allow traditional missionaries to even enter their country.

I wholeheartedly agree with all of these assertions. Business is an excellent avenue for Christians to have contact with unbelievers, to share their faith, and to bear witness to the holiness of God through their conduct at work. Business is also how we make money and with that money are able to financially support a plethora of good works. Without this revenue, it would be quite difficult for the church to do her job. It is a good thing that business is providing missionaries with unique opportunities to live in restricted countries and have contact with some of the most isolated people in the world, many of whom have never heard the name of Jesus or met a single Christian in their entire life.

Building a Weak Foundation

However, to use only these arguments to make a case for integrating business as a key part of missions would be to build a weak foundation. In fact, merely using this line of reasoning is why many people who are trying to integrate business in missions are having great difficulty. First of all, on the mission field, there is an ongoing debate among many missionaries about how much a missionary should work at a "secular" job to justify his or her visa. The idea is that the time used to justify the visa should be held to a minimum since this business work is a distraction to the real purpose of the missionary's presence in the country. Second of all, if producing revenue is the primary role of a business enterprise, it is hard to justify an ongoing business that is not producing money. Several missionary business endeavors are ended before they have really started, because the missionaries do not want to put too much time into the business and it is, therefore, not producing any financial benefits.

Using business in missions as a means to another end generally results in a loss of credibility. As one observer noted, "Professionalism can not be faked, however, and even the most zealous missionaries are recognizing that amateurism and deception, no matter how sanctified, is not a good model of Christian discipleship."[2] There are many good reasons to integrate business and missions. However, in order for business to become a credible, legitimate aspect of missions, the primary reason needs to be that we believe that business in and of itself glorifies God. Despite the amount of literature that has been published in the area of integrating business with faith, very little work has been done to address this specific issue. It seems that we frequently fail to focus on the primary issue and jump right in on addressing the secondary issues. This results in a weak foundation and disables the integration of business and missions when difficulties arise.

Building a Firm Foundation

The primary reason that God is glorified in business is that he is glorified when he sees his character reflected in our lives. We can imitate God in any number of ways, such as being faithful to our spouse, imitating how God is faithful to his bride, the Church. When we tell the truth, we imitate that he is truth, and when we honor our parents, we imitate how Christ, the Son, honored the Father. To love is to imitate the fact that "He first loved us" (1 Jn 4:9).[3] Another way we can imitate God is through our jobs. The most obvious way is to reflect his character in the job in the ways just mentioned. However, I would go a step further and say that work itself imitates God and glorifies God when done in agreement with his law and character. The first two chapters of the Bible describe how God created the earth and the first human beings. God created humanity in his image, meaning more like him than any other creature, but also being called to imitate him. Through the creation account, God is working. We are to imitate that aspect of his character. Furthermore, in issuing his first commands to humans, he said, "Fill the earth and subdue it. Rule over the fish of the sea and the birds of the air and over every living creature that moves on the ground" (Ge 1:28).[4]

The process was the following: God worked, he stated that men were created to imitate him, and then he gave a command to work. This command for Adam was to toil in the soil of the garden, name the animals, and so forth, but this command has expanded to every human being and is fulfilled when we engage in creation sustaining work of any kind. As Stan Reeves pointed out, "We are called to subdue the earth and rule over it. What does this look like? Genesis 2:15 tells readers that for Adam ruling and subduing meant cultivating and keeping the garden. The task for each of us would not necessarily be exactly the same as Adam's assignment. The world is a big place. The task of subduing and ruling encompasses every legitimate occupation. A plumber is called to use pipes, gravity, and principles of pressure to channel water and other things in ways that are useful to people. A factory manager is called to learn how his factory operates and coordinate others in applying their skills to subdue and rule. A teacher is called to pass along knowledge so that others can be equipped to subdue and rule. All occupations call us to subdue and rule in some fashion."[5] Business definitely fits into this category. Thus, we can say that business is not just a means to an end but an activity that imitates and glorifies God.

Dirty Water

The business world can be an ethical nightmare and as our headlines fill up with stories of Enron, Arthur Andersen and other companies involved in corruption, it can be easy to think that the world of business has nothing to do with ministry. This could lead many people to think that advocating the integration of business into the holy arena of missions is like trying to mix dirty water with clean water with the end result being it is all dirty. That is why I felt it necessary to include this brief section on how business and several issues related to business are not in and of themselves evil but are actually fundamentally good. They can provide the missions minded business professional tremendous opportunities to glorify God and be salt and light in a world that desperately needs it. It is also important to understand that business is more than a means to an end, but can actually be an end in and of itself. Business can be more than a way to obtain visas for missionaries in creative access locations. Business can be an opportunity to show a godless, depraved society how a good and loving God can take our ordinary talents and use them in a way to genuinely help people. Only when we understand the full encompassing power of business in helping others, glorifying God and doing good, can we build a firm foundation for the integration of business and missions.

Biblical Examples

Now, I would like to turn our focus to looking at some biblical examples of people using business skills in a cross-cultural ministry setting. The Old Testament contains many examples of followers of Jehovah, who were professionally active and had a big influence in the expansion of Kingdom of God in a foreign country. Perhaps the most obvious example is Abraham, a wealthy sheep farmer. He could be called the first missionary, as he was called to leave his homeland and start a new work for the Lord in a distant land. He took his profession with him and God used his talents to help him fulfill the work that God called him to do. Joseph is also an example of someone with exceptional skills who used them in a natural way to advance the Lord's work. He started off as a steward and despite a stint in prison, he worked his way to become Prime Minister of Egypt. Moses, Daniel and Amos are other examples of people who supported themselves financially through various professions while working for God in a foreign land.

In the New Testament, there is a mentioning of Lydia, "a seller of purple fabrics" (Ac 16:14). In her home in Phillipi, Paul established the first church of Western Europe (Ac 16:15). There are several examples in the Bible of people who were doing all types of different jobs and who also were engaged in some form of ministry. The use of business skills in a cross-cultural ministry setting for the advancement of the Kingdom of God has frequently been referred to as "tentmaking."[7] This is in reference to Priscilla, Aquila and Paul, who worked together simultaneously as ministers of the Gospel and as makers of tents (Ac 18:1-3).

Paul: Business Missionary

The finest example of combining a profession with active ministry is none other than the Apostle Paul. Despite this fact, he strongly defended the right of a minister to be paid for his work (1 Co 9). Peter, who had previously been a lifelong fisherman was, along with his wife, a donor-supported minister for many years (1 Co 9:5). In fact, Peter was clearly called by the Lord Jesus to leave his profession as a fisherman and become a full-time "fisher of men" (Lk 5:1-11). After the resurrection of Christ, Peter returned to being a fisherman and Christ met him on the beach and blessed him with a miraculous catch of fish. Christ then asked him three times if he loved him and commissioned him to quit fishing again and to take care of Christ's sheep (Jn 21). By Paul's note to the Corinthians, we know that Peter stayed faithful to that commission. Using this point and others, Paul makes a strong case for being a donor-supported minister of the Gospel and says at other points in his letters that he also received monies or food and lodging from supporters, albeit on rare occasions (See 2 Co 11:8, 9; Php 4:15, 16; Phm 22). He even stated that "the Lord has commanded that those who preach the gospel should receive their living from the gospel" (1 Co 9:4).[8]

However, it seems that Paul viewed this command more as permission to accept payment rather than an order to actually do so. As David Dungan says, "This alteration is based on the realization that this regulation was no longer appropriate in every case."[9] We are able to see that Paul clearly believed that a missionary could be financially supported through donations but obviously had reasons why he chose, for the most part, not to be. Paul states quite clearly on several occasions that he and his companions supported themselves. In 1 Corinthians 9:6, he states that he and Barnabas were supporting themselves on their journey to Cyprus and Galatia. In 2 Corinthians 11:12, while in Philippi, Paul says that he would continue to work so as not to be a "burden" to the Corinthians. In both of his letters to the churches in Thessalonica, he says that he and his companions worked "night and day" to avoid burdening them.[10] In Acts 19:9, it is mentioned that Paul ministered during the lunch hour in the lecture hall of Tyrannus for two years. F.F. Bruce observes, "It says much for the staying-power of Paul's hearers as well as of Paul himself if they frequented the lecture-hall daily during the heat of the day for two years. Paul for his part seems to have spent the early morning, and possibly the evening, in manual labour: 'these hands', he later reminds the elders of the Ephesian church, 'ministered to my necessities, and to those who were with me.'"[11] Because of Paul's strong defense for donor-supported ministry, many people have concluded that he simply made tents when money was scarce. However, the numerous references to Paul's self-support and the fact that three times he says that he did not receive financial support seems to suggest otherwise (1 Corinthians 9:12,15,18). Ruth E. Siemens points out, "The textual evidence seems to indicate that Paul and his team supported themselves on all three journeys as a matter of policy, and received no financial help from any source except for a couple of gifts from Macedonia. If Paul was receiving contributions from churches, his claims would be false and his arguments for self-support hypocritical."[12]

Why would the Apostle Paul make such a strong argument for donor-supported missionaries, and then turn around and spend time making tents to financially support himself when he could have used that time to preach and teach the Word of God? Was it to provide access to areas closed to him? The value of business missions today is usually seen in the fact that it provides missionaries creative access to countries that for one reason or another do not grant visas to or tolerate missionaries. While I praise God for the courage and creativity of my numerous colleagues who have and are continuing to engage in business for this reason, this was not the basis of Paul's strategy for his activity in business. Dave English says, "As a Roman citizen he could move freely throughout the empire. This means Paul found reasons so compelling that he voluntarily chose to work for a living rather than accept donor support...tentmaking was a complete strategy for maximum evangelistic impact and church multiplication."[13]   Paul had several reasons why he worked as a self-supported missionary. As F. F. Bruce says, "Paul scrupulously maintained this tradition as a Christian preacher, partly as a matter of principle, partly by way of example to his converts, and partly to avoid giving his critics any opportunity to say that his motives were mercenary."[14] He clearly did not see "business" as a time draining distraction to his ministry, rather as an enhancement to it.

Why Did Paul Work?

The primary reason for his use of this strategy seems to be that he was able to identify with the people he was attempting to reach with the gospel. Paul said, "I have become all things to all men, so that by all possible means I might save some" (1 Co 9:22). This quote comes in the conclusion of his explanation and justification of why he did not work as a donor-supported minister. This shows that Paul did not do this because he had to or because he wanted to, rather this was Paul's strategy! As English points out, "In context, this is Paul's final and climactic reason for working rather than taking support. He worked in order 'to become all things to all people.'"[15]

Identification

Like Paul, we can identify with people in numerous ways. He quoted Greek poetry to evangelize Athenian philosophers (Ac 17:28). He became like a Jew for the sake of the Jews (1 Co 9:20). While missionaries need to follow Paul's example and identify on numerous levels with the people to whom they are ministering, there is definitely a need in numerous situations to identify with them on the working level as well. It is even worth pointing out that Paul's working enabled him to identify with a group of people with whom he would not normally identify. Paul was a Jew and a Roman citizen of high education so he could easily identify with them. However, as Siemens says, "Paul had more trouble identifying with 'the weak' and the poor, the slaves, the day laborers."[16] His working as a business missionary was a deliberate strategy that enabled him to identify with a group of people with whom he would not have been able to do so in a natural way.

Credibility

Secondly, Paul gained credibility in the eyes of others. This showed that he cared more about his message than his money. He was also able to silence this accusation from his critics. As Siemens says, "It proved he was not a 'peddler of God's Word' nor a 'people-pleaser,' preaching what the audiences wanted to hear so they would give fatter contributions."[17] Despite the fact that Paul and Christ defended donor-supported ministry, in many parts of the world today, donor-supported missionaries still face this credibility problem. For example, as a missionary in Russia I earned a mere $300 per month and lived in a 600 square foot apartment. But on numerous occasions people questioned me why I had so much money and pointed out that I had the earning power of a manager in a Russian company. In Chile, I earned $1000 a month and lived in a seventy-year old house, that was smaller than the average US sized house and whose roof collapsed shortly after we moved out. Nevertheless, many Chileans argued that we, as missionaries, earned too much money. Chilean confidants told me that our standard of living was a matter of debate among the Christian community since we earned our living from the church.

There is no simple solution. Should we require missionaries to fully identify with the local culture, meaning live at a standard of living that is considered acceptable or average in that country? In this case, how would we account for the different standard of livings for a missionary in Switzerland and one in Mozambique?[18] Should we use the standard of living of the sending country? In this case, how would we account for the difference of living standards between the expatriate missionary and the nationals? How much should we concern ourselves with what people think? How much should we require missionaries to sacrifice?[19] What about the stress associated with living in a foreign culture at a standard of living well below to what one is accustomed?[20] This was, obviously, an issue and a basis for criticism that Paul was aware of and wanted to avoid and did so by not receiving his income from the church.

Modeling

Modeling was another purpose of Paul's tentmaking strategy. By working in a normal job, Paul was able to naturally model or bear witness a Christian lifestyle to the people around him. As we all know, it is easy to demonstrate a holy life within the confines of church, but much more difficult in the world. Paul was able to do just that. As Siemens says, "They needed a demonstration and Paul personally gave it. Without it they would have said, 'But Paul, you are demonstrating a holy life in church. But try doing it in the cesspool environment of my job!'"[21] Paul stated quite clearly that this was part of his strategy when he wrote, "Join with others in following my example, brothers, and take note of those who live according to the pattern we gave you" (Php 3:17).

In modeling a Christian lifestyle to the people around him, Paul was able to pass on three important patterns of behavior, which are difficult for donor-supported missionaries to do. First, he was able to demonstrate how a Christian could handle temptations to sin in the workplace. I am currently a donor-supported missionary working as a church consultant in Western

Europe. One of the struggles I have is that I feel like I do not have opportunities to practice what I preach before the people to whom I am ministering. I have no opportunity to treat a customer fairly, to practice financial integrity in a business setting, or to demonstrate how to handle difficult ethical situations that are commonplace in the contemporary corporate environment. Paul did not have this difficulty. The Corinthians had huge ethical problems, "Instead, you yourselves cheat and do wrong, and you do this to your brothers" (1 Co 6:8). He was able to show what it meant to not cheat customers. When ethical dilemmas presented themselves, Paul could show how a mature Christian should handle it. Obviously many of Paul's other disciples also struggled with many of the temptations common to business, "He who has been stealing must steal no longer, but must work, doing something useful with his own hands, that he may have something to share with those in need" (Eph 4:28). He was not limited to just telling his disciples what to do, leaving them shaking their heads and muttering, "Easier said than done." Rather he showed them and helped them see that it could, in fact, be done.

A second behavior pattern that Paul was also able to demonstrate was a quality work ethic. Laziness did not develop with the television, but has been around for a while. Although Paul had to admonish his readers not to be idle, he was able to back it up by pointing to his example. He wrote, "In the name of the Lord Jesus Christ, we command you, brothers, to keep away from every brother who is idle and does not live according to the teaching you received from us. For you yourselves know how you ought to follow our example. We were not idle when we were with you, nor did we eat anyone's food without paying for it. On the contrary, we worked night and day, laboring and toiling so that we would not be a burden to any of you. We did this, not because we do not have the right to such help, but in order to make ourselves a model for you to follow" (2 Tim 3:6-9). Paul was able to speak strongly and boldly because he was doing what he was calling on others to do. A lack of work ethic in many countries of the world today has led to poverty, an inability to produce, and a socio-economic quagmire that is not broken with mere speeches. As a missionary in Russia, I was able to see how seventy years of communism had produced a lackadaisical work ethic that in turn led to an economy that could barely sustain its people at a minimal standard of living. As one Russian economist said, "No amount of money or technical help will do much good in [Russia] without the recovery of a strong Judeo-Christian work ethic, which was destroyed during seventy years of Communism."[22] The breakdown of the Russian economy was so severe that many workers would go months without receiving wages. This resulted in the oft quoted Russian joke, "We pretend to work; they pretend to pay us." Of course, this is not limited to Russia, but is seen all over the two-thirds world. These poor, developing countries often need immediate and emergency humanitarian help. But to establish a long-term solution they need to have a self-sustaining and vibrant economy. This is only done with a strong work ethic. As Dave English said, "Infiltrating society with a moral work ethic is vital for development and creates a more productive, just system."[23] Paul did not need to merely preach this work ethic but was able to practice it as well.

A third behavior pattern that Paul was able to provide was a shining example for lay evangelism. Peter was able to commend his followers to "always be prepared to give an answer to everyone who asks you to give the reason for the hope that you have" (1 Pe 3:15). However, Paul was able to go a step further and demonstrate what evangelizing one's peers actually entails. Furthermore, Paul was able to pass on practical tips and applicable advice that only comes from having done the same work that he was calling his followers to do. To the Colossians, he said, "Be wise in the way you act toward outsiders; make the most of every opportunity. Let your conversation be always full of grace, seasoned with salt, so that you may know how to answer everyone." (Col 4:5-6) He knew what it was like to have to be around the same people everyday in the workplace, therefore he understood the importance of managing the relationships properly. Instead of telling people to boldly proclaim the truth, he encouraged them to be sensitive to their listeners. He had experienced how a Christian lifestyle in speech frequently led to questions, so he told them to watch their conversation and be ready to answer.

Despite many attempts to change this current aspect of American Evangelicalism, there is a tendency to emphasize donor-supported Christian workers in ministry as opposed to the laity. This has led to three problems worth mentioning. First, vocational ministers are frequently over burdened trying to do everything. Second, the laity are not engaging the people around them like they could because the vocational minister is paid to do that. This results in the vocational minister running around trying to be creative and make contact with people in order to evangelize them. These are the same people that the laity naturally see on an everyday basis. Third, growth is slowed down tremendously when new people come to Christ and are then removed from their natural environment before being empowered in ministry. Frequently, new Christians are encouraged to quit jobs because their job is viewed as a "distraction" to ministry or perceived "too secular."[24] Paul spawned a rapid, indigenous church planting movement across the Roman Empire (Rom 15:19-23). He did not do this alone, rather in conjunction with empowered laity who followed his example of natural marketplace evangelism.

Comparing The Models of Peter and Paul

So far I have listed several advantages to Paul's business ministry strategy and a few problems inherent with a system that heavily relies upon donor-supported ministers. After making such an argument, I could easily be asked why I work as a donor-supported minister or better yet, why did Jesus Christ our Lord commission Peter to work as a donor-supported minister? This is a good question, indeed, and one with which I have struggled. The answer lies in the nature of the particular ministry role.

In Luke 5:1-11, we have an account of Christ's calling Peter to follow him as a disciple. In this account Christ tells him that he will make Peter a "fisher of men," a seemingly evangelistic calling. He also calls Peter to leave behind his fishing and become a full time presumably donor-supported minister and disciple. After Christ's crucifixion, Peter returns to his fishing. After his resurrection, Christ appeared to several disciples, including Peter, on a beach while they were fishing. During this time, he reinstated and commissioned Peter. Christ asked Peter three times if he loved him. Each time Peter answered that he did and Christ responded, "Feed my sheep" (John 21). In the words of D.A. Carson, "The emphasis is now on the pastoral rather than the evangelistic."[25] We see through Peter's life that he maintained an emphasis in his ministry on the pastoral and saw himself as a shepherd. This is seen throughout the book of 1 Peter and primarily in the first four verses of chapter five. He calls himself a "fellow elder" and says elders are to be "shepherds of God's flock."

As mentioned before, Paul's reference to Peter in 1 Corinthians 9:5-6 lets us know that Peter continued living as a donor-supported minister. In 1 Peter 5:3 in his admonition to "fellow elders" he tells them not to be "greedy for money." This seems to imply that many of them were also working for the church as donor-supported ministers. However, Peter was clearly not simply a pastor of a local church as we have today. While his primary commission was to "tend the flock" as Christ had said at his reinstatement, he also fulfilled an evangelistic role in introducing the Gospel to the Jews. He was primarily an "apostle of the circumcision" (Gal 2:7-11), however this should not be construed to mean that his ministry did not also contain a cross-cultural component. He gave the message at Pentecost that was heard by people from all over the world (Ac 2:7-41). In a very real way he was also the primary instrument that opened the door to the mission to the Gentiles, as he authoritatively argued for their admission without submission to the Mosaic Law before the Jerusalem Council (Ac 15:7ff). He wrote the epistle, 1 Peter, to a predominantly Gentile audience.[26] There is also fragmentary evidence that indicates he later did missionary work out-side Palestine, beginning in Antioch and finishing in Rome.[27] Nevertheless, Peter had a very different commissioning from Christ than Paul did.

While Christ told Peter at his reinstatement to "feed my sheep", he clearly told Paul at his appearance on the road to Damascus that he was sending him to the Gentiles (Ac 26:17). While Paul still labored and prayed for his people, the Jews (Ro 9:1-3, 10:1), he was most definitely "an apostle to the Gentiles" (Gal 2:8). His ambition was not to "tend the flock" but to "preach the gospel where Christ was not known" (Ro 15:20). This is seen in his statement to the Romans, "But now that there is no more place for me to work in these regions" (Ro 15:23). As F.F. Bruce wrote, "The statement that 'no longer has any room for work in these regions' throws light on Paul's conception of his task. There was certainly much room for further work in the area already evangelized by Paul, but not (as he conceived it) work of an apostolic nature. The work of an apostle was to preach the gos-pel where it had not been heard before and plant churches where none had existed before. When those churches had received sufficient teaching to enable them to understand their Christian status and responsibility, the apostle moved on to continue the same kind of work elsewhere."[28]

Paul was a mover and shaker, a groundbreaker. He did not want to build on another man's foundation (Ro 15:20) and cautioned those who sought to build on his (1 Co 3:10). While there were other preachers to the Gentiles in his day, he was obviously the most significant. As F.F. Bruce put it, "[Paul] outstripped all others as a pioneer missionary and planter of churches, and nothing can detract from his achievement as the Gentiles' apostle *par excellence*."[29] Peter, on the other hand, was a shepherd of the flock, a preacher, and an unparalleled leader of the early church. As such they had different philosophies and strategies of ministry. Could it be that Peter's model of donor-supported ministry fits well in the context of "tend-ing the flock" and Paul's business ministry strategy fits well in the context of groundbreaking evangelism and church planting where there is no wit-ness? While there surely can and should be an overlap of these two distinc-tions, it seems that we continue to send out Peters to do the work of Paul.

Conclusion

The Bible starts out with God hard at work, then creating us in his image and calling us to sustain the creation that he had formed. Work and there-fore business is a vital means to glorify God. It is more than a means to an end, but actually can be an end in itself. It is more than a platform for ministry, but can actually be ministry. Any attempts to integrate business and missions should not omit this foundational truth. Furthermore, a careful analysis of Paul's missionary activity and letters makes it clear that Paul's business activity was a strategy Paul vigorously used and promoted in his apostolic work. Paul showed that he intentionally used this method and was not thrust into it for any other reason than that it enabled him to get quicker to his goal of seeing lives transformed and churches planted where there were none. Far from being a "distraction" to real ministry, Paul's business activity was an integral part of his overarching strategy in missions. After thoughtfully reviewing the biblical teaching on work, business and the way God has used several individuals along with Paul to use their God-given business skills to expand his influence in a foreign country, it is clear that there is a biblical basis for the integration of business and missions.

Discussion Starters

1. When and how does business bring glory to God?
2. How do you think Paul's business activities helped in his ministry?
3. If you were to develop a business with the purpose of integrating it with missions, what would be the primary focus of the business? Should it be profit, access, networking, interacting with locals, holistic support for your employees, evangelism, all of the above or something else?
4. What do you think of the distinctions between the models of ministry of Paul and Peter as presented in this chapter?
5. What are some areas of concern in dealing with the integration of business and missions?

Notes

1. Wayne Grudem, *Business for the Glory of God*, (Wheaton, IL.: Crossway, 2003), pp.11-12.

2. Steven L. Rundle "Preparing the Next Generation of Kingdom Entrepreneurs" in Tetsunao Yamamori and Kenneth A. Eldridge, eds., *On Kingdom Business: Transforming Missions through Entrepreneurial Strategies*, p.225.

3. Grudem, pp. 13-15.

4. All Scripture quotations are taken from the NIV.

5. Stan Reeves, "The Spirituality of Work", *Founders Journal* 56 (Spring 2004), p.15.

6. Grudem, p. 16.

7. Tentmaking is frequently defined quite broadly to refer to a disciple of Jesus Christ who is called by God to a cross-cultural ministry using marketable skills and service. This includes any variety of professions, including teachers, doctors, nurses, etc... and even sometimes students who study abroad. While these are legitimate expressions of skills in ministry, it should be noted that Paul's tentmaking was a business. However, due to the fact that the term tentmaking has been used widely with such a broad definition, in this paper I use the terms "business missions" and "business missionaries" to explicate to what type of tentmaker or tentmaking I am referring.

8. F.F. Bruce points out, "This 'command' appears in our gospel tradition in the Matthaean commission to the twelve (Matthew 10:10), 'the labourer deserves his food', and in the Lukan commission to the seventy (Luke 10:7), 'the labourer deserves his wages.' F. F. Bruce, *Paul: Apostle of the Heart Set Free*, (Grand Rapids, MI: William E. Eerdmans, 1977), p.107.

9. D.L. Dungan, *The Sayings of Jesus in the Churches of Paul*, (Oxford: 1971), p.32, quoted in Bruce, p.107.

10. In 2 Thess. 3:7 Paul even says that they did not eat food without paying for it. See also 1 Thess. 2:9, 2 Thess. 3:8.

11. Bruce, p.291.

12. Ruth E. Siemens, "Why Did Paul Make Tents?: A Biblical Basis for Tentmaking," *GO Paper* A-1, (1998), 14, available from www.globalopps.org/materials.html; Internet; accessed on 15 August 2004.

13. Dave English, "Paul's Secret- A First-Century Strategy for a 21st Century World", *World Christian*, (September 2001), pp.22-23.

14 . Bruce, p.220.

15. English, p.24.

16. Siemens, "The Vital Role of Tentmaking in Paul's Mission Strategy", p.124.

17. Ruth E. Siemens, "The Vital Role of Tentmaking in Paul's Mission Strategy", *International Journal of Frontier Missions* 14:3, (July-Sept. 1997), p. 123.

18. This is illustrated in the fact that our standard of living in Germany is actually much higher than in Russia or Chile, yet I have never been questioned about my pay. In fact, most of my friends have asked me why we seem to have and earn so little. However, the standard of living of missionaries in Western Europe has been a cause of tension with missionaries from areas where they live at a lower standard of living.

19. Paul Hiebert was my ministry supervisor while I was a student at Trinity. I remember one lengthy conversation that I had with him on this topic. He encouraged missionaries to try and identify as much as possible with the local culture. But he acknowledged the complexity of this issue. He cautioned against pat solutions and in particular encouraged missionaries with children to seriously consider the consequences of living in difficult situations. Some of his thinking on this matter is stated for the written record. See Paul G. Hiebert, *Anthropological Insights for Missionaries*, (Grand Rapids, MI: Baker Book House, 1985), pp.108-109.

20. The effects of stress from living in a difficult cross-cultural environment should not be diminished. The true story of a friend of mine, whom I will call, "John" brings this to light. John was an exceptionally talented minister of the Gospel. He had a proven academic and ministerial track record. He had a near perfect GPA in his Masters of Divinity program and had planted a church among an "unreached people group" in the urban heart of a large US city. His commitment to long-term missions was strong. He once said to me that a missionary who left the field after one term was a "loser." He felt called to take his family to live in an extremely poor Asian country and live among the poorest of the poor. He did not make this decision naively as he had been on several trips to this location. After two years in his "permanent" location, he and his family had to leave the country because he had a complete mental and emotional breakdown resulting from the never-ending stress of his chosen living conditions. It has been several years and it seems he is still not functioning normally.

21. Ruth E. Siemens, "The Vital Role of Tentmaking in Paul's Mission Strategy", *International Journal of Frontier Missions* 14:3, (July-Sept. 1997): p.123.

22. Ibid., p.123.

23. English, p.25.

24. In many cases this is a wise and justifiable decision. However, I have seen many people leave their jobs to pursue ministry and after finding a ministry job, they have had difficulty establishing contact with the people to whom they want to minister. These are the same people, with whom they previously had frequent and natural contact.

25. D.A. Carson, *The Gospel According to John*, (Grand Rapids, MI: William B. Eerdmans, 1991), pp.677-678.

26. Wayne Grudem, *1 Peter: Tyndale New Testament Commentaries*, (Grand Rapids, MI: William B. Eerdmans, 1988), p.38.

27. J. Van Engen, "The Primacy of Peter" in Walter A. Elwell, ed., *Evangelical Dictionary of Theology*, (Grand Rapids, MI: William B. Eerdmans, 1984), p.846.

28. Bruce, pp.314-315.

29. Ibid., p.18.

7

Nestorian Merchant Missionaries and Today's Unreached People Groups

Howard Owens

Travel well girt like merchants,
That we may gain the world.
Convert men to me,
Fill creation with teaching.[1]

"Why," you may ask, "do I bother with a study of Nestorian merchant missionaries?" The answer is simple. While the history of the eastward expansion of Christianity from Jerusalem is overshadowed by what students of missions know about the westward spread, the size of the church in Europe paled in comparison to the breadth of the church in Asia.

If the church in Asia reached such a scale, many Asians must have become Christians. Andrew F. Walls asserted that "the eastward spread of the Christian faith across Asia is still more remarkable than the westward spread across Europe."[2] John Foster made a similar point when he wrote, "Those who serve the Church in the East ought to have in the foreground of their thoughts a Church which was always universal, and which from the days of the Apostles onwards was always advancing eastwards. Western Church history will then take up its rightful place as a useful, indeed an indispensable, background."[3] I wonder, therefore, if Christendom is in the process of becoming deChristianized, was not Asia first deChristianized?

An appropriate objection to such pronouncements would be to ask, "Where is this church today?" One must readily concede that the regions east of Jerusalem are inhabited by some of the most unreached peoples of the present world. If, however, the spread of Christianity eastward was as extensive as some writers assert, who carried the gospel to Asia and were not some of the ancestors of these peoples "reached" at some point? How one responds to these questions has implications on contemporary missiology.

The Nestorian Church in Asia

In search of an answer to these questions, I will examine the missionary efforts of Nestorian missionaries. Their church has been variously known as the Syrian Church, the Nestorian Church, or the Church of the East. The latter will be avoided to preclude confusion with the Eastern Orthodox Church. These missionaries were largely from Syria, Persia, and Sogdiana.
As I progress through this inquiry, the reader will discover that, first, the primary actors in the spread of the gospel were merchant missionaries. These missionaries, who combined their business with their Christian mission, hardly resembled a contemporary missionary. They lacked ties to mission sending structures and to their sending churches that many of today's missionaries enjoy. These merchant missionaries must have appeared more as lay Christians who had a zeal for sharing their faith along the trade routes of Asia. Second, you will consider the impact these missionaries, along with their clerical and monastic colleagues, had on some of the people groups which are unreached today.

Nestorian Christology

When students of church history read of the Nestorian church, they probably think immediately of Christological controversies. A theologian named Nestorius, from whom the Nestorian church got its name, has been suspected of diminishing Christ's deity. Due to the limitations of this present study, the author will be unable to explore this debate. He, nonetheless, feels justified in proceeding with the development of his thesis. Today, it does not appear that Nestorius was as heterodox as was once thought. Paul E. Pierson, in his article in the *Evangelical Dictionary of World Missions*, "Nestorian Mission," stated that Nestorius' "Christology was probably orthodox, although perhaps not stated adequately."[4] Maintaining an unorthodox faith is far worse than being able to express accurately orthodox faith.[5] Due to the limitations of this paper, I will proceed by accepting that the Nestorians, as merchant missionaries, preached an unadulterated gospel.

In the Russian province of Semiryechensk, located in southern Siberia, were discovered Nestorian gravestones. In this cemetery, interred side by side, were the earthly bodies of individuals who had come from China, India, East and West Turkistan, Mongolia and Manchuria, Siberia, and Persia. The ethnic variety of these Nestorians allows one to suspect, as Alphonse Mingana suggested, that peoples across Asia were in constant dialogue.[6] They lived in an age when the church was planted in Asia. They lived in the age of the Nestorian merchant missionary.

Merchant Missionaries

Richard C. Foltz, in his *Religions of the Silk Roads*, told "the story of how religions accompanied merchants and their goods along the overland Asian trade routes of pre-modern times."[7] His thesis included three elements. First, he argued that ideas and trade were in continuous motion along the trade routes of Asia. He suggested that just as merchants managed a mixed inventory of imported or exported merchandise, so the people of Asia adhered to a mélange of local and foreign religious beliefs. He allowed that other factors attributed to the spread of religious faiths in Asia. He insisted, however, that trade was the main facilitator.[8] How were the merchants of these days able to wed business and missions?

Business and missions is the theme of the present meeting of the Evangelical Missiological Society. The theme may cover tentmaking as the means by which cross-cultural workers support themselves. This tentmaker would be akin to a bi-vocational worker. The theme may also cover the scenario of missionaries who use their business activities to justify their presence in countries that restrict the legal entry of traditional missionaries. In the case of Nestorian merchant missionaries, they appeared less like traditional missionaries. They were Christians who supported themselves by their business and who had a zeal for sharing their faith.

Merchant Missionaries and the Day of Pentecost

The Parthian converts of Pentecost were the first of these Asian merchant missionaries. Christianity began to spread among the Jewish diaspora in Asia. Luke recorded in Acts that the Parthians, Medes, and Elamites, who were in Jerusalem for Pentecost, were among the first converts to Christianity.[9] John Stewart believed that these men and women were either Jews or Jewish proselytes. These Asian converts were most likely merchants.[10]

Foltz argued that the Jews of the Persian diaspora turned to commerce for their livelihoods. He wrote, "[They] set up networks with relatives or other Judeans in other parts of the Persian Empire or elsewhere. . . . By the Parthian period, both Palestinian and Babylonian Jews were involved in the silk trade of China...Because Jews were spread across a wide geographic area spanning both the Parthian and the Roman lands, they were ideally situated to participate in trade between the two empires."[11] Given that the Christian faith was spread among Jews first, and given that the contacts that the Jews had with other peoples were essentially mercantile, Foltz later reasoned, "it can safely be said that Christianity's first link with the Silk Road was via the Babylonian Jews."[12] As with the Nestorian merchant missionary, the Jewish convert to Christianity did not conceive of his business as a facade for his missionary activity. His livelihood depended upon his business and not upon his evangelistic ministry.[13]

Merchant Missionaries and the Early Church

Per Beskow, writing in *Svensk Exegetisk Årsbok*, argued that Christian merchants continued to be the primary reason for the expansion of the Church in the second century. He explained that the spread of the Christian gospel was facilitated by a generally westward movement of merchandise and the westward emigration of Eastern populations, the Jewish diaspora, and the exchange of Christian slaves. "In both of these contexts," he concluded, "Asia Minor and Syria are of primary importance during the second century....Asia Minor and Syria were immensely rich and sent their merchants and ships around the Mediterranean with Oriental products." Beskow believed that, as incredibly as the thought may seem to the reader, merchant missionaries from Asia may have founded and provided the majority membership of the church in Gaul.[14]

Eckhard Schnabel, in *History of Early Christian Mission*, demurred on Beskow's insistence that Christian traders and the commerce of Christian slaves were the only explanations for the growth of the church in this period. Schnabel countered that Beskow based his reasoning uniquely on the absence of historical testimony supporting other explanations, such as "the sending of missionaries to foreign regions."[15] If the merchant missionaries were not the only traveling Christian evangelists publishing the gospel of Jesus Christ in other lands, they certainly played a significant role as the church spread to the west and to the east.

Nestorian Merchant Missionaries

Like the Jews before them, Persians who had placed their faith in Christ, were merchants. The close relationship between the business of Nestorian Christians and their missionary activity is confirmed by the metaphorical meaning of "merchants." Foltz noted that in Syriac, the language of the Persians, the word for merchant, tgr', was often used as a synonym for a Persian mission-ary. A fourth century Syriac hymn included the following stanza:

> Travel well girt like merchants,
> That we may gain the world.
> Convert men to me,
> Fill creation with teaching.[16]

The clergy of the Nestorian church also could be found among traders of their day. Paula Harris, who presented a thoroughly researched paper on the missionary heritage of the Nestorian church at the 1999 World Evangelical Fellowship's missiological meetings in Brazil, explained that the Nestorian missionary model included both the professional missionary and the lay missionary.[17] One may conclude that the professional missionaries were fully supported by their ministry activities. Stewart would not agree. He explained that the Nestorian church lacked the structure to provide for the material needs of its clergy. The Nestorian bishops supported themselves as Paul did through his tentmaking activities. They were merchants, carpenters, blacksmiths, and weavers. With humor, Stewart recalled how "sacerdotalists" objected that "the merchant could with ease lay aside his calling and become a monk or presbyter, and vice versa."[18] According to Mingana, some of the original priests in Persia were ordained by one "Aggai, a maker of silks, the disciple of Addai."[19] They were merchants from the start.[20]

Paul E. Pierson believed that these merchant missionaries, teamed with their monastic and cleric counterparts, formed "one of the most passionately missionary branches of the church."[21] Mingana considered the Persians to be the most "virile element" of the Nestorian missionary movement.[22] These Christians had the character to persevere through difficulty, the training to transmit the gospel message, and the social networks to encounter the men and women who had not yet heard of the Savior from Nazareth. These missionaries took the gospel to the extremities of Asia.

Sogdian Nestorian Merchant Missionaries

The Sogdians were the primary actors in this merchant missionary paradigm of the church in Asia. Foltz considered them to be the middle-men of trade and ideas.[23] "Sogdian merchants were the real masters of the Silk Road, whoever the ephemeral powers of the time might be. Under the rule of their fellow Iranian peoples, the Parthian and the Sasanians, Sogdian merchants moved easily in the Iranian lands to the west, where some of them were won over to the Christian message, just as other Sogdians, active in the former Kushan lands, had embraced Buddhism."[24]

Admittedly the Sogdians did not persist in their Christian faith. They were attracted to Manichaeism at the same time as Nestorian Chrisianity. Earlier they had been converts to Buddhism. As Foltz related their shifting faith, he insinuated a naive attitude in the Sogdians towards different faiths. Foltz allowed that the Sogdians never embraced Buddhism as a people, while he insisted that they were the primary Buddhist messengers east of their land.[25] If the Sogdians adopted Christianity in the late second century, the time during which an ancient Syriac document was written attesting to the presence of Christians among the Bactarians,[26] their Nestorian baptism came at least four hundred years after their encounter with Buddhism. They remained a Christian people until the eighth century, when they turned to Islam.[27] The Sogdians could have been a Christian people for between five and six hundred years. While their later abandonment of Christianity was complete, they were hardly flippant believers. Before their conversion to Islam, the Sogdians, because of their trade relations, were well situated to carry the Christian gospel along the trade routes of Asia.

The commerce of the Sogdians benefitted from a system of trails and roads which crisscrossed Asia. This system of overland trade routes was later called the Silk Roads. These itineraries were so denominated because of the predominance of the silk trade on these roads which connected Rome and China. The Nestorians established their churches in towns that lined these roads.

While there is much to contrast between Western and Eastern missions, they shared one common element: Antioch. Antioch was connected to the Roman Roads and the Silk Roads. From Antioch, Paul traveled into Asia Minor or Europe by traveling on Roman Roads, or by boarding a Roman ship. Nestorian missionaries, from Antioch, took the Silk Roads into Asia.

Foltz considered the Sogdians to be the most successful merchants of Asian trade and as such, "the major link connecting East and West."[28] Their ability to transmit the story of Christ, while they caravanned across Asia, was enhanced by their language, Sogdian. Sogdian was the Greek language of Asia. As the lingua franca for trade relations, Sogdian was the language of choice for the merchant missionaries as they traded their wares and communicated the gospel with their clients and associates.[29] The Sogdians also learned the languages of other Asian peoples as they had opportunity to trade with them. Their language abilities enabled them to serve as interpreters and translators. Sogdians were the primary translators of Buddhist, Christian, and Manichaeistic texts. Foltz asserted that Sogdian translators were behind the translations of religious texts "from Indian Prakrits (vernacular dialects), Aramaic, or Parthian into Bactrian, Tokharian, Khotanese, Turkish, or Chinese, either via Sogdian or directly."[30] These merchant missionaries were ideally suited for cross-cultural ministry because of their language skills.

Training Nestorian Merchant Missionaries

Nestorian merchant missionaries benefited equally from the training they received in Nestorian monasteries. The Nestorians had two primary schools, one at Edessa and the other at Arbel. Edessa's importance to Nestorian missions is unquestionable. Adolf Harnack, in *The Expansion of Christianity in the First Three Centuries*, described it as the headquarters of Nestorian missions and the nucleus of Syrian Christianity in the third century. From Edessa, Syrian Christian literature was disseminated. The Christian population even exceeded every other city of its day prior to Constantine. But it was no more than "an oasis." Harnack believed that "round it swarmed the heathen."[31]

East of the Tigris, Arbel was the second missionary center. It was the capital of the province of Adiabene. Mingana located the origin of the church's spread deeper into Asia at Arbel. He proposed that the missionary significance of neither city paled in light of the other city.[32] Nestorians were trained for three years in one of these schools, after which they departed to carry the message of Christ to the ends of the earth. Some established new monasteries in the lands of their sojourn.[33] The new monasteries became new Nestorian training centers.

These monasteries were the educational institutions for Nestorian children and youths. The primary subject of these schools was the Scriptures. While these schools were tuition free, per se, the parents were expected to provide a portion of the Nestorian monks' compensation. The students sought employment during their summer vacations to provide for themselves.[34] Future merchant missionaries were among the students in such schools. Aspiring merchants "were expected to study the Psalms, the New Testament, and to attend courses of lectures before entering on a business career."[35]

Ascetic Nestorian Merchant Missionaries

As merchants, the Nestorian Christians sought to maintain lucrative businesses. The future of their work and their own livelihoods depended upon profitable trades. Their desire for material gain must have been counterbalanced by the asceticism of their schoolmasters, the Nestorian monks. Alphonse Mingana related the tale of the Bishop of Arran who was accompanied by four presbyters and two laymen to the country of the Turks. They began their journey after the bishop had received a commission in a vision to evangelize Byzantine prisoners. Their daily rations consisted of a loaf of bread and a jar of water for each.[36] The merchants and missionaries who traveled the roads of Asia had to be accustomed to surviving on such meager sustenance.

The merchants would join a caravan for the trip to distant markets. Caravan members enjoyed a degree of safety due to the size of the traveling entourage and due to an eventual military escort. The caravan's professional guides knew the optimum routes for each journey.[37] Caravans still did not provide a trip of leisure. Merchant missionaries who were acquainted with the asceticism of a Nestorian monk possessed the stamina to survive the journey.

Often one may associate isolation from the activities and cares of the world with the life of the ascetic. If Samuel Hugh Moffett is correct, this impression originated from the reputation of the Egyptian ascetic, not the Nestorian ascetic missionary. In contrast to the ascetic tradition of Egypt, Moffett explained, "Syria..., with its travel and trading traditions, stressed mobility and outreach. Its ascetics became wandering missionaries, healing the sick, feeding the poor, and preaching the gospel as they moved from place to place."[38] Such missionaries brought the gospel to the Asian peoples of their age.

Nestorian Merchant Missionaries and Today's

Unreached People Groups of Asia

Mingana argued that the Persian missionaries, many of whom were merchants, worked to thoroughly convert the peoples they encountered. He wrote, "From the third century down to the time of Chingis [sic] Khan, the activity of the East-Syrian and Persian converts to Christianity slowly but surely worked to diminish the immense influence of the priests of the hundred and one cults of Central Asia, the most important of whom were the mobeds of Zoroastrianism and the wizards of Shamanism."[39] Foltz concurred that Christianity in Central Asia was "on the verge of displacing Zoroastrianism, on the popular level."[40] A Muslim scholar of the eleventh century, Abu Rayhan Biruni, wrote that "the majority of the inhabitants of Syria, Iraz, and Khurasan [were] Nestorians."[40] The Nestorians, at least before their decline, would not blend elements of their Christianity with those of another faith. When the Nestorians met these peoples, they sought to win them to Christianity.

The Keraits

The ancestors of the Uighurs were one of the peoples among whom the Nestorians worked when their church spread across Asia. They live today in the Xinjiang Uighur Autonomous Region in Northwest China. The Nestorian missionaries, while working in Central Asia, worked among the Turkic Kerait tribe, the ancestors of the Uighurs.

In 1007 C.E., the ruler of the nomadic Keraits was hunting at a high altitude and was surprised by a sudden snowstorm. He lost all hope of returning to his camp. While despairing, he saw a vision of a saint, who said to him, "If you believe in Christ, I will lead you to the right direction, and you will not die here." He gave his allegiance to Christ. After regaining his camp, he summoned the Nestorian merchants who were also in the camp, to seek their advice concerning Christianity. They emphasized his need to be baptized and they gave him one of the Gospels, which he read on a daily basis. They also taught him the Lord's prayer. The Kerait chief requested that a priest be sent to his tribe to baptize him and the two hundred thousand souls who had followed him to faith in Christ.[42] Moffett asserted that "during the twelfth and thirteenth centuries the whole tribe was considered Christian."[43] Of the Keraits, Paul E. Pierson stated that "in the eighth century their language was reduced to writing." He does not say it explicitly, but the scriptures may have been translated, knowing the practice of the Nestorians. Pierson goes on to say that this "was passed to the Mongols."[44] He alluded certainly to the Kerait orthography, and perhaps to the scriptures as well.

The Taklimakan Uighur and Lop Uighur

The Taklimakan Uighur and the Uighur Lop Nur are two other unreached people groups of East Asia. They too were in contact with the Nestorians. The latter are descendants of the "ancient Loulan people," who lived at the Lake Lop Nur. When it dried up, they had to move to Miran. Their contact with the gospel was through the Nestorian missionaries who "established churches in the villages along the Silk Road" between the eighth and thirteenth centuries.[45] The Taklimakan Uighur live today as a remote tribe in the Taklimakan Desert. Until 1990, when they were "discovered," they had lived in isolation for 350 years. Soon after their discovery, Nestorian manuscripts were uncovered nearby in the Dunhuang Oasis. At some point the inhabitants of this region, if not the ancestors of today's Taklimakan Uighur, were in the proximity of Nestorian missionaries. Today though, they are "the epitome of an unevangelized people group."[46]

Other People Groups

Nestorian missionaries, whether lay or clergy, influenced other people groups who are considered to be unreached today. The reader has already met the missionary band of a bishop, four presbyters, and two laymen who subsisted on a loaf of bread and a jar of water each day and preached the gospel to Byzantine prisoners, who were among the Turks. Nestorian missionaries evangelized the Mongols, the You Tai, the Central Tibetans, and the Sarikoli Tajiks. The Mongols at times were on the verge of embracing Christianity as a tribe. Nestorian missionaries won many Mongol converts between the seventh and fourteenth centuries. You Tai are Chinese Jews, who migrated to China between 500 and 1000 C.E. When Marco Polo passed through China, he found them among Nestorian Christians.[47] Concerning another group, the Nestorian patriarch in Baghdad, Timothy (778-820), referred to the presence of Christians in Tibet and expressed his willingness to send a missionary to them.[48] And finally, today's Sarikoli Tajiks are descendants of the Persians. Before the arrival of Islam in the tenth century, most Persians were Christians.[49] Are Sarikoli Tajiks the sons and daughters of these missionaries who originally brought the gospel to the peoples of Asia?

Nestorian Merchant Missionaries & Post-Christian Peoples

One result of recognizing the significance of the work of Nestorian missionaries in Asia, whether they were clergy or merchants, is that the church of today is returning to where it was once planted. Based on the preceding examples of peoples reached by the Nestorians, these peoples are post-Christian, even if ancient post-Christian. The criteria of apocalyptic group representation is met, as is the criteria of group accountability.

Criteria for Missions to Unreached People Groups

Paul Hattaway used these two criteria as he presented a case for the nearly 500 unreached people groups that he catalogued in *Operation China*. He first established that when Christ commanded the disciples to "go and make disciples of all nations,"[50] the Lord envisioned the nations to be the ethnolinguistic people groups of the world. Hattaway then considered the scene in Revelation of a multitude present before the throne of Christ from "every tribe, tongue, and nation."[51] He stated:

> If the ultimate aim of God is to redeem individuals from among every ethnic and linguistic representation of humankind on the earth, then everything must be done to learn who those people are so that the church may do everything in their power to see them won for Christ. This appears to be of such importance in the Scriptures that the final sign of the imminent Second Coming of Christ is linked to the completion of this task: "And this gospel of the Kingdom will be preached in the whole world as a testimony to all nations (*ethnae*), and then the end will come.[52]

Hattaway began with the necessity that the gospel be announced, so as to insure the comprehensive representation of all peoples before the throne of Christ. He established next the accountability criteria for the preaching of the kingdom. After the gospel has been preached as a testimony to an ethnolinguistic people group, the group becomes responsible for how it responds to the gospel.[53] He concluded, "In places like China there are whole races of people who have never had the opportunity to hear the gospel. Not only are these lost individuals, but they are lost ethnic representations of humankind."[54]

Hattaway pled with Christians to recognize the value that each of these peoples has in "God's sight." And rightly so. However, because of what has now been demonstrated, to say that some of these ethnic groups are without representation before the throne of God is difficult to defend. For one, a number of these groups were reached at some point in time. Second, the criteria of accountability also has been fulfilled as the gospel was preached "as a testimony" to some of these groups, or at least to their ancestors.

Ancient and Recent Post-Christian Peoples

Having recognized the contribution made by the Nestorian merchant missionaries to insure the representation of the peoples of Asia before Christ's throne and their accountability for the gospel, the first needed adjustment is with terminology. Some of these peoples must no longer be considered pre-Christian, at least based on how these passages in Matthew have been understood and how "nation" has been defined. According to this understanding, some of the groups must at least be seen as ancient post-Christian. The church is now going back to this continent to evangelize these groups again because of how precious they are in the "sight of God," to borrow Hattaway's words.

Denominating these groups as ancient post-Christian will enable a more instructive comparison to be made with the recent post-Christian people of the West. Christianity in a civilization once known as Christendom is in the process of waning, as happened to the Nestorian Church in Asia. Perhaps this deChristianization is happening for similar reasons. Future study based on a recognition of the similarities between the two situations will facilitate a better understanding of the scriptural mandate for missions on one hand, and a more realistic understanding of the history of the expansion of Christianity on the other. Post-Christian peoples must be understood in light of the scriptures. What missionary mandate remains for them?

Discussion Starters

1. What elements prepared the Nestorian merchant missionary for his secular and sacred tasks?
2. How did the sacred relate to the secular for the Nestorian merchant missionary?
3. How does the Nestorian missionary paradigm compare with your preferred paradigm? How would you critique the Nestorian paradigm? What lessons does the Nestorian merchant missionary offer you?
4. In addition to the criteria of representation and accountability, what biblical criteria for missions have I not listed?
5. As the church anticipates closure, the reaching of today's unreached people groups, what biblical motivation for missions will remain?

Notes

1. A Syriac hymn quoted by Richard C. Foltz, *Religions of the Silk Road*, p.62.

2. Andrew F. Walls, "Eusebius Tries Again: Recovering the Study of Christian History," *International Bulletin of Missionary Research*, 24,3 (July 2001): p.110.

3. John Foster, *The Church in the T'ang Dynasty* (London: Society for Promoting Christian Knowledge, 1939), p.vii.

4. Paul E. Pierson, "Nestorian Mission," *Evangelical Dictionary of World Missions*, Scott A. Moreau, gen. ed. (Grand Rapids: Baker Books, 2000), p.675. C. Gordon Olson considered the Nestorian view to be "weaker than the 'orthodox' view." C. Gordon Olson, *What in the World is God Doing? The Essentials of Global Missions: An Introductory Guide* (Cedar Knolls: Global Gospel Publishers, 2003), p.102.

5. Paula Harris recalled that these theological debates were taking place "in multiple communities and in translation to multiple languages." Paula Harris, "Nestorian Community, Spirituality, and Mission" in *Global Missiology for the Twenty-First Century*, ed. William D. Taylor (Grand Rapids: Baker Academic, 2000), p.496.

6. Alphonse Mingana, *The Early Spread of Christianity in Central Asia and the Far East: A New Document* (Manchester: University Press, 1925), p.41.

7. Richard C. Foltz, *Religions of the Silk Road* (New York: St. Martin's Press, 1999), p.7.

8. Ibid. Foltz considered the context of Central Asia to be pluralistic, precluding the possibility of finding monolithic religious traditions across the continent. He nonetheless described the conversion of "hundreds of thousands among the Eurasian steppe peoples... [to Nestorianism, which] appears centuries later like a bad dream to the first Catholic missionaries in China, who found it comfortably entrenched there as the recognized resident Christianity of the East." Foltz, p.8. While Christianity may adopt local forms that may lessen a sense of homogeneity on first view, the pluralism of these cultures did not exclude the possibility of attaching oneself to a particular faith over and against another.

9. Acts 2:9.

10. John Stewart, *Nestorian Missionary Enterprise* (Edinburgh: T. and T. Clark, 1928), xxv-xxvii. Foltz, p.1.

11. Foltz, pp.31-32.

12. Ibid., pp.64-65.

13. Foltz argued that their evangelism naturally followed their business. Their clients became familiar with both their Christianity and their commodities. Foltz, p.35. While Foltz's comments are beneficial for the present writer, he does take exception with other theses proposed by Foltz. For example, Foltz proposed that Persian influences were present in Jewish postexilic scripture. He argued that Ezekiel and Daniel borrowed their eschatologies from Persian beliefs. Foltz, p.32.

14. Per Beskow, "Mission, Trade and Emigration in the Second Century," *Svensk Exegetisk Årsbok* 35 (1970): p.108.

15. Eckhard Schnabel, *Paul and the Early Church*, vol. 2, *Early Christian Mission* (Downers Grove: InterVarsity Press, 2004), p.1555.

16. Foltz, p.62.

17. Harris, p.497.

18. Stewart, p.5.

19. Mingana believed that Addai was Thaddaeus, one of Christ's twelve disciples. Mingana, p.8. Moffett believed Addai was one of the Seventy in Lk 10:1-24. Samuel Hugh Moffett, *A History of Christianity in Asia*, vol. 1, *Beginnings to 1500* (San Francisco: Harper, 1992), p.33.

20. Bosch did not include in his "Missionary Paradigm of the Eastern Church" the role played by the merchant missionary. He accredited the spread of Christianity in Asia via Nestorian missions to Nestorian "monasticism, theology, and mission." David Bosch, *Transforming Mission: Paradigm Shifts in Theology of Mission* (Maryknoll, Orbis Books: 1991), p.204.

21. Pierson, p.675.

22. Mingana, p.39.

23. Foltz, pp.12-13.

24. Ibid., p.68.

25. Ibid., p.47.

26. Mingana, p.7.

27. Foltz, p.15.

28. Ibid., p.13.

29. Ibid., p.68. Syriac is often considered the language of the Nestorian church. Foltz explained the difference between Syriac and Sogdian. Syriac served as the language of the priest and Sogdian served as the language of the missionary.

30. Foltz, p.13. Foltz related how Nestorian missionaries of Persia taught the Turks the art of writing. Foltz, p.69.

31. Adolf Harnack, *The Expansion of Christianity in the First Three Centuries*, trans. James Moffatt (New York: Williams and Norgate, 1905), p.294.

32. Mingana, pp.5-6.

33. Stewart attested to the presence of "hundreds of monasteries in the land of Persia." Stewart, p.46.

34. Stewart, p.37.

35. Assemmani, *Bibliotheca Orientalis* 3, pt 2: p.941, quoted in Stewart, p.39.

36. Mingana, "Early Spread of Christianity," *Bulletin of the John Rylands Library* 9: 303, quoted in Stewart, pp.81-82.

37. Foltz, p.9.

38. Samuel Hugh Moffett, *A History of Christianity in Asia*, vol. 1, *Beginnings to 1500* (San Francisco, CA: Harper, 1992), pp.77-78. Bosch also contrasted Nestorian missionary asceticism with Egyptian isolated asceticism. Bosch, p.204.

39. Mingana, p.5.

40. Foltz, pp.66-67.

41. Abu Rayhan Biruni, *Chronology of Ancient Nations*, trans. E. Sachau (Lahore: Hijra International, 1983), p.282; quoted in Foltz, p.67.

42. This story is recorded in a 1009 C.E. letter written by a Nestorian metropolitan to the Nestorian Patriarch, John. Mingana, pp.14-16. See also Foltz, p.70.

43. Moffett, p.400.

44. Pierson, p.675.

45. Paul Hattaway, *Operation China: Introducing all the Peoples of China* (Pasadena: William Carey, 2000), p.529.

46. Ibid., p.530.

47. Ibid., pp.363, 564.

48. Arthur Christopher Moule and Paul Pelliot, *Marco Polo: The Description of the World*, 2 Vols. (London: Routledge, 1938), p.143; quoted in Hattaway, *Operation China*, p.511.

49. Hattaway, p.498.

50. Mt 28:19.

51. Rev. 5:9, 7:9. While conference participants and the writer discussed the themes raised in this paper at the South Central Regional meeting of the EMS in New Orleans, March 12, 2005, Mike Pocock astutely observed that in Rev. 7:9 the apocalyptic seer referred to the redeemed representatives of the world's people groups who came "out of the great tribulation." The writer afterwards added the reference to Rev. 5:9, for this multitude "from every tribe and language and people and nation" is the universal collective of men and women whom the Lamb purchased with his blood.

52. Hattaway, p.6.

53. Mt 24:14.

54. Hattaway, p.6.

8

North India's Need?
A New Expatriate Breed

D. D. Pani

The colossal magnitude of the West's five-century endeavor to expose the masses of India to Jesus Christ prompts the paradoxical questions: "Why is northern India, with its over 750 million inhabitants, still considered among the 'Final Frontiers' of missions?" and "Why in the year 2005 is India the home of over 30 percent of the world's un-reached people groups, making it the world's most un-reached country?"

Though the previous century is filled with analysis on this theme, the "conclusions" to date are at best obscure. Yet, the inevitable return of Christ demands that we in the West do not waste the precious time remaining in further rethinking our own failures and traditions. Neither should we squander time in fresh experimentation. Instead, much greater economy is to be found in learning from past examples of bona fide success. Among past examples of significance are the unfathomable 300-year triumph of the early western Church in reaching the Roman world, the unsurpassed 1000-year achievements of the Nestorian venture in raising up significant communities of believers throughout most parts of Asia (including India) before its own extermination at the hands of Islam, and several other success stories relevant to the present Indian scenario. Also, for India it is important to study the feedback of the Hindus and Moslems. Toward these ends five of the fatal stumbling blocks currently repulsing the Hindus' response to the gospel are given.[1] Further, some of the reasons appropriate to India for the victory of the Gospel in the Roman Empire and Central Asia are identified.[2] Herein an analysis of the rise of the Nestorian Church in North India is revisited. Also, two additional success stories appropriate to India are reviewed in brief together with several highly relevant world and Indian trends. Finally, based on a projected synthesis of all of this data, an adapted road map for conclusively impacting the leadership generating centers of India for Christ is provided.

Three Examples of Past Successes

The Performance of Colum in Scotland

Living under the supernatural power of the ruthless Druid priesthood, the Celtic Picts were so fierce and barbaric a people that even the powerful Romans elected to avoid further conflict with them. During the 2nd century they built a 70 mile east-west wall across the middle of the British Isles to keep the Picts out of Briton, and later another 30 mile wall of forts further to the north. These efforts proved ineffective. Yet, because of them, except for the many inconclusive battles that ensued, the ferocious Picts of pagan Dark Age Scotland remained isolated from the civilized world for several more centuries. Until the heroic efforts in the 6th century by Columcille (Colum) of Iona, the rightful heir to the throne of Ireland, they remained almost totally unreachable for Christ.

On an earlier Scottish raid, Colum's second cousin had been taken captive and (unknown to Colum) had been claimed by the High Druid priest of the Picts as his personal slave. Colum's first step was to establish a medium size settlement as his base on the small isle of Iona off the north-west coast of Scotland. Afterward he journeyed directly to the main King of the Picts's to demand an audience. At the time the land of the Picts was suffering under a severe food shortage. And though himself the heir to Ireland's throne, this Celtic prince-turned-scholar priest decided to assault the Picts king's ominous castle with only a staff, five reluctant monk companions and a bag of seeds.

In the account of the fearless Colum's conquest of the Picts, three dominant points stand out that have relevance to what is now needed in any *new breed* of Christian laborer in India. The first is Colum's faith. From a long distance away, the Arch Druid of the land could sense Colum's advent. Thus, before departing to perform an annual ritual he predisposed the king that the six travelers were deceivers who must not be allowed to enter his castle. As a consequence the little band was refused entrance. But even to Colum's great surprise, when he prayed in faith for an opening, the metal bars of the castle's gates melted!

The second point is the practical approach employed by Colum in attempting to reach out to the young Scottish King. The High Druid Priest returned from his ritual to find his vulnerable king in the company of the six monks. When he asked the purpose of Colum's mission, Colum fully disarmed his opponent by revealing the contents of his satchel. It contained only seeds: a gift of a specially developed barley variety, appropriate specifically to the comparable climates and soils of Ireland and Scotland. At the time Colum's secular gift represented the very physical thing this kingdom needed most.

The third relevant point (to India) that stands out is the appropriate way in which Colum went on to deal with the evil forces holding the king and his kingdom captive to the falsehoods of the Druid religion. At the time the high Druid priest of the land, Broichan, was serving in the role of father-mentor, royal advisor and spiritual authority to the young king of the Picts, Brude MacMaechon. The highly superstitious Picts were preoccupied with the great power of the Druids over the forces of nature. So complete was Broichan's authority in the land that as the Arch Druid he had earlier ordered and performed the blood sacrifice of the Brude's predecessor. So that the Pict's former king could make an appeal for better crops for their famine-ravished kingdom, Broichan had sent him ahead to the world of the dead. From one account[3] it is clear that when Broichan entered the banquet hall it had not been Colum's intent to appear to be playing the role of a wizard. But it is also clear that *God ordained the ensuing power clash to make Colum appear to be not only a wizard, but also a far more powerful wizard priest* than Arch Druid Broichan.

During the banquet, Broichan called his slave to serve him. When Colum recognized the slave girl to be his cousin and saw the cruel way she was being treated, he completely lost self-control. Later, as he stood by his boat on the shores of the Loch Ness not far from the castle, he repented in agony for his rage-ruined witness. During his outburst he had cursed the high priest, giving him only two days to live unless the girl was released. And as Colum stomped out of the banquet hall, his curse on the Arch Druid had been met with a counter-curse in the form of a test challenge. Broichan had declared that because of contrary winds the six would not be able to sail away. Soon after, upon seeing a small army charging out of the castle on horses in their direction, the six-some began to think that their doom was sealed. But instead, their faith was rewarded.

In sincere meekness the army's chief emissary beseeched Colum to return to *heal the high priest!* As he did he timidly explained that just after Colum had stomped out of the castle, Arch Druid Broichan had swallowed broken glass from his drinking vessel and was dying. Heeding this humble appeal, but in the manner of a wizard (as well as Christ), Colum preformed the healing miracle from a distance by sending a stone in the hands of two of his monks.

When his men returned with the girl they immediately attempted without success to set sail against the strongly opposing winds. Soon after the revived Arch Druid appeared on the ramparts of the castle and circled his staff. He chanted curses to strengthen the winds, however, as the six monks prayed in faith the winds reversed. And to the amazement of all, with Colum's cousin safely on board, they sailed away.

Not long afterward Colum was recalled and became King Brude's "foster father and soul-friend." King Brude MacMaechon allowed Colum to preach broadly in Scotland, teaching the people of his powerful God. Thus from Pictland many were added to the Kingdom of Christ. And in time ancestors of these peoples would begin to carry the gospel of Christ to the uttermost parts of the world; and some known to the author are in India still.

The Performance of the Nestorian Venture in Asia

The Nestorian Church was the main witness for Christ in Asia during the first millennium and during much of the first half of the second millennium. At the time of its apex in 1294 AD, it covered a far greater expanse and had more adherents than the combined Latin and Greek Churches of the former Roman Empire. And during most of the later half of the first millennium up until at least the later part of the 14th century, the epicenter of the Nestorian enterprise in India was in North India, rather than in the South. There are records to prove that the Nestorian regional leaders for India, called metropolitans, resided in northern India between the 7th and the 14th centuries.

After the Mongol Tamerlane's destruction of their ranks throughout much of Central and West Central Asia, and after annihilation in North India at the hands of first the Muslim Delhi Sultans and then the Muslim Mughals, the Nestorian remnant living in the safe haven of India's Hindu-dominated South became literally cut off. Yet, the strength of the earlier Nestorian presence in India is firmly attested to by the significant vestige of these believers that could survive in faith in such virtual isolation in South India for over a century. After 1500 A.D, in similar numbers these isolated Nestorians were recruited in earnest, first into the West-Syrian Jacobite and Roman Catholic enterprises and later into the Protestant movement. And from within these various new expressions the descendents of these former Nestorians have served as a major part of the foundation for the present Church in India today.

Perhaps the most important key to the success of the Nestorians in India and throughout Asia was the *heterogeneous constituency of its vanguard.* Moving ahead of or along side its monks were a host of professionals: merchants, teachers, physicians, administrators, translators, scribes, academicians, technicians, soldier-mercenaries and other professionals. There are even multiple references to Hindu kings employing large numbers of Christian warriors in their armies. In other parts of Asia, Christian administrators, translators, scribes, academicians and physicians were often found serving in the courts of kings. What is important is that this vanguard was typically able to possess highly credible degrees of utility at a variety of levels in Asian society, and thereby could deeply penetrate into the cultures of their advance, *in a most natural way.*

These non-clergy were self-supporting and thus, though they were foreigners, they did not face the suspicion that accompanies today's paid Christian workers. Further, because they usually worked hard to integrate into their new cultures rather than create new communities, their presence was normally not seen as a threat to the culture. For example, in Malabar, the most cast ridden place in India, the Nestorian Christians came to be viewed as another high-caste within the culture, and were given special privileges.

Many of the Kingdoms of Central Asia, including Muslim nations, employed Nestorians in government administrative roles. For example, not trusting the Chinese, the external ruler Genghis Khan employed many skilled Nestorians in the administration of his newly conquered China. This employment enabled the Nestorians to re-establish, for the second time, a major presence in China. Also, the Nestorians were the first to engage in medical missions and there was a long period of time in the Persian Empire when the majority of the medical doctors were Nestorian Christians. In Persia, they had the best medical schools. For a time also in Persia there was an established wisdom group of extremely well informed Nestorians with exceptional predictive powers upon which the Moslem rulers of the land relied heavily for guidance.

A more detailed description of the history and projected motif operandi of the Nestorian Church in North India is forthcoming.[4] For the sake of brevity, let us jump to at least one conclusion that can be gleaned from the foregoing discussion. Today, with large areas of North India currently devoid of living Christ witnesses, and with only a dismally low percentage of the North Indians having faith in Christ, there is an unprecedented need for yet *another expatriate vanguard.* However, rather than a vanguard of paid full-time Christian workers, this new presence of possibly 20,000 Western and South Indian Christians (in approximately a 1:2 ratio) must be similar in its consistency to the vanguards employed (perhaps sometimes unintentionally) by the Nestorians.

Performance of Sadhu Sundar Singh

The massive fruit that has resulted from the life and ministry of Sundar Singh makes him by far the most influential Indian Christian of the 20th century.[5] The son of a rich Punjabi Sikh facing the brightest of material futures, Sundar Singh fell more under the influence of his God-centered mother. And though a Sikh herself, his religiously tolerant mother exposed him to other streams of Hinduism. It was her dream that he grow up to become a Sadhu (ascetic Hindu "holy" man).[6]

By means of a special visitation at the age of 15, Sundar placed his faith in Christ. So powerful was this personal visitation of Christ that he could persist undeterred, despite all subsequent attempts by his family to dissuade him. When his family finally turned hostile he took refuge at a western missionary school, but found little true spirituality in his schoolmates. Thus, after submitting to baptism at the age of choice (16), he struck out on his own to preach Christ in the villages of northern India. And in deference to his deceased mother he took on the dress and manner of a Sadhu.[7]

In those days the life of a Sadhu was a hard one. Most who enjoined such a calling were older men, who, with their obligations in life already completed, lived their austere existences in the hopeful search for their own salvation. Unlike most Sadhus, to add to this austerity Sundar would never accept money or material possessions, but only food and a place to sleep. Thus he would frequently go without eating for many days. And because he was proclaiming Christ, his reception in many villages and towns was often filled with hostility. He carried only a blanket and Bible.[8]

The first of his journeys lead him to the Afghan boarder, where he began preaching to a Muslim crowd. These listened until they realized he was proclaiming Jesus as God. Driving him out, they forced him to spend a rainy night in the bitter cold of an open area reserved for caravan animals. Expecting to find him dead the next morning, they were shocked to find the well-built young man sitting half-clad beside a fire. He was drying his saffron (orange) robe. One of them bowed at his feet and confessed their intent to kill him if the exposure had not. Believing that Allah had preserved him, they took the tall bearded lad in. And for another week he lived in a leader's home, communicating Christ as best he could without knowledge of their language.[9]

Later, during one of his many journeys in route to Tibet, he became suddenly feverish. He could not walk and he faced a bitterly cold wind in the mountains. There was no place to take refuge. Worse, though a precipitous ascent of some seven miles lay ahead, the way back was further. Suddenly he realized that it was climb or die. Praying for strength, he continued on. In his exertion he was healed. Further on he came to a village where a large fair was in progress. In the center men with sharp knives were torturing a buffalo. Maddened by pain the creature ran around with its tongue hanging out. And as the animal suffered, the people rejoiced. They thought their sins were being forgiven. When it finally fell over they beat it to death with sticks and offered its blood to their deity. Clad in the apparel and tradition of a Sadhu, Sundar took advantage of the setting. During the remainder of the fair he had many good opportunities to preach the gospel. In like

manner, in numerous such settings in North India, his incredible impact for
Christ continued for many years.[10]

In his travels he regularly encountered the Lord's faithfulness in the
form of miraculous provisions and deliverances. In one village in Tibet the
head lama had Sundar thrown into a deep well and locked the iron grate
covering the well. Sundar was injured when he was thrown down into the
well filled with rotting flesh and dead men's bones. For a time it seemed
that there was no hope. Yet after several days he was supernaturally delivered, shocking the town and embarrassing the head lama who still had the
only key to the iron well grate. As he continued ministering in dependence
on God's strength and wisdom, he deepened his understanding of the Lord.
In his sufferings he learned the joy of the Lord. And in his prayer life, upon
which he was primarily focused, he began in time to experience the deep
presence of the Lord in a way to which only a very few have ever become
privy.[11]

In his later years Sundar was able to inspire many others, both Indians
and westerners, to the life of sacrifice for the Master. Through his many
travels and assorted writings He challenged the West and the westernized
Indian Church to deeper discipleship. After travel across the United States
Sundar Singh lamented that though the Christians of the West have for centuries been surrounded by Christianity, the Master's truth has not penetrated
them.[12] In 1929, at the age of 39, Sadhu Sundar Singh started his last journey to Tibet. He was never seen alive again.

Forsaking Paradigms Given Emerging Realities

My first extended tenure in India was spent attempting both to impact the
culture directly through a credible professional platform, and in working to
train other Indian Christian professionals to do the same. Because I was a
foreigner, I soon found that I was viewed by most of my new Hindu friends
as being outside the caste system. However, in time, because of my creden-
tials and my professional reputation, my high-caste Hindu friends began
treating me as having an equal, or sometimes higher, standing. I was
pleased to find that my workplace activities served not only to build
bridges, but also to melt barriers.

I am amazed at the gracious way in which many of my Hindu friends
would open up to me as a secular professional while we worked together. I
found myself able to build relatively deep friendships with individuals from
a variety of caste backgrounds. This follows from two reasons: (1) even
now in India's highly heterogeneous work place the barriers created by the
bias of caste keep many from true intimacy, and (2) as I neither projected
any bias for one's caste background, nor was viewed as having caste, my
friends could feel a greater freedom in my presence. Many of my high caste
friends viewed me as being one of them. Low caste friends simply viewed

me as they themselves *wanted to be viewed*, without caste. At times I found my Hindu friends even able to confide in me in ways they could not with each other.

Mistaken Paradigms

One intermediate "conclusion" of the rethinking effort of the 1960-80's was the idea that *the era of Western workers was over and that the manpower for influencing Northern India for Christ must come from South India* (where there is a relatively large concentration of Indian Christians). The acceptance of this new idea of sending South Indian Christian workers was fueled in part by the forced exodus of most of the fulltime western missionaries during the 1970's. Until this time period, the paradigm of sending the fully paid, non-professional, non-contextual, "full-time" western Christian worker to North India had prevailed. Unfortunately it is because of this earlier paradigm that the natural leadership centers of North India were never effectively penetrated. And spawned during this transition period, perhaps as a natural consequence of the western exodus, was the corollary that *the role of the Western Church should now be focused on the funneling of sufficient funds into the hands of these South Indian laborers.* These "conclusions" soon affected an intermediate paradigm shift that is still partially in vogue today.[13]

Unfortunately, the adoption of these deductions has contributed to further losses in the earlier momentum developed during the previous four and a half centuries of western missions. Not only have the results of this strategy been disastrous, but also the massive effort itself has been used to legitimately fuel a number of conspiracy theories by communal Hindu fundamentalists. One such theory being promulgated by a most credible former cabinet member of the Central Government of India is that the U.S. is using Indian Christians as its paid agents to effect a North American takeover of India.[14] This conspiracy theory, though certainly false, is a fabrication that does at least have the appearance of a factual premise. And unfortunately, far too many Hindus now believe it to be a fact.

More recently, and in consideration of the dismal results obtained through this intermediate strategy with paid South Indian workers, the emphasis has partially shifted instead to channeling western funds directly to the very limited supply of North Indian laborers themselves. It is this new approach that is responsible for an appalling series of fraud. Also, this policy has further fueled the conspiracy theories.

Fortunately, many western organizations have figured out that the practices of using paid Indians and fully-mission supported westerner nonprofessionals to present Christ to the North-Indian main stream is at best an incomplete stratagem because neither practice has delivered significant kingdom dividends. Unfortunately, many of these same organizations have shifted to using fully supported western "semi" and "pseudo" professionals.

Emerging Reality of Globalization

The mainstream Hindu has no respect for the "semi" and "pseudo" western professional who is attempting to minister in India while claiming to be a "true" professional. The middle and upper-middle class of India (230 million in North India) is generally well educated and sees right through this ploy. Thus, mission organizations that use this guise to obtain visas for their "fully supported" workers in the name of a contextual-ministry are only kidding themselves. Dependency on the part of those who can do work is not appreciated in India. Even Hindu spiritual workers are viewed by many Hindus as parasites who should be working for a living.

Though there can be exceptions, the most that a western Christian laborer entering India under such schemes can normally hope to do is find involvement in either dependency-based ministries or in culturally isolated ministries involving only Indian Christians. Normally such schemes can not place the western Christian laborer within the Hindu and Muslim mainstreams as an insider. Also, such schemes cannot take advantage of the powerful natural phenomenon upon which the Great Commission should be riding: *world globalization.*

World globalization is the integration of the economies of the world under a more uniform set of accepted rules and practices without national protective barriers to trade and information exchange. The first phase of world globalization took place in the era 1870-1914. Unfortunately, the great benefits of this era were practically wiped out by the two world wars. During the Cold-War period 1945-1980, world globalization was resurrected upon the backs of three key players: Western Europe, the United States and Japan. During this second era, 10 percent of the world's population controlled most of the world's economy and wealth. During the 1980's another roughly two dozen globalizing economies emerged on the peace dividends of the end of the Cold War, including India. Since 1960, due to these second and third world globalization phases, the world population has doubled, and the percent of those living in poverty has been cut in half.[15]

The sociological changes in India produced by globalization are massive, with the focus of the culture steadily shifting from the timeless universals of its ancient supposition system to the transient and the material. India is now producing 75 percent more engineers than the US per year—and these are good engineers! As a democracy rich in natural resources, and with a strong resolve to follow through on the economic reforms it launched more than one and a half decades ago, India is now positioned to take off economically on a scale perhaps equivalent to Japan in the previous century. One study shows India having the world's third largest economy behind China and the U.S. by around 2032 A.D., surpassing Germany by 2023 A.D. (Figure 1), and not extremely far behind the US in 2050 A.D.

Figure 1: India's Overtaking of the G6 Countries[16]

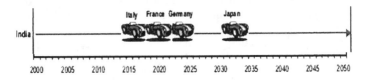

Because of its extensive use of English, India has many advantages in comparison to China. With more English speakers than any other country in the world, India has become the preferred site for outsourcing. The largest English newspaper in circulation in the world is *The Times of India*. Though the US is today outsourcing more and more low-level technical work to India, I can already envision the day when the reverse will be true.

Much more could be written here about India's growth potential, but what must be related instead is the need for the mission organizations of the U.S. (and other western countries) to start recruiting and sending more and more high tech and other highly qualified professionals to India. While the "fully supported" non-professional western Christian laborer may continue to find a place of ministry in rural settings of India, he or she can not be expected to be able to compete in a meaningful way for the attention of the Hindu-Muslim mainstream in the urban centers of India.

Emerging Reality of Urbanization

In the changing sociological dynamics of North India there is another force that is perhaps as powerful as globalization: *urbanization*. "Today, India's urban population is second largest in the world after China, and is higher than the total urban population of all countries put together barring China, USA and Russia. Over the last fifty years, while the country's population has grown by 2.5 times, in the urban areas it has grown by five times." The number of cities in India with over one million has increased from 1 in 1901 to 5 in 1951 to 23 in 1991, to an estimated 40 in 2001. This trend is expected to prevail. The decadal urban growth rate of 36.4 percent in 1991 increased to 40.1 percent in 2001.[17]

There are a number of factors driving the unrelenting wave of migration that is accelerating world urbanization. Among these are the skewed globalization developments that have led to the proliferation of commercial activities and job opportunities in urban settings.[18] In simple terms this globalization phenomenon can be described as being "the net result of the 'push' from stagnating rural areas and the 'pull' of more promising urban economic and social conditions."[19]

At this juncture it is necessary to ask the question, *What do the two complimentary forces of globalization and urbanization mean to the revised strategy needed to reach India in the third millennium?* Because of the speed of sociological transition being caused today by the above trends, the context of our focus cannot be on the present-day situation in India, but must necessarily be on the projected-future situation. The present-day situation would demand a continued emphasis on the extremely effective "unreached people group" paradigm currently being appreciated by many of the organizations now ministering Christ in India. And because some 65 percentage of India's population still resides in rural India today–this stratagem must necessarily be continued on for another several decades (or more). However, the above realities demand the evolving of a complimentary-parallel stratagem for the faster growing urban settings of India, which in people size will surpass the rural population in not many years from now.

In the emerging urban settings of India the "Indian distinctives" of the people group characterization (race, caste, language, culture, religious beliefs) are rapidly being dissolved by the far more powerful secularizing and enfolding forces of globalization. One Hindu Christ devotee friend has noted that: "It is the middle and upper middle class people who are working in most, if not all, the Multi-National Companies. The typical characteristic of this workforce is that they are skilled, talented, have ambition, come from various family /geographical backgrounds and mingle with each other far more than their counterparts in other jobs. Moreover, many of them have worked in other countries (including US) due to different assignments and truly want to stay in India. These are people who keep the economy humming. They have the potential to lead and many of them have vision. These are people, who of their own accord take initiatives to better the society around them and have open minds. *If they can be reached, the Kingdom in India will most certainly become much stronger.*" The various people groups resident in the cities interact with each other much more readily and heavily than they do in traditional rural settings. And this heavy interpersonal-"intra-caste" interaction is not only in the market place, but also in the many heterogeneous-residential settings (various apartment building, town house and condominium complexes) found springing up all over many of India's rapidly evolving large and mega-large cities.

Secularization, the message of globalization, is so powerful a force in itself that the powerful ruling BJP political party representing the Hindu-fundamentalist forces of India was soundly routed in the 2004 national elections of India by the country's traditionally secular Congress party. Though paradoxically, this result came about more because of the vote of the rural and the urban poor, who were not happy with the slower rate at which they themselves were being benefited (relative to the middle and upper-middle class) by the liberalization of the Indian economy (i.e., globalization). Seeing how these middle and upper-middle classes have benefited, the poor of India want globalization together with its secular message to move faster. Thus, in the large and mega-large cities of India, the barriers that would normally inhibit Christ's gospel message's transfer from one people group to another are evermore-rapidly evaporating. Yet those individuals who migrate to the cities normally maintain strong bonds with their rural family members. Thus the potential for impacting many of India's un-reached people groups in rural settings without "intentional" people group focusing is becoming ever more realizable. It is day-by-day becoming ever more possible to reach the rural villages via focusing on the urban cities. Without going into further details, the main strategic implications of these two powerful trends should now be fairly obvious to the reader.

Restoring an Effective Paradigm

Field reports from some of the newer semi-contextualized western workers in the North Indian state of Uttar Pradesh suggest that victorious power-encounters have preceded most of the recently meaningful openings for the gospel in the Hindu heartland. Such reports are most consistent with much of what is now being reported from China[20] and with the concise world-wide analysis of "divine signs and wonders."[21] They are also fully consistent with the earlier performances of Colum in Scotland in the 6th century and Sadhu Sundar Singh in North India in the early 20th Century.

Both Colum and Sundar Singh allowed themselves to be placed in harm's way for the sake of the gospel. And both gave up much in the material realm to be able to minister. Colum gave up a kingdom while Sundar gave up family and immense wealth. Yet neither of these men over-strategized prior to conducting their ventures. In both cases they simply submitted to going out into un-reached fields in the authentic guises that God had led them to assume. In general, the same can also be said for the Nestorians. Using the trade routes the Nestorians ventured into North India and other places all over Asia in an assortment of most genuine guises. And it seems that Sundar Singh, Columcille and the Nestorians were successful because of the fact that *the roles through which they chose to minister were ones upon which those they were attempting to reach placed strong focus.*

The exclusive focus of the Picts at the time of Colum was on the magic of the Druid priests. These dark wizards were men who could summon the forces of nature to their bidding, effecting control over the very laws of nature upon which the people's survival depended. Similarly, the focus of part of rural North India at the time of Sundar Singh was on their religious holy men. These hard-core ascetics were the inspiration of many in the rural settings of Sundar's time due to their ascetic life styles and supernatural activities. Thus, in the rural settings of Sundar's day, most took strong notice when a saffron robed holy man entered their village.

The models of Sundar Singh (as a superior Sadhu) and Columcille of Iona (as a superior wizard) are not as needed today in the urban areas of either the East or of the West. Instead in the face of globalization and the pre-eminence of modern science in urban India, what is needed today are individuals who are able to *stand squarely in the apexes of the varied practical-professional focuses of the urban secular-Hindu mainstream.* Needed are individuals who can stand in such focal points *with the same* strength *and* power of person as Sadhu Sundar Singh and Columcille of Iona.

It is at this juncture that it should be noted that it was *exactly this ability* that many in the Nestorians vanguard to India were best at in their time. It is reported that Islam was spread to Indonesia through merchants. These merchants were not fulltime paid missionaries, but men going out to do their jobs while bringing their religious beliefs with them everywhere they went. The same can be said for the Nestorian impact for Christ in Java, South India, Ceylon, Siam, Burma, Tibet, North India, and the many lands traversed by the Silk Roads (including China). Nestorian merchants were most often a part of the vanguards in these places. Monks, administrators, and many other professionals followed. Certainly, in some instances the monks lead and the others followed. But in most instances it was a heterogeneous effort. Because of this there could be power-encounters (supernatural demonstrations of proficiency, wisdom, knowledge, power, spirituality) at many levels of society. Nestorian merchants were found to be more trustworthy and enterprising, Nestorian medical doctors more competent and successful, Nestorian administrators more faithful and effective, Nestorian military mercenaries more fearless and skilled in war, and so forth.

Mobilizing the Sleeping Southern Giant

Using paid Indians and mission supported westerner non-professionals to impact urban North India for Christ is a failed stratagem. Similarly, using mission supported western "semi" and "pseudo" professionals (as many organizations are now attempting to do) is an equally futile stratagem. As mentioned earlier, the middle and upper-middle class of urban India, some 230 million persons in North India alone and growing, is generally well educated and can easily see through such guises. In like manner, with the bias of caste still existing in North India, even mobilizing bigoted south Indian professionals from lower caste backgrounds for the North's work place is a non-optimal approach. Certainly, none of these ploys can be starting points for the massive effort needed to reach the Final Frontiers of India.

The Initial Phase. Part of my earlier ministry effort as a professional in India was aimed at helping other South Indian Christian professionals to impact their Hindu friends for Christ. However, unlike my own direct success experiences with Hindus, here I found the effectiveness of the process through Indian Christians to be a mixed bag. While the professional environment provides a natural way to bring Indian Christian professionals into closer relationships with their Hindu professional counterparts, the process of friendship is still hampered by bias. Surprisingly, I found that this bias resides more with the Christians than with the Hindus and Moslems. Unfortunately, I discovered that my efforts to enfold these Indian Christians into this process were wasted. Thus, eventually I found myself working to weed out the bigotry of the Indian Christian professionals I was seeking to disciple. My model for this process[22] became the example of Christ as he prepared arrogant Jewish apostles to minister among the Gentile "dogs."

To a lesser degree I found that in the work place a bias also remains within the Hindus against Indian Christians who have come out of low caste or "no-caste" backgrounds through the efforts of the Western Missionary Movement. Thus, the witness of those Indian Christians having such a background is often still not quite as well received. The exciting exception to this is the reception by the Hindus of those Indian Christians who can naturally trace their ancestry back to the earlier Nestorian era in the Indian states of Kerala and Tamil Nadu. These earlier Christians were eventually absorbed into the caste structure in South India with a privileged status.[23] But more importantly it should be noted that this problem of Hindu bias against the lower-caste Indian Christian professional is really a problem of stereotyping, and is thus one that can be easily overcome if the South Indian Christian professional can himself become culturally sensitive while demonstrating great professional competence.

Initially, I concluded that, except for those with a Nestorian connection, *there is much greater economy in simply focusing on non-Christians professionals with a view to raising up a new generation of Christian laborers from the ranks of the Hindus and Moslems themselves.* This strategy is in any case what our Nestorian predecessors in India were initially required to do (not having a Christian community to start with), and with apparent success.

Thus, while efforts certainly need to be made to enlist this large legion of unbiased South Indian professionals, simultaneous efforts to mobilize a new breed vanguard from the West and S. Korea must be the main starting point. The size of this vanguard must be of an order of magnitude that is larger than the effective size of the Commission raised up earlier by the West to attempt to impact the former Soviet Union. India has more than three times the combined population of the former Soviet Union! And unlike the constituency used to fill the ranks of the Commission's work force, this North Indian vanguard must consist primarily of highly qualified and experienced Christian professionals. It must be made up of individuals who can competently work in the many secular fields needed by India.

Rather than coming to India as individuals, it would be best if most of those from the West would came as a part of larger ventures, either with Christian owned and operated companies, or better yet, with secular companies. And rather than carry on the traditional Western missionary function, the initial goal of this vanguard must be drastically different. Initially it must prepare the spiritual soil of urban North India for sowing. Thus, for a time these individuals should simply serve as points of light within the predominantly Hindu and Moslem culture. Their initial goal should be to simply make Hindu friends and to help shift the general stereotypes that Hindus have of Christians. Later on, its emphasis should shift to witness and planting a church among the Hindus that is Hindu in culture and Christ in focus. The same would be true for Muslims. To do this, the vanguard will at first have to avoid association with the ongoing unsuccessful traditional ventures of the older paradigms. And instead they must follow as closely as possible the overall successful modus operandi of the Church of the East.[24]

The End Game. The ultimate hope for the North lies primarily in a "new breed" of South Indian secular professionals serving as points of light and witnesses throughout the large urban centers of the North. To this end, the western vanguard is essential as the first step for a number of reasons. First of all, it is needed to affect the paradigm shift required to mobilize the South by irrefutably proving the effectiveness of the role of the professional *insider*. Perhaps as important, it is needed to help draw the South Indian legion of professionals north by serving as an example of this role.

Presently the South Indian Church and the South Indian professional have little vision and heart for the North. But in the past the Indian Church has been most teachable to the initiatives of the western Church and will likely continue to be so if/when the West takes the lead and demonstrates conclusively its effectiveness. Western professionals must first establish themselves as insiders in the Hindu culture of the North and begin an indigenous church planting movement. South Indian professionals shifting to the North to participate in this new paradigm must be properly enfolded. Thus, the initial Western vanguard must be large enough and the momentum strong enough to enable such assimilation. Starting with primarily all westerners the ratio should eventually shift in favor of the South Indians by perhaps a ratio of 2:1.

Considering the fact that a sizeable number of North Indian Hindus also seek work in South India in the early stages of their career, they too could be surrounded by culturally sensitive South Indian Christians during their tenure. The process of impacting North India for Christ could also take place in the South as well, and continue on when these Hindus return north.

Under the auspices of this new paradigm at some point the end game for the West will be to hand over the function of impacting North India to the South India Church. Only the Church of India has the personnel required to reach the 750 million and ever growing population of North India.

Figure 2: Third and a Half Wave

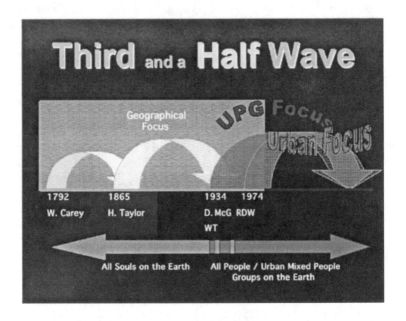

Conclusion: The "Third and a Half Wave"

In the West, Columcille was the best person the sixth century could produce–a prince, poet, scholar, soldier, holy man.[25] Similarly, Sundar Singh is
considered the most influential Indian Christian of the twentieth century,
"like a flower that blossoms on an Indian stem."[26] Twenty-first century India desperately needs a new breed of the caliber represented by these two
men. India needs the West's best. It needs an initial critical-mass of approximately 7,000 professionals *capable of producing professional power-
encounters* in all of the practical economic arenas upon which the middle
and upper-middle class peoples of urban Northern India are dependent.
Large numbers of businessmen, entrepreneurs, managers, computer-
scientists, specialized medical personnel, accountants, practical engineers
and professionals in many other areas are needed. Taking up both the vision
of Christ and the *modus operandi* of the Nestorians, this force must fully
penetrate the land by entering into the many and diverse urban workplaces

of India. In the rural areas, the church planting movements among un-reached people groups must continue. But as fast as the West can begin to raise up true professionals for this new paradigm, its focus should shift to starting secular-professional insider movements in the ever-growing urban settings of India. The overall change in strategy will thus involve a shift from an intentional primary focus on unreached people groups to an inten-tional co-focus that includes both the former and intensifying efforts to im-pact the natural leadership residing in the workplaces of urban India. This model thus calls for a continued shift away from a *geographic* focus and for an additional shift **to** *a merger of people groups* focus within the many globalized-secular settings of urban India. It could be called the "third and a half wave."[27]

We in the West cannot continue to quench our consciences by *paying others to do the Great Commission for us*. We must instead start executing our stewardship in a way consistent with the glorious efforts of the earlier Church of the East, the Nestorians. We must send out only our best and most qualified to "fight the good fight" in North India. And, in parallel with the work of this new vanguard, we must focus our efforts in South India (and in the Christian states of North-East India) on the raising up of a new type of *secularly professional* and *unbiased* Indian laborer who can ade-quately join ranks with their expatriate new breed counterparts.

Discussion Starters

1. What will the execution of this new paradigm mean in terms of the educational and training routes required the equip aspiring new-breed missionaries for urban India?
2. What type of new mission agencies will be required to raise-up, train and sustain the new breed missionary?
3. In what ways will the western churches have to be reprogrammed in order to be able to properly appreciate and support the new breed missionary (through prayer and other ways) as he or she ministers in North India?
4. How did Jesus go about training bigotry and bias out of His twelve disciples?
5. What will be the main hindrances put forth by the prevailing paradigms to this renewed initiative from the past?

Notes

1. D. Pani, "Fatal Hindu Gospel Stumbling Blocks," *International Journal of Frontier Mission* 18.1 (2001): pp.23-32; D. Pani, "The Devastating Role of Cultural Bigotry on Our Outreach to Hindus," *International Journal of Frontier Mission* 22.2 (2005): pp.57-68; D. Pani, "Resolving the Chemistry of the "Cultural Sins + Gullibility: Fatal Hindu Gospel Stumbling Block." Unpublished paper.

2. D. Pani, "Submission to Oppression in India: Lessons from History," *International Journal of Frontier Mission* 18.1 (2001): pp.33-41; S. H. Moffett, *A History of Christianity in Asia,* Vol. I., 1998; John Steward, *Nestorian Missionary Enterprise, 1928* (1979); John England, *The Hidden History of Christianity in Asia,* 1998.

3. John Desjarlais, *The Throne of Tara*, 1990.

4. D. Pani, "The Rise and Demise of the Nestorian Church in North India." Unpublished paper.

5. Eric J. Sharpe, *The Riddle of Sadhu Sundar Singh* (Intercultural Publications, New Delhi), 2004.

6. Phyllis Thompson, *Sadhu Sundar Singh*, 1973.

7. Ibid.

8. Ibid.

9. Ibid.

10. Ibid.

11. Ibid.

12. Kim Comer, ed., *Wisdom of the Sadhu, Teachings of Sundar Singh*, 2000, p.183.

13. K. P. Yohannan, *Revolution in World Missions*, 1986.

14. Arun Shourie, *Harvesting Our Souls,* 2000.

15. Tomas P. M. Barnett, *The Pentagon's New Map* (Putnam, New York), 1994.

16. D. Wilson and R. Purushothaman, "Dreaming with BRICs: The Path to 2050", Global Economics Paper No: 99, Goldman Sachs. http://www.gs.com/insight/research/reports/99.pdf.

17. Indiacore, "Urban Infrastructure" http://www.indiacore.com/urban-infra.html.

18. Ibid.

19. "'Security Demographics' PAI Report-Stress factor 2: Rapid Urban Growth," http://www.edcnews.se/Research/SecDemStress2-urban.html

20. B. Yun and P. Hattaway, *The Heavenly Man* (Monarch Books, Grand Rapids), 2002.

21. David Garrison, *Church Planting Movements* (Wigtake Resources, Bangalore), 2004.

22. D. Pani, Unpublished paper.

23. Leslie Brown, *The Indian Christians of St. Thomas*, 1956.

24. S. H. Moffett 1998; John Steward 1979; John England 1998; Ian Gillman and H. J. Klimkeit, *Christians in Asia Before 1500*, 1999; T.V. Philip, *East of the Euphrates, Early Christianity in Asia,* 1998; D. Pani, Unpublished paper.

25. Desjarlais 1990.

26. Friedrich Heiler, The Gospel of Sadhu Sundar Singh (translated into English from the 1924 German Ed.), (1996).

27. The emphasis on un-reached people groups (UPG) rather than on individuals within a geography was delineated by D. McGavran and W. C. Townsend and motivated into a current paradigm by R. D. Winter, etc. It is sometimes called the "third wave.

9

Seventeenth Century Puritan Missions: Some Implications for Business as Mission

Steven Pointer and Michael Cooper

In spite of all the snares of modernity, the modern missionary movement has made a profound impact on the way in which missions is conducted. Yet, as is common in evangelicalism, a sort of historical amnesia exists when it comes to the circumstances revolving around contemporary missiological practice. While the entrapments of colonialism are generally rejected, all the signs of a form of neo-colonialism are seemingly present in contemporary missions: the ideas of American cultural superiority, American ecclesiastic structures and polity, as well as American mission and ministry methodology.[1] With the suggestion that, "kingdom business will be the strategy of choice for the twenty-first century,"[2] a potential new entrapment of this neo-colonialism has been termed Business as Mission.

The purpose of this chapter is to examine historically and missiologically the Puritan missionary efforts in 17th-century New England. Specifically, it will focus on the manner in which commerce impacted the missionary activities of the Puritans in the New World. Through the lens of the Massachusetts Bay Colony the paper will study the motivation and impact of colonial business activities on the missionary movement. Ultimately, it will draw missiological principles from this historical context for consideration in the contemporary Business as Mission strategy. The hope is that an historical awareness of the past will be of assistance in the present and on to the future.

Understanding Business as Mission

Some have suggested that Business as Mission (BAM) is a relatively recent development in modern mission strategy. While many associated with the "new" movement have attempted to suggest that BAM is more like the ministry of Aquila and Priscilla than Paul,[3] there simply is insufficient biblical data for such an assertion. Nevertheless, the BAM issue group of the Lausanne committee provides legitimate rationale for the strategy. According to the issue group, 80 percent of the world's impoverished are situated in areas where Islam, Hinduism and Buddhism are dominant. It is in those areas where the countries' unemployment reaches from 30-80 percent. Not only is unemployment and poverty at issue, but these countries also represent the world's fastest growing populations.

BAM's strategy focuses on utilizing the skills and abilities of business entrepreneurs to enter creative access countries "legitimately." Contrasted with tent-making, Tetsunao Yamamori suggests that, "These businesses are not fronts to get into closed countries (with attendant ethical problems), but real enterprises that meet real human needs."[4] The objective is to create "kingdom businesses" having the goal of utilizing profits for "kingdom work." One motivating factor for BAM is its attempt to address the dependency created by Western missions for Western financial resources. History, however, testifies to the fact that this is by no means a unique strategy.

Case Study: The Massachusetts Bay Colony

Ask any schoolchild why the Pilgrims/Puritans came to the New World and you are most likely to get the answer: they came for religious freedom — and, to be sure, there is more than a germ of truth in this stock response. Much less likely would the reply be that they came as part of a commercial enterprise that was profit-driven. Yet, this aspect, too, is no less part of the story, albeit a less familiar one. The colonization of New England in the seventeenth century is characterized by the marriage of business and religious mission. As such, it represents a fitting historical case study for the new impetus in understanding Business as Mission.

The Plymouth Colony that was founded in 1620 was based on a business agreement between Pilgrim settlers and their financial backers in London. The understanding was that the "adventurers" would remain in England and provide the fiscal backing, the "planters" would re-locate to New England and provide the labor, and both groups would realize a profit — one from their investment of capital, the other from their investment of labor. The Massachusetts Bay Colony that followed in 1630 was organized upon the same investment principles. Indeed, it became an "established transatlantic settlement model in which the interests of settlers and financiers were combined in a single enterprise."[5]

Although all the New England colonies of the seventeenth century (Plymouth, New Haven, Connecticut, Rhode Island, and Massachusetts Bay) shared similar patterns, for the purposes of this case study we will focus only on the experiences of the Puritan Massachusetts Bay Colony in the first half century of its existence (1630-1680). That enterprise was a combination of distinctive Puritan beliefs and English culture at a particular stage in its development. Among the notable changes that England had experienced in the previous century of Tudor-Stuart rule were the convulsive religious upheavals of religious reformation, the effects of rising literacy and print media, a centralized nation-state with an identity that fused English nationality and Protestant faith, the still-emerging issue of absolutist monarchial claims versus the authority of Parliament, the growing commercialization of agriculture and spirit of capitalism, and expanding global colonial and commercial aspirations.

We need to see, then, that the Massachusetts Bay Colony, like its earlier predecessors in Tudor-Stuart England (beginning with the Russia Company in 1553, and also including the East India Company, the Levant Company, the Virginia Company, and the Plymouth Company) began as a trading corporation. Its charter of 1629 was a grant by the Crown of commercial concessions to entrepreneurs willing to assume the risks of exploration and settlement. In fact, these creative ventures for trading and colonizing distant parts of the globe represented new ideas in business practice that we now associate with the modern corporation: ideas such as limited liability for stockholders, the use of management committees, and the payment of dividends.[6] Amazingly, King Charles I allowed the charter for the Bay Colony to be brought to the New World, where this commercial document was transformed into a quasi-constitutional one, as company meetings in New England became the basis of a representative government.

To these economic and cultural factors, we must also add the distinctive Puritan beliefs that fueled this enterprise. Reformed theology combined with the Reformation principle of vocation to produce the Calvinist work ethic in its purest form. New England represents the only historical case where Puritanism served as the dominant cultural model and the foundation of the social order. To be sure, English Puritans, as "the hotter sort of Protestants" (in Patrick Collinson's apt phrase), had national, social, ecclesiastical and spiritual aspirations for the Mother Country. But, except for the revolutionary interlude of the 1640s and 1650s, Old England usually thwarted the Puritan culture of discipline and reform, as a succession of monarchs proved unresponsive and the Anglican establishment too often hostile to such designs. Ironically, however, the Anglican agenda (especially under Archbishop William Laud) of "resacralizing the church...had the effect of desacralizing the workplace," and the Puritans of Massachusetts Bay responded with ever greater resolve that "plows and shop counters — not to mention spinning wheels, gristmills, and fishing boats — did indeed remain sanctified means for seeking God's glory."[7] They were adamant that it was labor that gave meaning to life and dignity to the worker. As Perry Miller has asserted, that everyone should have a calling and work diligently at it was a cardinal belief of Puritanism. "Everyone has a talent for something, given of God, which he must improve."[8]

Thus, the ideas of calling and improvement made work in seventeenth century New England as much a spiritual expression as it was an economic function. However, contra Perry Miller's interpretation of New England society as initially pious and communal and only later materialistic and individualistic as the commercial aspect of the enterprise overwhelmed the religious, John Frederick Martin argues convincingly that the twin impulses of business and mission were present in the New England experiment from the outset. Having been launched by a business corporation in the colony's birth, its subsequent reproduction in the form of founding additional towns also took on the same character. All the important decisions made at the start of the colonial period reflect this: to embrace a pro-development ethos regarding the wilderness, to rely on business entrepreneurs to accomplish that, to organize towns upon business principles, to exclude non-shareholders from land divisions, and to encourage individuals to profit from landownership as the reward for helping to develop the frontier.[9]

Initial impressions of New England suggested that economic prosperity would never be a temptation for the settlers. Endowed with meager resources, a short growing season and harsh winters, even the friends of the Puritans back home described New England as "poore, cold, and useless."[10] It is all the more remarkable, then, that within a generation of its founding, the Bay Colony had a flourishing, diversified economy which included fishing, shipbuilding and commerce.

So, in point of fact, fear of starvation and concern for survival quickly gave way to the more persistent lament, that economic success would produce spiritual decline. In countless jeremiads from the second and subsequent generations, Puritan ministers bewailed the formula of declension: piety leads to industry that produces wealth that leads to worldliness. As Cotton Mather (1663-1728) put it succinctly, "Religion begot prosperity, and the daughter devoured the mother."[11] Such warnings, Stephen Innes argues, helped provide "a cultural counterweight" and "the moral ballast" to this fledgling capitalist commonwealth, and ensured that the ethics of the marketplace never went unchallenged.[12] That the Puritans endorsed "material opportunity" and the workings of the market is clear, but they also worried about prosperity and its implications for religious fervor.

If we have revealed something of the business character and success of this enterprise, what about its sense of mission? What was this "errand into the wilderness" to accomplish? Historians have rightly seen John Winthrop's famous lay sermon of 1630, "Model of Christian Charity," as articulating that collective sense of mission from the outset. Evocatively presenting the new settlement to be a "city upon a hill," Winthrop frames his discourse around the concept of covenant. A people in covenant with God will enjoy his favor, provided that they remain faithful to the conditions of that covenant. Such fidelity will require subordination of individual self-interest to the good of the community, and the leavening rule of that community by truly regenerated saints.[13]

Over the next several decades the particulars of that mission would be worked out on several fronts. First, the planting of churches, properly reformed according to the "Congregational Way" (as the new system was called), was a very high priority. An ecclesiology, assumed to be the biblical model, dictated that the local church was the equal of all other congregations and was a covenanted gathering of true believers, who were able to give testimony to their regenerated status, and were led by a minister whose ordination and office existed only in relation to that congregation. Did such a system raise the bar so high for church membership that many persons who would have been welcomed into other Protestant churches found themselves excluded in the Bay Colony? Such concern was common; one minister wrote to John Cotton in 1642 to report that "many [are] murmuring that we come to make Heathens rather than convert Heathens to Christianity."[14]

Second, as important as the church was, the Puritan vision and sense of mission was much more comprehensive. Nothing less than the creation of a godly commonwealth was their goal. To that end, these "visible saints" labored to frame the institutional structures of civil government, education, family life, economic activity, and social ethics, guided, as ever, by their reading of scripture. This "Puritan canopy" over all of life surely represents one of the most ambitious efforts by Christians to implement a biblical worldview in the history of Christianity.[15]

But third, and for our purposes of most interest, what about mission in the sense of evangelistic outreach, in particular to Native Americans? There is some evidence to suggest that this missionary purpose was important to the Puritans. After all, the very charter that John Winthrop brought across the Atlantic with him stated that "the principal end of this plantation [was to] win and incite the natives of [the] country to...the Christian faith," and the founders of the Massachusetts Bay Company had commissioned a seal depicting an Indian uttering the Macedonian plea: come over and help us (Acts 16:9). However, it seems that such language was quite conventional at the time and does not reflect the true priorities for the founders. Indeed, until the mid-1640s virtually nothing was done to promote the evangelization of the natives.[16] Why, we ask?

Richard Cogley, in the best study of Puritan mission work among Native Americans, puts forth several possible explanations. Puritan missionary theology did not employ a direct form of evangelism, but rather what he terms an "affective model." Given the presumed linkage for the English between "civility" and religion (and usually in that order), it was assumed that growing familiarity by the natives with English ways would automatically create a desire to embrace both the culture and the faith of these newcomers. Of course, quite apart from the ethnocentrism of this model of evangelism, it also meant that such a mission would not begin until the natives requested it![17] Complicating the task even more were the difficulties of overcoming the language barriers, the philosophy of English colonization (and the assumption that all aliens — whether Native Americans, Irish, etc. — must be pushed beyond the pale of English settlement), and the particulars of millennial eschatology whereby some Puritans expected minimal native conversions until after the national conversion of the Jews.

The event that precipitated a change in Puritan-Indian relations in Massachusetts was the submission of six sachems to the authority of the Bay Colony's General Court in 1644. Thereafter, John Eliot (1604-1690), minister of the church in Roxbury and destined to be known as the "Apostle to the Indians," began his mission to the coastal natives in 1646, and proceeded to learn the highly inflected Algonquian dialect of Massachusett. By the time of the outbreak of King Philip's War in 1675 (which, not surprisingly, severely affected mission work among the Indians), the missionary enterprise on the mainland of Massachusetts included two Native American churches and fourteen "praying towns" where Christian Indians lived together. In addition, another missionary project was begun in the 1640s on the island of Martha's Vineyard, thanks to the work of Thomas Mayhew, Jr. and his first native convert, Hiacoomes.[18] In many ways Mayhew, Congregationalist minister at Great Harbor on Martha's Vineyard, was the more effective missionary. Cogley writes that Mayhew "lived in greater proximity to natives and was a more perceptive student of their culture."[19] Nonetheless, these two missionaries pioneered and dominated New England evangelistic efforts in the seventeenth century.

Most germane for our purposes is to note the means of support for this evangelistic mission. In 1649 the New England Company was incorporated in England to provide the funding for this project. English ministers and their congregations were solicited to collect donations for the work among these New World natives. To keep this work fresh in the minds of English Christians, Eliot (and others) supplied a steady stream of reports that were published and well-circulated in England. For example, in the fifth of this series, "Tears of Repentance" (1653), Eliot described the first stage of forming a Native American church in Natick. With the restoration of the Stuart monarchy in 1660, this corporation was dissolved, but replaced in 1662 by the Company for Propagation of the Gospel in New England and the Parts Adjacent in America. Both corporate charters (1662 and the earlier 1649) asserted that the Mother Country would have to fund these missions because New England could not afford to do so! Whether true or not, in 1649, Cogley contends that this claim was "manifestly false in the 1660s."[20] We can only speculate why New Englanders shirked this opportunity to be involved, if only financially, in this mission work.

Furthermore, representatives of the several New England colonies (Commissioners of the United Colonies) served as the intermediaries between the corporation and the missionaries, making decisions about allocating goods and moneys. John Eliot's relations with these commissioners were often strained, since their primary responsibility was intercolonial defense, not Indian missions. Thus, Eliot lamented in 1652 that they were "not so well informed or persuaded" about these evangelistic endeavors.[21] Still, an estimated 75-80 percent of the allocated funds before 1675 went either to the Eliot or to the Mayhew missions, financing the expenses of these missionaries and their co-workers, underwriting the publication costs of Eliot's works in Massachusetts, and paying for the English-language education of natives. Nonetheless, the half-hearted involvement of the commissioners in this work was compounded by their likely dishonesty in appropriating these funds as well.[22]

By the time that Eliot began his mission work, the Indians of eastern Massachusetts had already become dependent upon the English economy through selling their lands to colonists and by participating in the fur trade. With the establishment of the praying towns, Indian proselytes improved their economic standing through paying jobs, apprenticeships, new cottage industries, and the various consumer goods supplied by the New England Company.

What observations, then, can be made about the relationship between business and missions in the seventeenth century Bay Colony? First, we may note that the relationship was a thoroughly intimate and integrated one at all levels. Englishmen were enamored with the promise of business principles, the prospects of mercantile capitalism, and especially the allure of the potential of corporations. To that, Puritans added their distinctive valuation of individual calling and commitment to improvement through industry and thrift. Combined in the New World context where the wilderness became the enemy to be subdued, Puritans unleashed an entrepreneurial energy that brought economic success and, simultaneously, the means of fulfilling their divinely-appointed mission. Yet, second, we also note that the collective ownership of the mission to plant churches and create a Christian commonwealth required the acknowledgement that economic success was a double-edged sword: it signaled both divine approbation and covenant blessing, but also served as perpetual temptress. Whatever one thinks about the accuracy of the declension motif in Puritan history, a significant number of Puritans believed that spiritual apathy was a reality and yearned for a fresh visitation of God's Spirit. Such yearnings were to be realized in the Great Awakening.

Finally, the absence of collective ownership of the mission to the Indians is most evident. Cogley contends that John Eliot was probably no different than other colonists when he began his work among the Indians in 1646, but that he "was transformed by his exposure to the natives: he learned to appreciate their humanity and to sympathize with their problems."[23] Sadly, his fellow ministers and colonists never experienced a similar transformation. Instead, the mission was delegated to a handful of missionaries, who, regardless of how committed they were in their labors, were always to be handicapped by congregational polity (which precluded their fulltime appointment as missionaries to the Indians; Eliot and Mayhew always continued as ministers to their congregations, with other ministers rotating in to fill their vacancies when they were away); by the delegation of the financial responsibility for the mission to England from New England; and by the bureaucratic difficulties of support discussed above. In sum, if the glory of New England Puritanism was its audacity to envision a thoroughly Christianized society, its shame was its lack of commitment to mobilizing its abundant resources to achieving an inclusivist version of that dream.

Implications for Missions in the 21st Century

It was Marcus Cicero who was credited with saying that "Not to know what has been transacted in former times is to be always a child. If no use is made of the labors of past ages, the world must remain always in the infancy of knowledge."[24] The Roman orator understood the importance of historical awareness. While a reflection of the Puritan mission in New England is interesting and compelling, the implications of this study for the contemporary strategy of BAM are significant and insightful.

Business' Affects on Religious Fervor

First, it should be of no surprise that the pursuit of material wealth often leads to the decline of religious fervor. The Puritan desire for religious freedom of expression was soon overcome by the need for physical sustenance. While it is understandable and necessary to provide for the well being of a community, it was not long before the provision was looked upon as a means to an end. Undergirded by the Reformation conviction of calling as much a material as a spiritual notion, the Protestant ethic soon became the driving motivation in the service of God. According to Max Weber, "Waste of time is thus the first and in principle the deadliest of sins"[25] in Puritanism. Concomitant with the Protestant ethic was the decline of religious fervor. Weber would call it "the problem of the secularizing influence of wealth."[26] The Puritans help us to see that over time missionary zeal could be replaced by the material concerns of this life. Henry Bowden noted, "In missionary work in early New England there was thus a wide gap between declared intentions and actual accomplishments."[27] Business, in essence, has the potential to take the place of missions.

Colonialism and the Western Way

Second, Stephen Neill notes that colonialism holds the idea of bringing Western civilization to the uncivilized.[28] Commonly represented as the three "Cs," Christianity, commerce and civilization, colonialism was inherent in the mission of the Puritans. David Bosch noted that there was little difference between "mission" and "colonialism" from the 16th century onward.[29] Mission societies had a dual mandate, one to evangelize and one to civilize.[30] As seen in the Puritan mission, civility came first and as Paul Hiebert has noted in regards to colonialism, "to become Christian" meant "to become civil."[31] In fact, as Bowden observed, the Puritans shared the Englishman's sense of cultural superiority.[32] This tendency continues as one result of the Protestant ethic.

Rose Wu has recognized that global capitalism appears to be the new colonialism. As industrial nations seek their market share the cost is often the exploitation of people in terms of some loosing jobs and others acquiring them all for the sake of the bottom line.[33] She notes, "the ideology of the free market today has assumed god-like proportions."[34] BAM seems at points to suggest that Western capitalism is not simply biblical, but God's strategy for bringing the gospel to the unevangelized of the world.[35] While there might be some degree of truth here, it must be careful to not equate material gain with spirituality. As we learned from the Puritans, the Western way is not necessarily the right way outside the context of the West.

Deliberate Disciple-making as Non-negotiable

Third, as previously noted, the missionary strategy of the Puritans was summarized as the "affective model." It was assumed that the natives would convert once they saw the benefits of English civility. As the historical record makes clear, this did happen, but unfortunately only on a minor scale partly due to the emphasis on survival. While the mandate to "wynn and incite the natives of the Country to the Knowledge and obedience of the only true God and Savior of Mankinde, and the Christian fayth," formed a part of the Massachusetts Bay charter it was more common to look at the "poor savage" as a hindrance to colonial expansion.[36]

Ralph Miller has correctly noted that the emphasis of the Great Commission (Matt 28:18-20) is disciple-making rather than the oft-translated imperative "go."[37] While the Puritans had this perspective, the emphasis was on making disciples in the image of English Puritanism. This is a natural and often unfortunate tendency for those on a mission and would presumably be a tendency for BAM as well, not to mention many other evangelical missions' endeavors. However, the Puritans help us understand the essential nature of missiological and theological education. While BAM is said to offer business people more legitimacy and opportunity to receive long-term visas it must not do so at the expense of cross-cultural educational preparation.

The Rule of Gold

Finally, while the center of Christianity has shifted from the northern hemisphere to the southern, Western countries continue to be leaders in the missionary enterprise. According to *World Christian Encyclopedia,* the West sends more missionaries and missions moneys than any region of the world. The United States, most notably, sends more missions moneys per capita than any other country.[38] Along with the great wealth of the United States comes the notion of responsibility. BAM offers tremendous potential for utilizing that wealth for the benefit of the unevangelized.

Added wealth, however, brings added suspicion. The Native American response to the Puritans, while initially positive, turned negative due in part to the perception that the colonizers simply wanted land without regard to the people already inhabiting it. No matter how pure the motives for evangelizing the unevangelized, capital often becomes a motivating factor for the missionary or businessperson and the national. The unfortunate response is often one of suspicion. This is not unique; in fact, Jonathan Bonk has noted this instance in the London Missionary Society in Central Africa and Central China.[39] Ruth Tucker, reflecting on the time period, notes that the greatest reason for the unsuccessful evangelization of Native Americans was, "the intense conflict between the two cultures for supremacy over the land."[40] Nevertheless, the ministry of the Mayhews provides an example of the importance of respect for people's rights and their cultures.[41] As BAM considers new opportunities in foreign lands, economic ventures must take existing social and economic structures into consideration and strive to work within them rather than imposing western economic principles out of context.

Conclusion

Lesslie Newbigin suggested that Western Christianity was one of the greatest secularizing forces in the world.[42] While work is as much an act of worship as ministry,[43] undoubtedly one of the issues that contributed to this secularizing force was business. This chapter has suggested through the historical lens of the Massachusetts Bay Colony that there are inherent dangers to focusing on business as a means to missions. As suggested, historical awareness and application of lessons learned in contemporary missions strategy will help to assure that the same mistakes are not repeated.

Weber concludes his classical treatment of the effect of industry on religion with a lengthy quote from John Wesley. After observing the effects, as well as the necessity, of business and religion, Wesley grew increasingly concerned. In no less than four sermons over a period of a few years, Wesley drew the attention of Christians to the dangers of riches. Weber noted that Wesley's understanding of the struggles of the material world summed up well the entire thesis of his book. Wesley was particularly concerned for the increase of pride, anger and love of the world that were concomitants of increased wealth. His solution was simply to give away all that is possible. He states,

> What way, then I ask again, can we take, that our money may not sink us to the nethermost hell? There is one way, and there is no other under heaven. If those who gain all they can, and save all they can, will likewise GIVE all they can, then the more they gain, the more they will grow in grace and the more treasure they will lay up in heaven.[44]

This is a timeless reminder for us as we consider the next "strategy of choice for 21st century missions."

Discussion Starters

1. The chapter suggests that the pursuit of material wealth often leads to the decline of religious fervor. How can BAM balance the two?
2. How might BAM guard against exporting the superior notion of Western capitalism as God's economic plan and the concomitant effects of "civilizing" a culture?
3. The chapter suggests that the growing familiarity by natives with English ways would automatically create a desire to embrace both the culture and the faith of the Puritans. What lessons for contemporary missions can be learned from the successes and mistakes of the Puritan mission?
4. What other historical examples illustrate this missions strategy of commerce impacting the missionary activities of their day?

Notes

1. Michael T. Cooper (2005) "Colonialism, Neo-colonialism and Forgotten Missiological Lessons." *Global Missiology*, vol. 2, p.2.

2. Tetsunao Yamamori, Preface in Tetsunao Yamamori and Kenneth A. Eldred, eds., *On Kingdom Business: Transforming Missions Through Entrepreneurial Strategies* (Wheaton, IL: Crossway, 2003), p.10.

3. Yamamori and Eldred, eds., 2003, p.9; Peter Tsukahira, "The Integration of Business and Ministry" in Yamamori eds., 2003, pp.124-126.

4. Ibid., 2003, p.10.

5. John Fredrick Martin, *Profits in the Wilderness* (Chapel Hill, N.C: University of North Carolina Press, 1991), p.35.

6. Stephen Innes, *Creating the Commonwealth* (New York: W. W. Norton and Co, 1995), p.206.

7. Ibid., pp.12-13.

8. Perry Miller, *The New England Mind: From Colony to Province* (Boston: Beacon Press, 1953), pp.40-41.

9. Martin, *Profits in the Wilderness* (Chapel Hill, N.C: University of North Carolina Press, 1991), pp.3-5.

10. Oliver Cromwell quoted in Innes, 1995, p.8.

11. Cotton Mather quoted in Innes, 1995, p.26.

12. Ibid., pp.30-31.

13. David D. Hall, ed., *Puritans in the New World: A Critical Anthology* (Princeton: Princeton University Press, 2004), pp.164-170.

14. Sargent Bush, Jr., *The Correspondence of John Cotton* (Chapel Hill: University of North Carolina Press, 2001), p.372.

15. Mark Noll, *America's God* (New York: Oxford University Press. 2002), pp.31-50.

16. Richard W. Cogley, *John Elliot's Mission to the Indians Before King Philip's War* (Cambridge, Mass: Harvard University Press, 1999), p.2.

17. Ibid., pp.5-18.

18. Hall, ed., 2004, p.244.

19. Cogley, 1999, p.173.

20. Cogley, 1999, p. 209.

21. John Eliot quoted in Cogley, 1999, p.215.

22. Margaret C. Szasz, *Indian Education in the American Colonies, 1607-1783* (Albuquerque: University of New Mexico Press, 1988), p.106; Cogley, 1999, pp. 216-223.

23. Cogley, 1999, p.249.

24. Source unknown.

25. Max Weber, *The Protestant Ethic and the Spirit of Capitalism* (London: Routledge, (1904 [1922]), p.104.

26. Ibid., p.118.

27. Henry Warner Bowden, *American Indians and Christian Missions: Studies in Cultural Conflict* (Chicago: University of Chicago, 1981), p.112.

28. Stephen Neill, *Colonialism and Christian Mission* (New York: McGraw-Hill, 1966), p.12.

29. David Bosch, *Transforming Mission: Paradigm Shifts in Theology of Mission.* Maryknoll, N.Y: Orbis, 1991), pp.303-305.

30. Donald A. Jacobs, Contextualization in Missions in James M. Phillips and Robert T. Coote, eds., *Towards the 21st Century in Christian Mission,* (Grand Rapids, MI: Eerdmans, 1993), p.237.

31. Paul Hiebert, *Anthropological Reflections on Missiological Issues* (Grand Rapids, MI: Baker, 1994), p.76.

32. Bowen, 1981, p.122.

33. Rose Wu, Standing With the Poor or With the Powerful? *International Review of Mission* 87, Iss. 345 (April 1998), pp. 213-214.

34. Ibid., p.214.

35. See for example Ralph A. Miller, "Key Concepts and Lessons Learned" in Tetsunao Yamamori and Kenneth A. Eldred, eds., 2003, p.281.

36. Ruth Tucker, *From Jerusalem to Irian Jaya: A Biographical History of Christian Missions* (Grand Rapids, MI: Zondervan, 1983), p.84.

37. Miller, 2003, p.283.

38. E. Michael Jafferian, The statistical state of the missionary enterprise. *Missiology: An International Review* 30 no. 1 (January 2002), pp.15-32.

39. Jon Bonk, The Role of Affluence in the Christian Missionary Enterprise from the West. *Missiology: An International Review* 14, no. 4 (October 1986), pp.437-461.

40. Tucker, 1983, p.104.

41. Ibid., p.89.

42. Lesslie Newbigin, *Honest Religion for Secular Man* (Philadelphia: Westminster. 1966).

43. Wayne Grudem, How Business in Itself Can Glorify God in Tetsunao Yamamori and Kenneth A. Eldred, eds., 2003, pp.127-152.

44. Weber, 1904 [1922], pp.118-119.

10

The Integrative Role of Business in Islamic Daw'ah

William Wagner

In the fall of 2000, I became interested in why some major religions and churches were growing and others were not. Theological considerations did not seem to make the difference, rather it seemed to come down to methodological considerations. There were some groups that have experienced rather rapid growth during the last two decades while others were either retaining the status quo or decreasing. Why were some growing? What strategies were they using that produced such grow?

After making a preliminary study I decided to focus in on six growing groups. Four could be considered to be denominations (however I do not think that two of them would like this designation) while one was a world religion and the other was more a philosophy or a way of life. The six growing groups included the: Southern Baptists, Assemblies of God, Jehovah's Witness, Mormons, Muslims, and homosexuals.

My major concern was not their belief systems or their organizational structure. I was not concerned how they identified themselves. The only criterion for choosing the six was that each had a history of growth, both in numbers and in influence. What was of interest was their overall strategies and methodologies. One of the basic questions asked of the six was *how did they use business for the furtherance of their cause*. This chapter will concentrate on the Muslims' use of business in their missions strategies with some references to the other groups when deemed pertinent.

Before addressing the major theme, observe how one Islamic scholar perceives the topic. Kherviam Mural identifies three levels at work in the creation of a global Nation of Islam. They include:

1. The macro level: the level of overall *ummah* and Muslim societies and states.
2. The intermediate level: the level of very large groups, institutions, and structures.
3. The micro level: the level of the individual person and small organizations.[1]

Islam works on all three levels in its strategy. In my studies I felt that only three of the groups named had developed complete strategies at all three levels: Mormons, Muslims, and Homosexuals. The other three did a good job at the first two levels but found lacking in the third, that of trying to influence a whole nation.

For example, the Mormons are well known for their two-year missionary service during their college years, usually between their sophomore and junior year. Much of their work consists of doing missions on the intermediate and micro levels. Going from door to door and building relationships with people of their target group is one of their specialties. Here they are enjoy great success, especially in the Americas, but possibly the greatest success in the long run will be at the macro level. In studying their program, one can see that they not only want to send their young men out to do the micro work, but also to prepare them for the macro task. Upon completion of their two-year service, the young men return to college to finish their university degree. When the recruiters for international business and government agencies, like the FBI, the CIA and the State Department come to interview, they are often impressed that the Mormons already know another language, are a little older and have international experience. The results are that a large number of government and business recruiters seek out the Mormons. Today there is an inordinate number of Mormons working in international business, the FBI and the CIA. In a recent article from the Baptist Press their success was given:

> The Latter-Day Saints population in greater Washington has reached 50,000 and Mormons are key figures in the Treasury Department, the Peace Corps, and the Bureau of Land Management, ...Mormons oversee the White House legal office and advise Congress on international affairs, religious freedom, Social Security, housing, land use, educational reform and matters of war...Mormons are disproportionately represented in the Central Intelligence Agency....a designated 'employment specialist' shares computer lists, phone numbers and job openings to help the LDS population further penetrate the government.[2]

The Mormons are probably the best of all the groups in infiltrating businesses to further their religious beliefs on the macro-level. Homosexuals are also quite adept at this and have proven to be successful in getting business interests to support their national agenda. It seems that evangelical Christians are only at the beginning of developing a mega-strategy that will influence the whole social structure.

The Overall Islamic Strategy

In studying the overall strategy of Islam in today's world, there are four pillars that support the achievement of their aims. These are: (1) Daw'ah (missions), (2) jihad (holy war), (3) mosques (presence), and (4) immigration.

Influence Through Business

Islam does not separate different activities into pigeonholes as is done in the West. Thus, it will help us to see that the use of business is a part of all four pillars.

The first pillar, Da'wah, is the silent revolution that is possibly the most successful of the four in today's world, and is one of those Arabic words that have several valid meanings. Jane I. Smith, professor of Islamic Studies at Hartford Seminary in Connecticut, in her book, *Islam in America*, gives three different definitions for the word Da'wah:

1.   The active business of the propagation of Islam with the end of making conversions
2.   The effort to bring those who have fallen away from Islam back to active involvement in the faith
3.   The responsibility to simply live quiet lives of Muslim piety and charity, with the hope that by example they can encourage wayward coreligionists as well as others that Islam is the right and appropriate path to God.[3]

The second pillar, jihad, is generally and traditionally defined in English as "holy war." The role of business for jihad, as well as the third pillar, mosques, is primarily to provide funding for weapons for Holy War and the construction of expensive mosques. It is necessary to understand that Islam has a great amount of money to use for its aims of world conquest. Let me give an example. A physician friend who had worked for five years in Saudi Arabia stated that all one needed to do was a little mathematics to see the enormous wealth that countries like Saudi Arabia have. He stated that

Saudi Arabia pumps ten million barrels of oil a day. At this writing the price of oil is approximately $50 a barrel. Of this amount the government retains $40, which means that they receive $400,000,000 a day from its oil revenue. This goes on every day of the year with the revenues flowing into a country with only six million citizens. I have discovered that they give about one fourth of this revenue for the furtherance of Islam. The exact distribution of the funds is kept secret, but recently the Saudis donated most of the $8.5 million to build a mosque for south-central Los Angeles and five other major mosques around the country.[4]

Immigration, the fourth pillar, also has its roots in the business world. When a Muslim goes to a designated city to live, funds are provided to find a home and start a business. And they are interest-free. Once the business is up and running, relatives will come to the same area and the first man has the obligation to help them start similar businesses. Soon they are established in the area and new areas are sought out for similar business start-ups. In London whole Boroughs have been taken over by Muslims employing the same strategy. Some think that this is just a natural way of life without realizing that this is often well planned.

Influence Through the Media

Muslims are no longer willing to sit back and allow the Western media elite to cover world events unchallenged; rather, they are taking the initiative in bringing the news to a global audience. Of course their news is biased, but they reply that the Western media is also biased; therefore, what is the difference? *Al-Jazeera,* the Arabic television and press agency, is well known worldwide for upstaging the illustrious CNN with its coverage of the American wars in both Iraq and Afghanistan. Its exclusive access to Osama Bin Laden has given it such a high profile that it launched an English-Language channel in Europe and increased its Washington D.C. bureau staff from 6 to 24. The Western media is actively seeking Muslim input. CNN, not to be outdone in the Muslim world with its large audience, has launched CNN-Arabic in an attempt to reach the vast Muslim television audience worldwide. Following the September 11 events, the British Foreign Office established an Islamic Media Unit to "focus on the Arab media to which it reaches out through personal interaction for an exchange of views."

The Islamic world also focuses firmly on spreading Islam through the use of mass media and governmental organizations. One of the primary ways this occurs is through the Islamic relief organizations. Dr. Roushdy Shahata, a professor at Halawan University in Egypt said, "The journalists must always have a good Islamic bias." Also, being a religious journalist, he can write to his subjects from an Islamic point of view. "He assures that the goal of the journalists must first of all have causes."[5] The main organization that promotes the use of the media is the World Islamic League. It also has an alliance with several other large media organizations, including the *Middle East Newspaper*. In a recent conference in Jeddah, Saudi Arabia concerning ecumenical (Islamic) media, Dr. Thraky emphasized once again the importance of the mass media in the spread of Islam. They agreed on a plan of cooperation to proclaim Islam and display it in a better light. Thraky also said that all the mass media must cooperate with the Daw'ah organizations.[6]

There appear to be five components in their unprecedented attempt to communicate their message to the West. These components include:

Component 1: "We are not...." This is an attempt to change the negative stereotypes of Muslims in the Western world by the emerging Muslim media Mongols. For a century the Arab has been seen as a rather dim-witted fellow living in an inhospitable part of the world. When there was the need for comedy relief in a film, the director could generally do well by inserting an Arab into the script. With the emergence of political correctness, all minorities benefited from the new unwritten rules concerning stereotypes. For the Arabs, petrodollars along with some very capable men gave a new impetus toward bringing about this change in how the media works. Several organizations were formed that had as a part of their purpose statement the influencing of the media. One such organization is the Council on American-Islamic Relations (CAIR), a Washington-based institution founded in 1994. Daniel Pipes has written: "CAIR presents itself to the world as a standard-issue civil-rights organization whose mission is to 'promote interest and understanding among the general public with regards to Islam and Muslims in North America and conduct educational services.'"[7]

CAIR has proven to be a very active organization that has been involved in defending Islam especially in the media. In its short history, it has been involved in various means to intimidate news organizations that portray Islam in a light that they cannot accept. Among their targets have been writers such as Steven Emerson, Daniel Pipes, Shaykl Palazzi, and a host of others who dare to take issue with Islam today. Among organizations that have heard from them or felt their criticism have been *The National Post, New Republic, Los Angeles Times, Dallas Morning News, The Weekly Reader's Current Events* (a children's magazine), and many others too numerous to name.[8] In some cases CAIR will picket the offices of the targeted news organizations or organize a letter-writing campaign. In some undocumented instances, there have been threats addressed to the personnel in the organizations and the facilities where they are located. Whenever there is a terrorist attack or a Muslim is on trial, the news media will have a representative from CAIR or one of the other Muslim organizations defining their faith.

The movies and television have proven to be a problem for Islam. In the past, several movie producers have suggested making a movie on the life of Mohammed. There was fierce opposition to this because Muslims believe it is a sin to make an image of their leader. One producer decided to make the movie without an actor playing Mohammed, in which the space the actor would normally occupy would be left free. This also did not meet the approval of the Muslim community. A few years ago another attempt was made to chronicle the life of Mohammed, "presenting the story of the seventh-century Islamic prophet to an American audience largely unfamiliar with the religion he founded."[9] The producers went ahead with filming and did not show the face of the prophet. The film was about two-thirds finished when the events of September 11, 2001, took place. They were about to cancel the project when it was suggested that it be made into a two-hour documentary entitled, "Muhammad: Legacy of a Prophet."

The documentary told the story of Mohammed together with the interviews with scholars and modern-day U.S. Muslims. The Public Broadcasting Service first aired the project on December 18, 2002, right before Christmas. Rather than just being a film about the Prophet, it became a tool for Muslim propaganda. It received raves from the secular press but was considered by many to be a film seeking to win converts to Islam. It is of interest to note that, "the largest source of funding comes from the Corporation for Public Broadcasting, a private, non-profit corporation created by Congress that in fiscal 2002 received $350 million in taxpayer funds."[10] The same network aired another documentary in 1998 on the life of Jesus where the main emphasis was from critical scholars that questioned much of the historicity of Jesus. Islam has shown that it need not be afraid of films today but rather can use them to its advantage.

Muslims did have a setback in the early 1990's when the film "Not Without My Daughter" was produced. It chronicled the life of an American woman and her daughter who were taken back to Iran, the homeland of the husband. She was not allowed to leave and basically became a slave in a Muslim context where the women have little or no rights. She finally did escape over the mountains into Turkey. One Muslims author wrote, "This film was a setback for our cause but we are now much more abreast of the media and it will not happen again."[11]

Islam has been very successful in the last ten years in redefining who they are and who they are not. But before the Muslim community can communicate positively to its skeptical Western audience, it must first convince them that Islam is not all bad, and that the Islamic faith is not the same as Palestinian suicide-bombers or women-abusers.

Another outlet that Muslims have used is the press. Recently there was a report in the English-language paper, *Gulf News,* on the Islamic Affairs Department of the government of Dubai, a member of the United Arab Emirates. The goal of this department, according to its manager, is to "project real Islamic teachings and correct faulty notions. Many non-Muslims and even Muslims maintain devious impressions about the religion. Thus, our task is to correct the faulty understanding."[12] An entire article in the *Washington Post* was devoted to the Muslim efforts to shake off negative stereotypes, chronicling the lives of three American Muslims who work for the U.S. government. "All said their jobs help break down stereotypes about Muslims." [13]

It is amazing to see how big a change has occurred in a little over a decade on how Americans view Islam and Muslims. This was no accident but is the result of a well-planned strategy that only now is becoming very effective. I doubt that there will be many articles, TV productions, movies, or magazine statements that are negative towards Islam. This will definitely not be the case with portraying Christians and the Church.

Component 2: "We are..." The first element of the Muslim media message is to dispel negative views of Muslims by projecting positive ones. As much as possible, the desire is to show that Muslims, particularly American Muslims, are decent, hard-working, loving, kind people. In short, American Muslims are just as Western as any other ethnic group in the great American "melting pot."

This, in fact, was the clear message of a series of public service announcements produced by the Islamic Media Foundation that aired to more than two million viewers across America in November 2002. The series, entitled "Your American Muslim Neighbors," showed American Muslim families in quintessential American activities: Little League games, visiting Mount Rushmore, going to worship together (albeit to a mosque), etc. The images were altogether wholesome, positive, patriotic, and serene. This production was also shown overseas in an attempt to show to Muslims living in the Middle East that Muslims have it good in America. Some commentators have ridiculed this attempt as being totally out of place in that area of the world. However, it has experienced much success in the U.S.A.

The Islamic Media Foundation has also run series of public announcements that are in keeping with the group's objectives of "letting others know our contributions to the well-being of this society."[14] Adds *The Muslim News:* "Muslim communities across America are on a PR mission to explain what their religion is all about...from political fundraisers and food drives to open houses at mosques."[15] Once again it is clear to see that their message is that Muslims, far from being bomb-bearing fanatics, are in fact paragons of charity to their American neighbors.

Component 3: "We believe..." Muslims have found that in this atmosphere of multiculturalism in America, schools are an excellent place to bring in their propaganda. At the same time that Christians are fighting the ACLU to regain basic rights in the schools, Muslims seem to have an open door to come in and proselytize. One textbook used in a California school presented Islam in a very favorable light and suggested that the students might want to dress up like Muslims and experience such activities as eating Muslim food and praying. The students often were asked to take Muslim names and role-play being a follower of Mohammad. If this were done in a Christian context, there would be many lawsuits immediately, citing the separation of church and state as the reason.

Recently one of the principals of a California school gave me a letter from the Islamic Speakers Bureau that was addressed to all principals and district superintendents. In the letter, there were announcements suggesting that the teacher have the student tune into the aforementioned TV film, *Muhammad: Legacy of a Prophet,* as well as other TV programs that were showing in their area. They also offered "An Arts and Crafts Kit for Presenting Ramadan and Eid during the Winter Holiday Season." In the letter were suggestions that all teachers and administrators attend a staff development training entitled, "Staff Development Training for Educators and Administrators: Incorporating Islamic Cultural Studies in the Curriculum and Interacting with Muslim Students." They offered to send speakers to the schools to teach courses for the classroom for grades 7 to 12 entitled, "Orientation on Islam and the Muslim Worlds in the Context of World History and Social Science." Another course for grades 10 to 12 was "Women in Islam."[16] My friend told me that those sending the letters have received many requests for speakers. For Islam in America today, schools are a potential rich harvest field because of their emphasis on multiculturalism.

The five government-employed Muslims interviewed by the *Washington Post* said clearly that they each felt obliged to reach out to non-Muslims and educate people about Islam, especially at the start of Ramadan. Ramadan, in fact, is a frequent starting point for Muslims educating non-Muslims about their faith through the media. Muslims observe it worldwide, similar to the Christian observation of Christmas or Easter in terms of its universal proactive and high importance to each faith's followers. Thus, it is an obvious conversation starter for education, even within the media. WBAY TV, an ABC-affiliated station in the Green Bay, Wisconsin area, included a brief explanation of Ramadan in a recent broadcast about the local Muslim community:

> Muslims from around the Fox Valley gathered to celebrate the beginning of Ramadan. Ramadan will last for one month. It required Muslims to fast from sunrise to sunset for the next month and to refrain from several vices listed in the Koran...Ramadan is the time for prayer and fasting. It's also a chance to show the world what Islam is all about...It's an ongoing effort to change the way Americans view the Islamic faith.[17]

The Muslim News adds: "Many of the nation's approximately 7 million Muslims will use the month of fasting and spiritual renewal...to continue their quest to make inroads into the mainstream."[18]

It is not only during Ramadan that the push for education takes place. The online version of the Saudi Arabian English daily *Arab News* has a hyperlink to a long feature on the life of the prophet Mohammad for the benefit of its English readers who may wish to know more about the Muslim faith. It is likely that there are few, if any, Arabic-language newspapers in the West that would include a link to a feature of any length on the Christian view of Jesus Christ.

There are numerous books on the market, following September 11, written by various "experts" which purport from various perspectives to educate its readers on Islam. *The Christian Science Monitor* reviewed one of these, *The Heart of Islam*. Jane Lampman wrote: "In *The Heart of Islam,* a renowned Muslim scholar offers to people interested in authentic Islamic teaching, as well as its external expressions in law, history, art, and community."[19] Glowing reviews such as this further the educational thrust of the Muslim identity through use of media. In short, the message is clear: "Let us tell you what we really believe." They do, however, report only the side that Westerners want to hear.

Component 4: "Come and see..." As Muslims correct and improve their image and educate Westerners about their faith, their next step is to begin to convert others to Islam. As Yusuf Mohammed, an attorney in the U.S. Labor Department, says, "There is a great opportunity forced on us by 9/11. A lot of people have become curious about Islam and want to know more."[20] Adds Anwar Hansan, founder and president of the Maryland-based Howard County Muslim Council, "We're trying to reach out to the community now, to remove the fear and ultimately make America a better place."[21]

While this kind of encouragement to reach out to community may take place Friday after Friday in mosques around the United States, it means little to the wider public until it is published in mainstream media. What is significant is the way local Muslim leaders are now being interviewed, quoted, and highlighted in print, radio and television reports. Through Muslim use of media, readers, listeners, and viewers who were already curious about Islam are more exposed to this faith and could become prime candidates for future conversion. Omar Al Khateeb, manager of Dubai's Islamic Affairs Department, is clear about his office's role: "We try to attract non-Muslims to our religion, which was created for any time or place." In short, the message has reached the point where it is "Come and see for yourself what we really are all about."

Component 5: "Let us tell you..." Overarching each of the other components of the Muslim message is the desire to have an active voice in the mainstream media, to be heard loud and clear in every discussion of issues that relate to faith, particularly to the Islamic world. This is the strategy behind much of the Islamic Media Foundation, which provides training and resources to help local Muslim leaders become sources for the mainstream media. In an article supported by the foundation it was written:

> To inject Islam's solutions into national forums of debate it is
> imperative to have a Muslim resource group that knows how to
> handle the media, so that mainstream media can have easy ac-
> cess to Islamic scholars and specialists whenever they need an
> Islamic perspective or need commentary on situations involving
> Muslims.[22]

To that end, the Foundation has organized the Islamic Media Access
Network, a grassroots structure consisting of Muslims interested in media
activism. This organization has plans to establish an Islamic Broadcasting
Network. It also produces *On Sight*, a weekly news magazine program that
can be used by communities on their local television station. *On Sight* reports on events and issues from a Muslim perspective.

Muslim communities around the world are catching this wave. *The
Muslim News* touts itself as:

> ...the only independent monthly Muslim newspaper in the UK–
> it is neither backed by any country nor by any organization or
> party. It is financed by subscriptions, advertising and British
> Muslim businessmen...*The Muslim News* reports on what the
> mainstream media refuses to report.[23]

Many other newly-created Muslim media groups are being organized
in order to propagate the faith. *Al-Jazeera* is the most dominant today, but
others will be heard from in the future.

Not only are there Muslim entities attempting to influence the news but
there is also the potential that Islamic interests will soon be influencing the
mainstream media even more. In an article in *Newsweek*, the writer Micael
Isikoff interviewed Prince Al-Walid bin Talal, the multibillionaire investor
who made headlines when he offered $10 million for the 9/11 victims and
was turned down by Rudy Giuliani. During the interview, the Prince complained about how the Zionists had "infiltrated" every part of the U.S. government. What infuriated him most was the "Jewish lobby's power over the
media." As Isikoff continued he noticed behind bin Talal's desk the em-
blems of the many U.S. corporations of which the prince has part ownership: AOL-Time Warner (his stake: $1 billion), NewsCorp ($1 billion), and
Disney Corp. ($50 million), not to mention his $10 billion stake in Citicorp,
the banking giant. Isikoff suggested, "But still...Surely, prince, given your
holdings, you've got a little influence with the American media yourself."
"Oh yes, he told me; he talks to the top executives of these firms all the
time. 'I try to tell them not to be biased,' he said."[24]

Influence Through Economics

Today's global economic system is both centralized and yet greatly diffused. Gigantic multinational corporations control an ever-increasing share of wealth and influence but are susceptible to boycotts organized by dissatisfied consumers. In most cases boycotts, some of which are publicized, have little or no effect on the large corporations, due in part to their size. If, however, a significant homogeneous group does seek to bring pressure, it must be heard.

In the 1970's, 1980's and even up through today, there have been attempts to have all Muslims boycott brands that are sold in Israel. Their purpose was to deny Israel the more commonly used products of the contemporary world. Varying degrees of success were achieved in that some companies' products (soft drinks being one) had to make a decision whether to sell to Israel or the surrounding Arab states. Those boycotts would ebb and flow depending on a number of issues and were not always related to politics. Businessmen seemed to always find a way around the boycotts so that their own interests were satisfied.

During and after the second Gulf War, businesses and even nations were jockeying for use of the world situation for their own benefit. The American public was called upon to order "freedom fries" instead of French fries and to stop buying French perfumes, wines, and automobiles as a way to show displeasure with Frances's lack of support for the American businesses, such as McDonalds. One source of this economic battle has been the growing influence of Islam in France.

The war caused a variety of commercial protests against America. Some of the reported protests include:

- Almost one out of four people in the Asian-Pacific region said they have avoided purchasing American brands.
- German bicycle maker Reice and Mueller has canceled all business deals with American suppliers.
- The Quibla Cola Company, a soft drink maker based in Great Britain that markets to the Muslim community, called for a boycott of United States global brands.
- Consumers in Europe and the Middle East have snapped up 4.5 million bottles of Mecca-Cola, an anti-American soft drink launched in October 2002. Mecca-Cola - with the motto that translates as, "Don't drink stupidly, drink responsibly" – has orders for fourteen million more bottles. The cola is also sold in Middle Eastern Neighborhoods in the United States: in Detroit and soon in New Jersey.[25]

Later in the same article the following was reported:

> Mecca-Cola founder Tawfik Mathouthi also plans to open Halal
> Fried Chicken restaurant, to be called HFC, a jab at the KFC
> chain. His aim: "People will stop eating and drinking American
> products and using American goods," he says, "and that will in-
> crease the social problems in the United States and increase job-
> lessness, and Americans will awake from their long sleep and
> maybe ask the United States government to respond."[26]

Muslims will continue to attempt to leverage their increasing large purchasing power to both increase their own wealth and, in many cases, to
damage American culture and even global Christian witness.

Influence Through Politics

All minorities in America now feel that even with their small percentage of
the total population they can influence public opinion through politics. Recently the announcement was made that the largest minority group in America is Hispanics, now approximately 13% of the population. If the statistics,
put out by the Muslims who claim they now have 7 million in the United
States, are correct then they would have about 2.8% of the population. It
should be noted, however, that the real figures are approximately one-half
of that estimated by Muslims. Because of the parity between the Democrats
and the Republicans, this small amount can make a large difference. The
more they grow the more political power they will have. Many Muslims
have claimed that they put George W. Bush into the presidency because
they overwhelmingly voted for him in Florida.

Radicals within Islam have learned very well how to use Democracy to
their own end. As already stated they have had some success in countries
such as Malawi in Southern Africa where a minority population was able to
win the election mainly through the investment of tremendous amounts of
funds into the electoral process. In other countries their efforts have been
thwarted, not because they did not have the votes, but because of fear of
what would happen if radical Muslims did take over the government politically. Both Algeria and Turkey are examples of countries where the funda-
mentals came close to succeeding.

The political process is much more advanced in Europe than in the
United States. In England there is now a shadow government that has been
created by the Muslims to act on their own issues, but also to be prepared if
the opportunity ever comes to take over the government. In Belgium, an
Islamic delegation arrived in the country to hold a meeting with the government and, in turn, the whole of Europe (since Brussels is fondly called
the heart of Europe). Dr. Thraky, from the World Islamic League, said,
"The European parliaments are a very good way to reach within the coun-

tries." He also said that there are many Muslims in the parliament of Belgium and that this is good because it is making good progress in the proclamation of Islam. Because of the good relationships between the Muslims in the Belgian government and the country, the World Islamic League was able to accomplish the following on their trip. They were: (1) granted permission to teach the Islamic religion in Belgium's schools, (2) granted permission to have a prayer room in the Brocksel airport, (3) granted permission to build a new Islamic Cemetery, and (4) able to have some laws changed, allowing Muslims to practice their religious commitments.[27]

In the Netherlands there are seven Islamic parliamentarians in the Parliament. Many of these are members in Dutch political parties. Dr. Marzouk, the president of the Islamic University in Holland said, "The Muslims in this country must be ready to govern Holland because of the increasing numbers of Muslims and the decreasing numbers of the original people of Holland." [28]

A successful part of their mega plan is to bring both educators and politicians to the Islamic faith. Here are some examples of their success:

1. Alexander Cronemar is a filmmaker who is involved with American foreign affairs. He has a Master's degree in Comparative Religion from Harvard University. He has also worked in the Middle East. He married an American Muslim woman and became a Muslim himself. He was the producer of the recently shown film on the life of Mohammad.[29]

2. Dr. Kasper Ibrahim Shahin, who became a Muslim on June 10, 2002. He is a scientist, economist, and professor of Technology at a state institution in the United States. He is also the president of this institution and is very well-known by former presidents George W. Bush and Ronald Reagan. He became a Muslim as a result of the influence of his Islamic friends. It was stated that he too wants to bring Islam to other scientists and prominent people in America by the use of mass media, but first he wants to bring his family into Islam.[30]

3. Dr. Hofman Murad, the former German Ambassador to Algeria, is reported as saying that he found Islam as the logical religion and one that was very close to the human mind. He found that Christianity is a faded religion. He is using all of his influence to spread Islam in Germany and around the Globe.[31]

4. The son of the President of the BBC became a Muslim, married a Muslim woman, and changed his name to Yehia Beart. It was reported that his goal is to spread Islam in the UK and help his family embrace Islam.[32]

These are just a few of the names of prominent converts as reported in the Middle East Newspaper. Islam sees the need to concentrate on the main policy-makers. One of the many rumors surrounding the death of Princess Diana was that she was killed by the Secret Service because she was considering marrying a Muslim, thus allowing the possibility of the future Queen Mother becoming a Muslim. The rumor was probably false but the concern about this possibility was real.

Conclusion

Islam claims it is the fastest-growing religion in the world. This is debatable but it is certain that they are growing rapidly. One of the reasons for their growth is its well-planned, integrative strategy of using business to finance its work and to influence people in high places. Those who have the task of developing strategies for Christian missions could learn much from the success of Islam' s integrative strategies and methodologies.

Discussion Starters

1. As Islam seeks to dominate the world, how is business an integral part of their overall strategy?
2. How does public relations and business mesh in Islam's strategy?
3. How does Islam use business as a tool for missions in a better, more effective way than Christianity?

Notes

1. Khurram Murad, *Da'wah Among Non-Muslims in the West* (London: Islamic Foundation, 1989) p.3.

2. *Baptist Press.*

3. Jane I. Smith, *Islam in America* (New York: Columbia University Press, 1999) p.160.

4. Marsha S. Haney, *Islam and Protestant African-American Churches* (San Francisco: International Scholars Publications, 1999), p.109.

5. Islamic News Article 200.08.2002-09-06 6. This was opened in the Middle East and was in Arabic. This was the only information available in identifying the source.

6. "Islamic Cooperation," *Middle East Newspaper,* March 3, 2003.

7. Daniel Pipes, *"How Dare You Defame Islam,"* p. 3. http://danielpipes.com/article/321,4.

8. Bassam Za'ar, "Insight: Projecting True Picture of Islam," *Gulf News,* online, edition, November 2002.

9. *US Filmmakers Tread Carefully in Mohammed Biography* http://tv.yahoo.com/news/va/20021212/103972897200.html.2.

10. Daniel Pipes, "PBS Caught Recruiting for Islam" *Baptist New Mexican* (January 25, 2003).

11. Osma Gull Hasan, *American Muslims: The New Generation* (New York: Continuum, 2000) p.100.

12. Bassam Za'ar, "Insight: Projecting True Picture of Islam," *Gulf News* online edition, November 2002.

13. Caryle Murphy, "Muslim U.S. Workers Hope to Break Image" *Washington Post,* November 6, 2002.

14. Internet, www.islamicmedia.net/mission1.htm.

15. Ursula Owre Masterson, "American Muslims Launch PR-style Campaigns to Defend Islam" *The Muslim News* (Harrow, Middlesex, UK), November 6, 2002.

16. Letter dated December 2002 sent to schools in California from the Islamic Speakers Bureau. The founders of the Islamic Speakers Bureau are Maha El Genaildi and Ameena Jandali. Telephone: 408-296-7312.

17. "Muslim Ramadan Begins, So Does Acceptance" WBAY TV (Green Bay, WI) November 8, 2002.

18. Donna Gehrke-White, "Moving Beyond the Mosque: Muslims Seek to Enter Mainstream" *The Muslim News* www.muslimnews.co.uk/ramadan.

19. Jane Lampman, "A Muslim Scholar Builds Bridges to the West" *The Christian Science Monitor,* November 7, 2002.

20. Caryle Murphy, "Muslims U.S. Workers Hope to Break Image" *Washington Post* November 6, 2002.

21. Ursula Owre Masterson, "American Muslims Launch PR-style Campaigns to Defend Islam" *Muslim News* (Harrow, Middlesex, U.K.), November 6, 2002.

22. www.islamicmedia.net.

23. www.muslimnews.co.uk.

24. Michael Isikoff, "It's All A Matter of Bias" *Newsweek* December 30, 2002 / January 6, 2003, p.14.

25. Noelle Knox and Theresa Howard, "Anti-war Protests, Take Aim at American Brands" *United States Today* April 4, 2003, 2B.

26. Ibid.

27. Muslim Holland http://www.islamway.net.

28. "Meeting in America About Islam" *Middle East Newspaper* Religion May 8, 2002.

29. *Middle East Newspaper* Religion June 23, 2002.

30. Ibid.

31. Ibid.

32. Ibid.

Part 3

Case Studies

11

A Case Study for African Self-Sustaining Churches

Tom Stallter

For as long as I can remember, it has always been the goal of missions to plant indigenous churches. At first this was referred to as the three-self theory (Henry Venn and Rufus Anderson) and more recently better thought through as the four-self theory: self-governing, self-supporting, self-propagating, and self-teaching or self-theologizing. But we have not always done so well at accomplishing our goal of indigenous churches. There is a certain dependency between these elements for a truly indigenous movement that we have not taken seriously. For example, only the fourth self can make the other three aspects of the theory truly indigenous. For our purposes here, only the amelioration of debilitating poverty can make self-support possible. We have generally ignored these relationships in our cross-cultural church-planting endeavors.

We want the African church to be indigenous, but few missions have stepped out into the territory of self-theologizing or poverty elimination among the churches they have planted. The purpose of this article is to present an example of one type of poverty elimination that will help national churches be truly self-supporting, and therefore, self-sustaining in their governing, theologizing, and multiplication. We helped to plant the church. Now we expect it to grow and develop in its cultural context. What is wrong that they do not catch the vision? A main reason is their poverty. We must seek ways to empower churches for development and ministry in the poverty of urban Africa. To do this we need to facilitate vocational training and employment for Christians.

Poverty in the Republic of Chad, Africa

Forty-eight percent of the population in Chad is under 14 years of age and 80 percent of the population is below the poverty line. Poverty is a leading cause in people not receiving health care in a timely fashion and contributes to an average life expectancy of 46 years with one in five children dying before they reach five years old. More related to our topic, poverty in urban Central Africa is a leading cause in keeping church members from supporting a pastor, sending missionaries, and training young people for ministry. This poverty is not related to worldview concepts but to the objective reality of the lack of vocational training of the people and the limited job market. Eighty percent of the national labor force is found in subsistence farming, herding and fishing, which are rural occupations. But in urban centers there is very little commercial, industrial or technological employment, and very few who are trained for the few possibilities that exist.[1]

Economy and Survival

When we think about the economy in a country and its affects on the church, a few observations are in order. First and most obvious, a functional economy is essential for social structure and social survival. Secondly, employment is essential to personal survival in any society. This is something we take for granted when most of the members in our churches in the U.S. come from double income families. We should easily be able to make the final observation that employment of church members is essential to indigenous ministry survival. Paul talks about this necessity for our Christian testimony in 1 Thessalonians. 4:11-12. But are we prepared to deal with the problem in the 2/3 world where in some cases only a few of the people in the congregation have any income at all? We must be committed to dealing with this problem if we believe indigenous ministry must be self-supporting.

Since societies are integrated systems of five main institutions, societal needs are served by each part. Christian life and ministry takes place in this environment and is serviced by those institutions to one degree or another (Figure 1). In this case study we emphasize how it is served by the economic element.

Government – Education – **Economy** – Religion – Family

Figure 1. Social Needs Served by Economics

The church is an institution of society that fits the "religion" slot of secular social theory. How much influence it has for the maintenance of the society is decided by developing societal values, but in the holistic African society it is of central importance. If the church is to be indigenous, it must also have these elements within itself, and, for this reason, it mirrors the secular model. In the indigenous church terminology it might be seen as follows (Figure 2).

It is easy to see how ministry survival (training of leaders and mission outreach) and personal survival of the church community (Acts 2) are related to the ability to be self-supporting. Poverty is directly related to dysfunctional ministry and personal survival, causing it to be dependent on outside help.

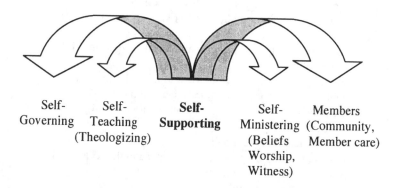

| Self-Governing | Self-Teaching (Theologizing) | **Self-Supporting** | Self-Ministering (Beliefs Worship, Witness) | Members (Community, Member care) |

Figure 2. Self-supporting Central to an Indigenous Church

Poverty and sociological principles, seen through local cultural systems, and acted on by contextualized Evangelical mission endeavor, should become missiological praxis. The process should result in Enterprise for Vocational Development (EVD), or Micro Enterprise Development (MED), and so forth. We think that contextualized Enterprise for Vocational Development among committed Christians is one of the best ways to act on the problem of poverty. Love in Action International (LIAI) bends its every effort in that direction; it is all about employment and vocational training for African Christians in a way that helps Christians grow churches in the Republic of Chad.

EVD uses vocational and ministry training through viable businesses to accomplish its goal. Some of the endeavors supported by LIAI include: bicycle mechanics, construction, tailoring, metal fabrication, computer processing, and micro-enterprise development.

Vision Principles of Love in Action International

Certain principles that represent a vision for the accomplishment of the goal through the enterprises are listed below. We refer to these as vision principles. If those involved do not feel ownership for these ideas they are not really a part of the process. The principles take into account the following:

1. The church in the 2/3 world is crippled by poverty and Christianity in the West has a responsibility to help.
2. Authentic relationships with God through Christ are foundational to successful self-help programs among poor peoples.
3. Poverty is only overcome on its own soil.
4. Poverty elimination methods must be adapted to the context.
5. Vocational training through viable business is a multiplication solution to poverty.
6. Training on all levels, from vocational skills to management, is best accomplished through apprenticeships.
7. Management must be able to train apprentices for local ministry.
8. Management must feel ownership.
9. Subsidies are only used for startup capital; occasional gifts are used for encouragement.
10. People in the partnerships must:
    -   be authentic in their faith and Christian worldview,

- possess the skills and aptitudes necessary,
- be committed to the vision of LIAI and hard work.

11. The purpose of LIAI is to empower local churches. Local churches are central to the vision but not owners of the businesses.

12. Local opinion leaders must advise the cultural aspects of the projects.

Market Potential Criteria for the Enterprises

Every enterprise for vocational development must meet one or more of the criteria listed below in its production in order to stay in business and either train people to have a share in the market through personal vocation or to be marketable to the employment available. These are illustrated in the examples given.

- High Demand/Volume Product
- High Demand Skills
- Outsider Skills in Demand
- Rare Product with Fixed Niche
- Felt Need Satisfaction
- Quality Niche
- Outside Market Availability

Examples

Metal Fabrication

The LIAI metal fabrication shop is a local business with market driven and high demand products to which outsider skills are applied to meet a quality niche in the market. At this time metal grillwork for doors and windows, metal window shutters, as well as ox carts are the main products. One expatriate instructor and nine apprentices comprise the shop. Future metal fabrication products may include a tricycle for the handicapped, a rare product with a fixed niche and felt need satisfaction. That is, they are hard to find and though the demand is limited the need is ongoing. As with all LIAI projects there is an African consulting committee to provide the cultural advice needed when expatriates are part of the project.

The African apprentices also receive instruction in evangelism and discipleship and go on outings to reach villages for Christ. A local pastor assists the missionary in this training. Last year the four second-year apprentices shared their faith in black African and Muslim villages with substantial results.

Bicycle Mechanics

Bicycle mechanics is a mobile vocation that has a small capital investment in initial tools and training. These mechanics are in high demand since most families own a bicycle and pastors all travel on bicycles for ministry and conferences. Often a mechanic travels with the pastors to meetings and conferences since the quality of the bicycles is poor and it assures their arrival. When they arrive at a conference, the mechanic spends the time putting all the bikes back in shape for the trip home. Tricycles for handicapped people take the same skills for maintenance and afford the mechanic further employment.

Sewing Center

The Sewing Center was the first business begun in Chad, and, as a prototype, helped us learn how to do business in the Central African culture. It began in 1993 and was fully indigenous by 1995. By 1997, the African instructor-manager owned 100 percentage of the business. The sewing center uses two national experts who train three to four apprentices every two years. Over twenty people have been trained while the trainers benefited from employment. It has a very marketable product in that the clothing is a high volume commodity that meets felt need satisfaction by being affordably priced and offered at a discount to church leaders. The Center owns a quality niche by producing a better product, and something totally unheard of in Central Africa, it offers quality assurance. One more criterion sets this business apart; it has an outside market in the U.S. where womens dresses in particular have drawn American attention.

Last year's graduates from the Sewing Center program reported on the first year out in the market place. One apprentice was able to rent a sewing machine after his training. His work created sufficient income to buy his own machine and a pair of oxen, which has made farming a lot more productive to support his family. A second apprentice was able to rent a sewing machine as well and has already been able to acquire his own. A third used the income of his work to pay the dowry for his wife and they were married. This is a big accomplishment considering the abuse of the marriage custom of dowry in Chad.[2] The business of this apprentice is doing so well that he has been able to buy a second sewing machine and has two apprentices working for him.

The letters received from these graduates all expressed deep appreciation to the Sewing Center and Love in Action International for their commitment and resources to help them learn this valuable skill. The Sewing Center currently has four apprentices, including a lady from an area where the churches are heavily involved in church planting among the unreached.

Instruction in Construction

Construction teams are trained to bring in high demand, outsider skills to fit a quality niche. Projects are built with indigenous materials and labor, but with skills that come from experts outside the situation. A percentage of funding for materials for projects is negotiable depending on the nature of the project. This area of EVD receives a lot of public attention since it does construction for community health and development like medical dispensaries in neglected areas and bridges to keep roads open. This also brings attention and credibility to the Gospel as members of the team speak in the villages. The construction team is also involved in the building of churches and Bible schools. Instead of bringing in outside short-term building teams from Europe or the U.S., construction training has been provided so the labor can belong to nationals needing the employment. All of the buildings used in the projects and businesses, as well as those that service the churches, are built by Africans.

The African owner of the company is both the instructor and manager. In addition, he is the main evangelism trainer for church planting, and has built a two-story training center for that purpose.

Essential People in 2/3 World Vocational Training

The people essential in the enterprise to be used must meet qualifications that fit the vision principles. Briefly put, all individuals involved must first have an authentic faith in Christ and a Christian worldview, and they must have a commitment to the vision of Love in Action International. Other qualifications are as follows:

Instructor/Manager

- An expert in the business to be used
- Intercultural training and above average adaptability aptitude for expatriates
- Aptitude for business management and ownership for nationals

African Consulting Committee

- An understanding of the effects of the culture on the business
- Must be made up of opinion leaders with influence in the wider community
- Able to participate with managers in decisions

Apprentices for Vocational Training

- Necessary aptitudes
- Respected in the Christian community
- Willingness for ministry

Mike Retterer Training Center

The Mike Retterer Training Center (MRTC) is a place where outsiders come to train African Christians in high demand skills. These may be other Africans who are specialists or expatriate specialists. It is also used to train people in discipleship. There is an accompanying guesthouse for EVD trainers so that the training can be concentrated even though trainers may come from a distance. Both the MRTC and the guesthouse were built by the EVD construction team.

The MRTC will also be used for word-processing of outsourced Christian literature projects from France. This will provide both employment and training in computer skills that will make individuals marketable to other areas of employment in the urban centers.

Summary

The necessary elements of vocational training for the African church are not optional if the endeavor is to be indigenous and survive to help churches become self-sustaining in Central Africa.

- A vision for enabling the national church and their participation in it
- Market potential for the product of the training business (seven criteria)
- Finding African experts or outsiders with expertise for training nationals
- African structure and resources for the venture
- Respected, influential Africans committed to the venture who can give cultural advice

- Apprentices with an authentic faith, an aptitude for the training and African business

Enterprise for Vocational Development can help produce vibrant, self-sustaining churches in Africa. Love in Action International <www.loveinactioninternational.org> exists to use enterprise toward this goal.

Discussion Starters

1. Why is self-support so important to indigenous churches in the 2/3 world?
2. How might the sending of short-term teams to build projects for 2/3 world Christians be counter productive to self-sustaining churches?
3. Why is a Christian worldview essential for all involved in EVD for those in urban poverty in Africa?
4. What does the author mean by "Poverty is only overcome on its own soil?"
5. Why is an "African structure for the venture" and "cultural advice" important to the success of EVD?

Notes

[1] The statistics in this paragraph come from both the CIA *Facts on File* located on their Web site at www.cia.gov, 2005, and the 3D World Atlas, Xamba Software, 2003.

[2] Insights are offered into this critical problem in the article "Payment of Dowry and the Christian Church," by the Theological Advisory Group in *African Journal of Evangelical Theology*, 15:2, 1996.

12

Tying the Knots:
From Macrame to Multi-millions

Meg Crossman

How would a woman with no business background, no college training, no commercial experience, and no financial backing turn her artistic abilities from macramé into a productive, multi-million dollar, international organization? It would only be possible with the driving energy of an unselfish dream and continual reliance on the Lord. The passionate desire to find ways to support indigenous missionaries carried Crystal Alman a long way.

YWAM From the Beginning

Crystal grew up in a YWAM family. Her parents, Wedge and Shirley Alman, are credited with founding YWAM bases throughout Latin America. She learned to live on an amazingly thin financial shoestring in the years when they received as little as $6 a week for pastoring. "Home," the family said proverbially, "was wherever Mom's suitcase was." Yet, by watching her parents seek God and trust Him for every provision, she observed undeniable demonstrations of God's faithfulness.

Crystal learned to sew at the age of 11, and from that time on made clothes for herself and her Mother. Few people encouraged her in her artistic endeavors and the family called her "the mess-maker" because of the art that continually flowed out of her. Her gifts and enthusiasm for color and design seemed to have no place in a ministry intensely focused on evangelism.

Developing Support for Colombian Nationals

Although Crystal was not living for the Lord in her late teens, she still was concerned by a need that she saw at the YWAM base in Bogotá, Colombia. The difficulty Colombian national workers faced in finding viable means of support troubled her. They came from poor fellowships that thought, "Only Americans can be missions workers." Their churches had no vision to support Colombians joining YWAM. Who would provide for them?

While praying with others at the Base for these needs and how to meet them, the Lord spoke to her, "What do you have in your hand?" When working summers at a YMCA camp in California, she had learned to do macramé. She could teach this to others. Crystal began to train YWAMers to make Macramé pot holders and wall-hangings. Selling these provided useful income. Could this be a way for Colombians to support themselves? That "Word from the Lord"—the same one He gave Moses, concerning his staff (Ex 4:2) became a recurrent principle throughout her journey.

Using two aged sewing machines and $20 from a supporter in Switzerland, Crystal made a sweatsuit—a new kind of garment worn by Colombians. She trained others to produce them, using nothing but scissors and the ancient sewing machines. Cutting them out, her fingers became bruised and blistered!

After staging a YWAM fashion show, Crystal found the sewing ministry beginning to prosper. Their first workshop was on a patio under transparent acrylic sheets—burning sun poured in, suffocating them by day; by night (and they often worked late in the night), the air at almost 9000 feet was viciously cold. Working with no table for cutting material, owning no patterns to work from, they still learned to construct many kinds of garments. They bought a Coca-Cola stand and set it up outside the YWAM base. The outfits sold and the income realized did provide for the workers.

Taking the sweatsuits with them, YWAMers could go on their door-to-door evangelistic rounds. Even if the person they were talking to would not accept the Lord, they very well might buy a sweat suit! Eventually, they produced garments of many kinds for men, women and children.

Crystal was insistent that YWAM workers learn to do things the right way. If something was sloppily produced, she'd insist that they "Tear it out and do it again." Integrity in construction was a bedrock standard.

A Really Big Order

One day, a German man walked in and showed her a picture of a particular Macramé wall hanging. "Can you make that?" he asked. "Of course," she responded, "and a lot better than that!" "Can you make 1000 by next month?" "Absolutely!" she answered, in spite of having *no* idea as to how that could be accomplished. In fact, though they had to work day and night to do it, the order was successfully filled. Quickly, more orders came in from the German contact and from others who saw her work.

Crystal Had to Find Out

At last, under her own father's ministry, Crystal made a radical commitment to the Lord. She never looked back. Shortly after, she told her folks, "I'm not going to really grow until I find out that He's my God, too." She knew she needed to detach from the provision she had experienced in an on-going way under her folks, and test her own ability to trust and hear from God.

She moved to Brazil and a YWAM evangelistic work among the poor. There she *did* learn to hear from God, finding that her obedience led to His provision. In the 1978 outreach at the World Soccer Games in Argentina, Crystal joined a team sent from the Brazilian base. When hepatitis laid her low, she had to press into God and step up to handle the responsibilities of providing hospitality for all the leaders.

Moving to Toronto, she studied two years under Colin Harbinson (well-known playwright who wrote *The Toymaker's Dream*) in his YWAM School of Creativity. There for the first time, she found her imaginative and inventive gifts affirmed and valued. Crystal returned to Colombia, now equipped to start a School of Creative Arts and help her parents.

Using Her Gifts To Serve

Her artistic gifts and her organizational ability were both put to use as she served on the leadership team and decorated the entire base. Little by little the sewing business flourished. When she married a Colombian man with entrepreneurial ideas, he clearly saw ways to make the work economically viable. They were able to buy better quality cutters and commercial grade sewing machines.

By 1981 they were making all kinds of sweat suits and dresses of knit fabric. Long sleeved, belted or straight; simple, but elegant, the garments continued to sell. Crystal's focus and desire continued to be giving liberally to YWAM.

She designed elaborate wall hangings. She began weaving unique backgrounds for them. She made her own beads in exotic ways. Nothing was wasted—Crystal's background in missionary frugality made her skill-ful at recycling anything and everything. The decrepit sweater from the missionary barrel, too dilapidated to give away even to the poor, could be unraveled and rewoven into a wall hanging. The leftover cuttings from other factories could be combined with glue, baked in the oven, and made into exotic beads or buttons!

By now she was producing jackets with fringe and beads that matched. The jackets were made with exotic detachable front and back panels from matching scraps left over in the construction the jackets (very arty, like the wall hangings). Scarves were created to match them. She added skirts and blouses, as well.

Crystal found that people did not respond well to the idea that these lovely garments were made by third world people. It carried a connotation of sweatshops with unskilled or underpaid workers or merely a missions handout for poorly produced products. She decided to put her own name on them, marketing her creations as "Crystal Handwovens." She also realized that pricing them cheaply made buyers think they were poor quality. She made them expensive and sales climbed.

As the Lord began to connect US markets to the company, they were blessed and helped by a wonderful group of Christian businessmen and women. These committed brethren from San Jose, California, met with her once a week at 6 AM to pray and give counsel. A gift of $5000 from an-other man gave her the seed money to establish her first showroom.

One day, Crystal dressed herself and her kids in the clothes she'd made and walked into Nordstrom's in San Francisco. A saleswoman pleaded with her to talk to a buyer who just happened to be in the store at that time. As a result, Nordstrom's began to carry her line! That opening led to others: Bloomingdale's, Neiman-Marcus, and a number of upscale boutiques were now carrying Crystal Handwovens.

The Business Paradigm Does Not Fit

However, while the business grew in productivity, Crystal faced a different problem. YWAM simply contained no organizational model to suit either her artistic gifts or her business prototype. She fundamentally did not fit with the way YWAM operated. She did not know if there was a biblical basis for her business. Some people around her feared that to do this kind of work was probably "un-spiritual." Often, Colombians suggested her efforts smacked of capitalism (in the most exploitive, negative sense).

Crystal struggled with these difficulties:

- Should missionaries be making a profit?
- Should people give up evangelism to earn money?

- Was this work pulling people away from God's
  real design for them?

She wrestled with these troubling questions.

At last, YWAM's top leadership came to her and said "Crystal, you need to run this company as if it were your own." The tensions were too great. YWAM, with an ingrained commitment to evangelism, could not comprehend organizationally how to oversee a business. It deeply hurt Crystal, who had known nothing in her Christian life but YWAM, but there was no alternative. In 1987, she put the company completely in her own name and arranged to buy the equipment from YWAM. Surprisingly however, once the business *was* in her own name, God prospered them even more.

Moving On and Moving Up

They settled to the town of Chia, with a population of about 15,000 people. Unbeknownst to her, it was a center of weaving. This really allowed her to develop her first love: using manual handlooms and weaving. She would wait on the Lord for creative ideas. He might tell her, "This year, I want to express My joy," and show her colors and designs to do so. She would weave several meters of fabric and give it to the women to replicate. Crystal's major contributions were these creative designs.

Though she kept her operation very low key, still wanting simply to be a servant to YWAM and it's work, some newly positive relationships arose. The move to Chia proved to be a fruitful connection with people who had background in traditional weaving skills. Most of the women were single heads of household who had been employed in the "hot houses" exhausting and exploitive work with flowers for export. The Lord gave Crystal Isaiah 23:18 in relation to her work:

> "The money she earns by commerce will be dedicated to the
> Lord. She will not store it away, but those who worship the lord
> will use her money to buy the food and the clothing they need."[1]

By now, they operated with commercial equipment, electric cutters, and industrial level sewing machines. Beyond that, however, the factory developed every step of the process from production to shipping. She was able to hire many people from the town to handle each part of the system. All details of the work took place under Crystal's organization. She trained many people, starting from her housemaid, who became a skilled manager and trusted co-leader. All in all, they had about 200 workers on various levels.

This was a quality operation, in a niche market, rather than a huge manufacturing production. In a year, they might produce about 22, 000 garments. The artistic jackets would often take 6-7 days to construct. Then pants, tops, skits, sweaters, even jewelry, would be made to accompany the jackets.

As Crystal began to display her garments and wall hangings at Apparel Marts in the US, the operation flourished. Her tags said, "Created for you by the Master Designer." She did so well she was able to hire sales reps all across the US. She won prizes and awards of many kinds. Eventually she was given the highest honor as the Featured Designer at the Chicago Apparel Mart. In her acceptance speech when receiving that top award, she honored the Lord, shared the Gospel, and told how "God gives me my designs."

The work provided a rich milieu for developing creativity. Colin Harbinson had taught her that when a culture turns away from idolatry, the Lord restores its creative ability. She saw that theory in operation, not only in her own life, but also in the Colombians. The business maintained a positive environmental impact as she continuously invented ways to recycle and revamp items that would otherwise be discarded.

Transformational Initiatives

In all levels of the factory, people came to know the Lord. When they moved to Chia there was a Catholic church and one small evangelical church. Eventually, there were more than a dozen thriving evangelical works. YWAMers did not turn out to be productive factory workers, but they were excellent at winning the factory workers to Christ. Yearly Christmas parties were events where Crystal could have her Dad preach and clearly present the Gospel. Many were saved, not only workers, but also their extended families. Crystal herself personally led many of her supervisors and legal advisors to the Lord as well.

The workplace was a first-rate center to practice discipleship. People would learn not only about the Lord in a hands-on way, but also how to live and work with integrity, how to pray for the needs of one another and the company, as well as how to emulate models of others living for Christ. Of course, it was also an economic boon for the town of Chia.

Crystal's passion remained the support of people and projects in YWAM. One year alone, the company gave more than 60 percent of the profits to missionaries and mission work—and this from a company that was making a 20-30 percent profit, where many others might make no more than 3-5 percent. On top of this, much of her giving was off the books, such as outfitting missionaries with her beautiful clothes or giving away samples, or the profit from the sales of samples. The more she gave, the more the Lord blessed.

The Road Through Valleys of Darkness

The road was by no means one with continual successes. Over the years, she encountered serious setbacks.

- Within the company, those who seemed loyal often dismayed and betrayed her.
- Scam artists worked their way in and took the company very low.
- Missionaries who came on board to work with her proved to be unskilled in doing the detail work they contracted to carry out.
- A manager fired all her sales reps and worked for other companies while charging her for his expenses.
- A supervisor woman embezzled in a major way until the Lord gave Crystal two dreams about this person's dishonesty.

By trial and error, she learned many management lessons. She eventually had to put a certain structural distance between herself and her workers, whom she had previously treated with a motherly attitude. Those who professed faith could become embittered with God if she had to let them go. The loving gifts she had given over the years began to be sources of strife: "She loves you more; she got you a nicer watch!" Even the bread and cake she baked for coffee breaks had to be discontinued for similar reasons. Finally, she gave everyone Bibles at Christmas and provided only black coffee for breaks. Then people complained that she no longer loved them!

Continual problems arose from imitators or copiers who would take her designs, then produce and market them as their own. She entered into agreements with advisors in the States who proved to have a different vision than she did. Intense issues arose from the spiritual warfare problems. Colombians frequently feel that since the Conquistadors robbed them, they are only taking back what is theirs when they steal from their company. Even loyal friends and workers had to be searched by security guards—not only when they came and left but even when they went on coffee breaks! These kind of unbroken cultural strongholds brought about persistent struggles.

Terrorists and narco-trafficers in Colombia were an ever-present threat. Crystal was careful not to ever put a sign on the outside of the factory identifying who and what they were. "Vacunas" or protection money was publicly demanded by guerillas from any business of over a million dollars. Her life and home were under peril, but the Lord protected her until the day He directed her to move. She obeyed. Within 24 hours after she left, the guerillas arrived.

The greatest tragedy took place when her marriage fell to pieces. After years of abuse, Crystal's husband left, tried to take the whole business, and relentlessly assaulted her reputation. For the third time in the life of the company, she was reduced to nothing but her trust in the Lord. She has now sold everything, turning the business over to the people she trained. She is waiting on the Lord for the next steps.

Lessons and Learning

Much of what Crystal learned, she learned in the "School of HK & BE" (Hard Knocks and Bitter Experiences). With no business background or theory, much of what she did was simply "on the job training." The principles of Great Commission Companies were unknown to her. She had no idea how to copyright her designs. She began with no seed money—she started from nothing, with nothing—yet her utter trust in the Lord was unshakeable.

Amazingly, it seemed that in the darkest times, she would see her Colombian workers reach out to the Lord, praying for her and for the company as never before. God redeemed these painful circumstances in astounding ways! YWAM leaders, in due course, came and asked her forgiveness, grateful for her generous spirit and her perseverance. The reconciliation meant a great deal to Crystal.

Now, opportunities are arising not only for new spin-offs of the business, but even for teaching the principles she's learned in other nations. It is not easy or painless to run a business with a mission purpose and intent. It must BE a business! Yet, it can have profound and significant effects for the Kingdom even while it is realizing a profit.

Part of the challenge of assessing this account is deciding how we evaluate success. Some of Crystal's positive outcomes would include:

- Empowering an impoverished people.
- Enhancing their skills and teaching them new levels of creativity.
- Winning many to the Lord and seeing new works raised up in the town.
- Using the workplace as a laboratory for discipleship.
- Developing a self-supporting business that generated millions of dollars.
- Using profits liberally to support missionaries and mission endeavors.
- Learning to operate in a situation of terrorism and spiritual warfare.

• Bringing about some levels of community transformation.

Many questions are still challenges in this field:

• Can a prayer base be developed when a company is running a $500K profit?
• In what ways could a business be linked to a missions agency?
• How will reliable people be identified and trained?
• What transformational concepts can be expanded?
• How can cultural creativity be enhanced and supported?
• What unique business challenges must be met in different countries and cultures?

Crystal Alman is still learning ways to "tie the knots" and help others do so as well. There may need to be innovative measures developed to appraise Kingdom success in the creative work God is giving her to do. She has opportunities now to help similar works start in several other countries. Most clearly she has seen the Lord take her to nothing and lift her up again, always teaching her His love in amazing and enriching ways.

[1] Source: *Good News Bible.*

Discussion Starters

1. Can ministry be part of a company that is running a $500K profit?
2. How can a business be linked to a missions agency? What are the issues?
3. Why do not all missionaries make good business people? Why do not all business people make good missionaries?
4. What transformational concepts can be expanded?
5. How can cultural creativity be enhanced and supported?
6. What unique business challenges must be met in different countries and cultures?

13

Unleashing the Brazilian Missionary Force

João Mordomo

It has become increasingly recognized in the Christian missions movement over the past three decades or so that a monumental shift, what Lamin Sanneh of Yale Divinity School refers to as a "Copernican Shift," has taken place in the global center of gravity of Christianity. In the 1970's, Catholic missiologist Walbert Buhlmann wrote of the coming of the "third church," the church of the third world in the third millennium,[2] with the Mediterranean church of the first centuries after Christ being the "first church," and the northern and western European (and later the North American church) being the "second church." Among Protestants, Andrew Walls of the University of Edinburgh has been at the forefront, since the 1970's, of the study of the emergence of this so-called "third church," which he refers to as "New Southern Christianity."[3] Only slightly more recently did missiologists begin to ponder the astounding missiological consequences. For example, in 1986, Tracey K. Jones, Jr. wrote that

> Fifty years ago no one would have anticipated that much of the intellectual and moral leadership shaping the Christian mission in the world today would

> come out of the churches of Latin America, Africa,
> and Asia; it has been a shock to the Christians in
> North America to discover that the numerical center
> of Christianity is shifting from the northern hemi-
> sphere to the southern hemisphere.[4]

More recently, scholars like Samuel Escobar,[5] Philip Jenkins[6] and Dana Robert[7] have documented and commented convincingly on the importance of the shift to the south.[8]

David Barrett's "Annual Statistical Table on Global Mission," which has appeared in each year's January edition of the International Bulletin of Missionary Research since 1985 projected that by 2000, 62.6 percent of global Christianity would be comprised of adherents from Latin America, Africa, Asia and Oceania; that is to say, the "third church." Adherents in Europe and North America would comprise a mere 37.4 percent of global Christianity. In his 2000 table, he reported that the percentages were actually 60.3 and 39.7, respectively. He was only two points off! Larry Pate and Lawrence Keyes observed back in 1986 that,

> It is becoming clear to most missiologists who look
> across the mountain ranges of the future that the
> "feet of those who bring good news" are rapidly
> changing color. New streams of brown, black, yel-
> low, and red feet are joining with the white to pro-
> claim the salvation message. The gospel no longer
> masquerades as a white person's good news about a
> white, Western imperialistic God. It is Koreans-to-
> Nepal, Singaporeans-to-Nigeria, Brazilians-to-
> North Africa good news! More and more, the news
> is spreading from every people to every people.[9]

While Christianity in much of North America and Europe stagnates, vibrant new churches are taking root around the globe, and increasingly providing the next generation of cross-cultural "good news" bearers. The Brazilian Evangelical church is an excellent case in point. According to Larry Kraft, a specialist in Brazilian church growth, Brazil was only about 1 percent Evangelical in 1900.[10] By 1970 that figure had grown to just over 5 percent, and by 1990, just over 12 percent.[11] By 2000, according to the Brazilian Census Bureau,[12] Evangelicals comprised over 15 percent of Brazil's population, for a total of over 27 million people, making it the third, fourth or fifth largest Evangelical church in the world.[13] While the absolute numbers differ considerably from other emerging churches, the percentages do not. And the percentages reveal phenomenal church growth.

In addition to this emerging pool of potential cross-cultural missionaries, there are numerous qualitative reasons to consider Christians from emerging churches as potentially *better* missionaries than North Americans and Europeans. Consider the following reasons to mobilize Brazilians to join in God's global mission:

- **Ecclesiastically:** With over 27 million adherents, the Brazilian Evangelical church is a huge force to be mobilized.

- **Spiritually:** Brazilian believers are vivacious and spiritually attuned, both to God and to other realities of the spiritual world.

- **Culturally:** Brazilians are relational, gregarious people who generally have much more in common culturally with the unreached peoples of the world than do the traditional sending nations from North America and Europe.

- **Ethnically:** Brazil is an ethnically diverse country. From the early miscegenation of the "big three," the indigenous peoples, the Iberian peoples and the African peoples, to the more recent arrival of millions of immigrants from the Middle East, Japan, China, Italy, Germany, Poland, Ukraine, Russia, Latvia, etc., Brazilians are accustomed to living in close proximity with people from diverse ethnic backgrounds.

- **Historically:** Brazil was never a colonizer, but rather was colonized, holding this in common with many unreached nations of the world.

- **Politically:** Brazil is traditionally a neutral country and has caused very little offense around the globe.

- **Economically:** Despite recent small economic setbacks, Brazil is an increasingly strong player on the global scene.

- **Biblically:** We must remember that God has called *all* His people, His *global* family, to take His glory to the nations.

- **And don't forget:** Brazilians are the best soccer players in the world, and the world loves soccer, "the beautiful game," as Pelé called it. Soccer opens doors of opportunity in places.

How is the Brazilian Evangelical church doing on the cross-cultural missions scene? There is good news to be found. The church increasingly recognizes the special role in world missions to which God has called her, along with other Latin American churches. This realization was perhaps best expressed by Luis Bush, then president of COMIBAM, the Ibero-American Missionary Cooperation,[14] at the March 1987 COMIBAM congress, which took place in São Paulo and united more than 3000 delegates, about a thousand of them from Brazil. In his opening comments, Bush declared that "From a mission field Latin America has become a mission force."[15] This missions awareness can further be seen in the advent of the Brazilian Congress on Missions (four congresses to date). The first, in Caxambu, Brazil, in 1993, was influenced by the Third Latin American Congress on Evangelization (CLADE), which took place the year before in Quito and whose final document declared that "the Holy Spirit has developed a new missionary awareness in Latin America," and that "the church in Latin America must assume its responsibility in world evangelization fully and without delay."[16]

Perhaps the best indicator of the growing awareness of, and involvement in, cross-cultural missionary activity, is numerical, and can be seen in the growth of the number of Brazilian evangelical mission agencies and missionaries. Although a handful of Brazilian "foreign missionaries" were sent during the first seven decades of the 20th century, the Brazilian Evangelical missions movement is generally considered to have been born in the 1970's.[17] In that decade, when the first evangelical cross-cultural missionaries began to trickle out of the country, they often found themselves in the position of a William Carey or an Adoniram Judson, having to establish the very mission agencies that would send them.[18] Also in that decade, the first two genuinely Brazilian interdenominational mission agencies were founded, Betel Brasileiro in 1972, and Missão Antioquia in 1976.[19]

By 1984, there were enough agencies that the Association of Brazilian Transcultural Missions (AMTB) was founded[20] to foster vision and a spirit of partnership for cross-cultural missions. The most recent available data by researcher Ted Limpic,[21] indicates that today there are approximately 100 associated member agencies (most, but not all, of which truly work cross-culturally, and some of which are actually international mission organizations that have operations in Brazil). That is up from 88 in 1996.[22] Together, as of 2001, these organizations fielded 2803 cross-cultural workers (up dramatically from 1796 in 1996,[23] and 880 in 1989)[24] with 2055 working outside of Brazil. In addition, there are dozens, if not hundreds, of other small agencies not associated with the AMTB, as well as numerous local churches that send missionaries directly or employ a "church-to-church" sending model. Patrick Johnstone puts the total number of Brazilian mission agencies at 132,[25] with the total number of Evangelical missionaries being either 4754, which he reports in the Brazil section of *Operation World*, or 5925, which he reports in the Brazil section of the *Operation World* database, contained on the *Operation World* CD-ROM.[26] Of the 5925 missionaries reported in the database, 4160 of these work cross-culturally, with 2229 of those working in Brazil, and 1931 outside of Brazil.

The good news is that there are very possibly *over* 150 Brazilian cross-cultural mission agencies fielding *over* 4000 cross-cultural missionaries, reflecting a significant increase over the past 15 years. This can by many standards be considered positive and exciting news, especially in light of Brazil's political and economic realities over the past three decades. But the bad news is that there are *only* about 150 Brazilian cross-cultural mission agencies fielding *only* about 4000 cross-cultural missionaries, and according to Limpic's data, only about 420 of those, less than 15 percent, are working in the 10/40 Window.

Should Brazil be further along? Very possibly. After all, 150 agencies and 4000 missionaries is paltry for a church of 27 million people. According to Johnstone's data,[27] the Brazilian Evangelical church ranks sixth in sending cross-cultural missionaries in absolute terms, but only thirteenth if the measurement is the number of churches necessary for the sending of each missionary.[28] *Could we be further along?* Absolutely! And *Brazil will be* as it increasingly develops and employs better contextualized ministry models that take into consideration both the developmental/historical realities of the Brazilian Evangelical church, and the economic realities of Brazil itself. It is my intention, then, to propose a model that will propel the Brazilian Evangelical missions movement further and faster.

After a decade of helping build a Brazilian cross-cultural sending agency that focuses on the Turkic, Kurdish and Arabic Muslim world, I would like to suggest that the answer to this question has to do in large part with wineskins. Old models that do not fit the Brazilian context are presently being used in a new reality. In all fairness to the Brazilian Evangelical missions movement the missionaries that helped establish Evangelical Christianity in Brazil over the past 150 years did a less than stellar job in equipping the fledgling church to be what Alan Tippett and others have called "self-theologizing."[29] There is no comprehensive Brazilian Evangelical theology of missions to be found.[30] Neither did many of the foreign missionaries effectively practice what Hiebert calls "critical contextualization,"[31] at least not when it came to facilitating the development of contextualized models to enable Brazilians to do effective cross-cultural ministry. Venn and Anderson's Three Self model[32] that included "self-propagating" and "self-extending" is foundational to a biblical, healthy, indigenous church planting movement.

The 150 or so mission agencies, most of which have only a handful of workers and are struggling for their very existence, have the historical cards stacked against them. They are attempting to overcome huge obstacles using a model that is simply not working. Granted there are exceptions, but they are derived from the same fundamental model, the "Professional Missionary Model" (PMM). Mike McLoughlin provides a helpful description of the PMM:

> The well beaten path of the modern missions movement is the way of the supported worker. One often hears inspiring testimonies of zealous Christians who "laid down" their secular employment to enter missions "fulltime." The professional missionary with a Bible School diploma and technical training in development is the epitome of a successful missions strategy. He or she is also the spiritual icon of the Church, held up as an example of counting the cost and a model of spirituality. However, in the history of the Church the professional missionary is a recent phenomenon. During its first four hundred years of existence, the Church grew from being an obscure religious sect of Judaism to the dominant religious influence of the world principally through people who lived their faith in the marketplace.[33]

I would add that there is very substantial evidence to support the contention that Christians who took the Gospel to "the ends of the earth" throughout the Middle Ages (the Nestorians, for example) and right up through the Reformation period (the Moravians) and into the 19th century (the Basel Mission), like the Christians of the first four centuries, also did so in connection with their business and trade endeavors.[34]

Any Brazilian missionary who seeks to serve in the PMM mold faces an uphill battle and runs a significant risk of never achieving critical financial mass and finally being able to serve among the people to whom he or she is called. And any Brazilian mission agency that chooses to perpetuate this model will very possibly continue to struggle year after year to place even a single worker or family in a cross-cultural ministry.[35]

The PMM is unworkable for the Brazilian and other emerging missions movements both from a contextual and practical standpoint, as well as questionable from a biblical and theological standpoint. It simply is not the best model to enable and unleash these missions forces to overcome the major obstacles they face and function as active participants in the *missio Dei*. I see the Pedro's and the Claudia's and the Andre's and the Maria's, people who are equipped and ready to serve the Lord among the least-reached peoples of the world, but cannot do so because they simply do not have, and cannot find, the financial resources to do so. Or perhaps even worse, those who have left Brazil because they were amazingly able to raise their own support (perhaps through partnerships with North American or European Christians and organizations), but are floundering in ministry as traditional profile missionaries employing the PMM, or possibly struggling with the internal and external pernicious effects of certain duplicitous tentmaking models.

Four major obstacles result in hopelessness for potential Brazilian cross-cultural workers. These include: getting out, getting in, staying in and sinking in.

Getting Out

Brazilian missionaries many times simply cannot get out of the starting blocks due to a lack of financial resources. This is partly a developmental and cultural issue. The Brazilian church is simply young and has not had much time to develop a pattern of giving to cross-cultural missions. But the issue is also partly an economic one. Poverty, corruption and inflation have plagued

Latin American countries. Recent economic indicators for Brazil are less than encouraging:

- Brazil, while being the fifth largest country in the world, ranks 11th in the world in GDP in terms of purchasing power parity,[36]

- However, Brazil ranks a mere 92nd in the world in GDP per capita[37]

- Brazil's real growth rate is only 74th globally, at 5.10% annually, [38]

- Unemployment in Brazil ranks 107th in the world.[39]

- Brazil ranks 177th in the world in annual inflation rate.[40]

Economics plays a big role in hindering the *sending* of Brazilian cross-cultural missionaries. Even when cross-cultural workers do manage to reach the field, it is often for economic reasons that they *return home prematurely*. According to Limpic's research, "Brazilian agencies cite 'lack of financial support' as the greatest single cause of missionary attrition."[41] This is a heartbreaking reality. Even as I write, in the past month I have been involved with families confronting both situations. By God's grace, the family that has already been at work among Muslims for more than five years has momentum and an outstanding ministry track record and should be able to raise more support in order to return to work among their people group. I have strong doubts, however, that the second family that has spent years in basically a holding pattern will ever be able to raise enough support to reach the people group to which they are called. And the great tragedy is that this family is very well prepared and would certainly make a tremendous, eternal impact among a huge Muslim people group *if only* they had funding. These types of stories are encountered over and over again throughout Brazil.

But the issue is not only economic; it is also one of vision and stewardship. I cannot count how many times I have heard comments such as the one a Brazilian missions colleague of mine heard at his church: "Forget this idea pastor! This business of missions is not for us in the Third World. Mission is for the churches of North America and Europe who have tradition in this area and financial resources."[43] I have heard the following addendum even more: "And what about all the needs right here in Brazil? What about the poverty? What about the educational needs? What about the regions of Brazil where there are not many Evangelicals? How can we invest our money in people and places far away when the needs are so great right here?" But the most frustrating posture of all can be summarized thus: "What? You mean it's going to cost nearly $2000 for a family of four to live in Istanbul or Cairo, or...? Our *pastor* only makes half that amount! How can we justify paying the missionaries twice as much as the pastor? The pastor serves us everyday, but the missionaries don't serve us at all. And the pastor is the pastor; the missionaries are, well, merely missionaries." The vision is often limited, distorted, introverted, ethnocentric, anthropocentric, egocentric and, in some cases even unbiblical. There is often an utter lack of comprehension of the most compelling theme of Scripture that He desires and deserves to be known, loved and worshipped by representatives from all the peoples of the world.

Church hierarchy and pecking orders are no excuse for not sending or adequately supporting missionaries. Neither is poverty an excuse. Even if all 27 million Brazilian Evangelicals were poor God could do abundantly more *if* Brazilians practiced stewardship. But they do not. This begs the question, Should Brazilian potential missionaries be disqualified from serving the Lord cross-culturally simply because their churches do not have a fully biblical vision concerning God's mission to all peoples? Because Brazil and the Brazilian church face continual economic difficulties? The obvious answer is *no!* A more appropriate model, one that can utilize God's global resources for God's global glory, is needed.

Getting In

Stories about people like Brother Andrew and George Verwer and others who are willing to risk life and limb in order to briefly infiltrate Communist or Muslim contexts to share Christ or encourage believers challenges me. I thank the Lord for people like these and pray that He will increasingly raise up others. I also thank the Lord for the thousands of cross-cultural workers from around the world who with the same sense of calling and conviction seek to enter countries in North Africa or the Middle East or Central Asia as tourists or students in order to stay for months or a couple of years to advance God's cause. These are viable means to enter restricted access nations, but they do not

provide credible long-term solutions. Very few people, even
Brazilians, are able to enter many of these geopolitical contexts,
even as tourists or students. And even if they can manage to enter in these ways, the fact is that many unreached peoples live in
regions that tourists and students do not normally go, and are
immediately suspect if they do. Certainly there is a better way to
get into closed contexts.

Staying In

If getting in is difficult, staying in can prove to be nearly impossible, especially on a tourist or student visa. They are not *credible* for a long-term presence or impact. Who ever heard of a
tourist in Turkmenistan or Saudi Arabia who has been in the
country for several years, rents his own apartment and speaks
fluent Turkmeni or Arabic? Even if the worker manages to reside in the country for years, he or she has long since lost credibility. People are much less gullible than we think. In our experience, the more cosmopolitan nationals will realize fairly
quickly that the worker in question is a missionary. The rest will
very possibly assume that he or she is a spy for a foreign government (probably the U.S., even if the worker is obviously Brazilian). After all, who else besides a church or government institution could possibly be paying the bills for someone who apparently never has to work?

Sinking In

Of course, staying for decades among a people group does not
guarantee effective ministry, changed lives, multiplied churches,
or transformed societies. Rwanda in 1994 serves as a case-in-
point where some 700,000 Christians were killed by *other Christians* in a matter of months. Cross-cultural Good News bearers
must find mechanisms by which they can penetrate social networks and make a fully-orbed Gospel proclamation in word and
deed. They must penetrate to the core worldview level. The best
way to do that is by rubbing shoulders with real people everyday, empathizing with their struggles to make ends meet and
deal with the existential issues of life. The PMM more often than
not neither encourages nor allows for this kind of "in the
trenches," "in-your-face," "down and dirty," incarnational ministry to take place. The Word who became flesh and dwelt
among us was not a religious professional! He could empathize
with people because He faced the same issues that they did as

part of His human existence, and that included working for a living, for most of His life. He understood and practiced in the truest sense a theology of presence. Certainly that should receive more than token attention from His co-laborers as we seek to emulate Him by sinking into the cultures we wish to reach.

The Brazilian church has a calling and has certain distinct and unique qualifications that equip her to be at the forefront of taking the Gospel to the ends of the earth, but *not* with the models that have been handed down to her. A new model is required.

The Business as Mission Model

The business as mission model (BAM) could serve the Brazilian church well into the 21st century, unleashing them for effective, holistic, God-pleasing frontier ministry. BAM is perhaps uniquely qualified to help cross-cultural Brazilian workers get out, get in, stay in and sink in.

What is BAM?[43] How does it work? Why is it relevant not only for unleashing missionary forces, but also for *reaching* the least-reached peoples of the world?

BAM has a Kingdom perspective. Kingdom businesses start from the theological premise that God desires to be known, loved and worshipped among all peoples of the world. Kingdom businesses recognize that all Christians have a calling to love and serve God with all of their heart, soul, mind and strength, and to love and serve their neighbors. Kingdom businesses further recognize that God calls some people to work for His kingdom in business just as certainly as He calls some people to work in other kinds of ministry or mission ventures. Kingdom businesses take seriously the biblical mandates to reach the unreached and to serve the poor and oppressed. The business of business is business. The business of business as mission is business with a Kingdom purpose and perspective to fulfill the King's mission.

BAM is premised on holistic mission. Holistic mission attempts to bring all aspects of life, ministry and godliness into an organic biblical whole. This includes God's concern for such business-related issues as economic development, employment and unemployment, economic justice and the use and distribution of natural and creative resources among the human family. Sadly, evangelism and social concerns are often still addressed as though they were separate and unrelated. This assumes a divide between the sacred and spiritual or the secular and physical. The biblical worldview, rather, is one that promotes an integrated and seamless holistic view of life. BAM is an expression of this truly holistic, integrated paradigm.

BAM is different from but related to marketplace or work-place ministries. Marketplace ministries focus primarily on taking the gospel to people where they work (usually in a monocultural setting), preferably through the witness of co-workers and professional colleagues. These ministries encourage the integration of biblical principles into every aspect of business practice for the glory of God. BAM naturally includes these elements. When a workplace ministry is initiated in a business owned by believers to intentionally advance the kingdom of God, there will be substantial overlap. But whereas workplace ministry can choose to limit its focus solely "within" the business context itself, business as mission is focused both "within" and "through" the business, generally in a cross-cultural setting. It seeks to harness the power and resource of business for intentional mission impact in a community or nation at large. Whereas workplace ministry may occur in any setting, BAM is intentional about the "to all peoples" mandate, and seeks out areas with the greatest spiritual and physical needs

BAM is different from but related to tentmaking. Tentmaking refers principally to the practice of Christian professionals who support themselves financially by working as employees or by engaging in business. In this way they are able to conduct their ministries without depending upon donors and without burdening the people they serve. Tentmaking infers the integration of work and witness with an emphasis on encouraging evangelism by lay Christians rather than clergy and ministry professionals. Where tentmakers are part of business ventures that facilitate cross-cultural mission goals, there is substantial overlap with business as mission. However, although a tentmaker might be a part of a business, the business itself might not be an integral part of the ministry as it is with BAM. BAM sees business both as the medium and the message. BAM most often involves job-making as an integral part of its mission. Tentmaking may involve this, but is more often simply about job-taking, i.e., taking up employment somewhere in order to facilitate ministry.

BAM is different from business for missions. Profits from business can be donated to support missions and ministries. Likewise employees can use some of their salary to give to charitable causes. This can be called business for missions. This is different from BAM. While this should be encouraged, none of us would like to be operated on by a surgeon whose only ambition is to make money to give to the church! Instead, he is expected to have the right skills and motivations to operate with excellence and professional integrity. Likewise, a BAM business must produce more than goods and services in order to generate new wealth. It seeks to fulfill God's Kingdom purposes and values through every aspect of its operations. A BAM model can reinforce the false sacred/secular, clergy/laity construct, limiting businesses and business people to a role of funding the "real ministry." While funding is an important function, BAM is about for-profit businesses that have a Kingdom focus.

BAM does not condone non-business or non-missions. Two approaches to business, among others, do not fall within the scope of BAM in any sense. The first is fake businesses that are not actually functioning businesses, but exist solely to provide a platform and/or cover for missionaries to receive visas and enter countries otherwise closed to them. This "missionary in disguise approach"[1] model has little redeeming value. It is often employed by people who have little interest in business, and who seek to do the least possible amount of genuine work. As Rundle and Steffen point out, using business as a cover is not nearly as original or clever as we might imagine. "Spies and terrorists also have trouble operating openly in most countries, and they too have discovered the usefulness of the business platform."[44] It is simply dangerous for a missionary to employ such a duplicitous strategy, and very few churches have been started this way.

Secondly, businesses that purport to have Christian motivations but which operate only for private economic advantage and not for the Kingdom of God cannot be classified as BAM. Neither these, nor businesses run by Christians with no clear and defined Kingdom strategy, are considered BAM. BAM has not only an excellent business plan, it also has a "Great Commission plan."

BAM pursues profit. Kingdom businesses must be built on viable business plans, produce goods or services that people are willing to pay for, and be financially sustainable. Sustainability implies that the activity is profitable. Without profit the business cannot survive and fulfill its purposes. Accordingly, BAM businesses are *real* businesses that genuinely exist to generate wealth and profits. BAM does not view profits as inherently evil, bad or unbiblical. Quite the contrary, profits are good, desired and beneficial to God and His purposes, as long as they are not derived from oppressive means, or from gouging customers, or selling products and services that do no honor Christ and His

Gospel. Temporary subsidies may be utilized to establish a
BAM initiative. Permanent subsidies or financial support without expectation of ultimate profitability are closer to charitable
or donor-based ministries than BAM-based enterprises.

BAM is innovative and creative. The business and ministry
plans, methodologies, and strategies used, are intentionally creative and diverse, just as God created us in an amazing array of
shapes and sizes and colors. BAM seeks to develop and deploy
innovators and risk-takers, call them Kingdom entrepreneurs,
people who, in Rundle's words

> ...are *authentic* businesspeople with proven compe-
> tence in at least one area of business administration.
> They are spiritually gifted much like traditional
> missionaries, but are called and equipped to use
> those gifts in a business context. Kingdom entrepre-
> neurs have a genuine desire to see communities of
> faith spring up in the spiritually driest places, and
> are willing to live and work in these places to make
> that happen. Rather than perceiving the business as
> a distraction from their ministry, kingdom entrepre-
> neurs recognize it as the necessary context for their
> incarnational outreach. The daily struggles – meet-
> ing deadlines, satisfying customers, being victim-
> ized by corruption – are precisely the things that en-
> able kingdom entrepreneurs to model Christian dis-
> cipleship on a daily basis.[45]

BAM comes in all shapes and sizes. Does the size of the
business matter? Yes and No! Christian micro-enterprise programs exist that help provide necessary income for families and
individuals resulting in community development, churches being
planted and discipleship taking place. Christian micro-enterprise
development has been well accepted and is effective for the
Kingdom. It has a legitimate place in the broader definition and
practice of BAM. However, BAM focuses on larger scale business, generally small to medium sized enterprises. To tackle the
enormity of the challenge before us business people need to
think and act bigger, beyond micro to small, medium and large
enterprises.

What might one of these Kingdom enterprises look like? In
Rundle and Steffen's conception,

> There is no limit to the forms a Great Commission
> Company can take. Nevertheless, there are some

> basic characteristics that they all have in common,
> which enable us to define a Great Commission
> Company as "a socially responsible, income-
> producing business managed by Kingdom profes-
> sionals and created for the specific purpose of glori-
> fying God and promoting the growth and multipli-
> cation of local churches in the least-evangelized and
> least-developed parts of the world."[46]

For the past two centuries, education and health have been
the handmaidens of the modern missions movement. However,
virtually every country in the world today has a ministry of education and a ministry of health whose leadership more often than
not frown upon the thought of any outsider telling them how to
educate or care for their people. In the 21st century, business fills
the void left by education and health. Business opens doors in
even the most tightly shut nations like Turkmenistan and North
Korea, and business people replace (in a sense), traditional missionaries. As Neal Johnson puts it,

> ...the business community, because of its enormous
> power base of influence, resources, and expertise is
> in a unique position to undertake mission for Christ:
> worldwide and next door. This mission can be done
> effectively and efficiently by Christian believers in
> the business community. The heart of mission is
> helping hurting people holistically through the love
> of Christ. And what matters is not who does it, but
> who receives it; not who does it, but how and why it
> is done. In these instances, it is the business com-
> munity itself that is replacing the traditional "send-
> ing agencies" of earlier Christian mission para-
> digms. It is the business community utilizing the re-
> sources God has placed in their hands to become a
> major part of *missio Dei*.[47]

The BAM model is perhaps one of the most biblical, sensi-
ble and effective models for cross-cultural frontier ministry today for emerging missions in developing countries, such as Brazil. It is a balanced and integrated approach in that:

- with one model it can overcome the four most significant obstacles (getting out, getting in , staying in, sinking in),

- it does not separate sacred and secular, spiritual and material, clergy and laity, nor demean or overrate the secular and the laity,

- business and ministry activity become one in the same for the Glory of the Father. It is not just good theology, it is good missiology and doxology,

- it is both theocentric, motivated primarily by a desire to see God glorified among all peoples, and anthropocentric, because it is secondarily driven by a desire to meet the needs of people,

- the cross-cultural Good News bearer has one identity, no duplicity, no dishonesty,

- it unites economic activity with social and justice concerns and plugs them into church-planting movements,

- it unites emerging missions movements like that of Brazil with the peoples where the name of Christ is never or rarely heard.

The BAM model can and should increasingly become the missions model of choice for the 21st century, especially for emerging missions movements. It serves as a catalyst to inspire and encourage people to get into business and to stay in business, to get into missions and stay in missions, especially at the frontier of missions among the least-reached peoples in the developing world. It envisions and enables the laity, the 21st century missionary personnel, to go to the 85 percent of the world where "professional missionaries" cannot and where the PMM model does not work. It unleashes emerging missionary forces like that of the Evangelical church in Brazil.

Discussion Starters

1. Do you feel that the so-called "Copernican shift" in the global center of Christianity's "gravity" – to the developing Church in the developing world – is truly significant for world evangelization, or has the author overstated the case?

2. If your heritage is within a long-established North American or European church tradition, how do you feel when you consider the contention that your church's global influence and relevance is waning? Do you consider the shift good or bad for world evangelization? What can/should you and your local church, or mission agency or educational/training institution, do in response to the shift? What changes do you need to make, attitudes do you need to rethink, partnerships do you need to develop, etc.?

3. Identify the strengths of the "professional missionary model" (PMM)? Now detail its weaknesses. Do the same for the "business as mission" (BAM) model. Should the global missions movement be leaning more toward one or the other? Which one? On a scale of one to ten, with one being purely PMM and ten being purely legitimate tentmaking and BAM, where, ideally, should the global missions movement be focused?

4. In Steve Rundle and Tom Steffen's conception, *"There is no limit to the forms a Great Commission Company can take. Nevertheless, there are some basic characteristics that they all have in common, which enable us to define a Great Commission Company as "a socially responsible, income-producing business managed by Kingdom professionals and created for the specific purpose of glorifying God and promoting the growth and multiplication of local churches in the least-evangelized and least-developed parts of the world."* With which portions of this statement do you agree or disagree, and why?

Notes

1. Lamin Sanneh. "Global Christianity and the Re-Education of the West." *Christian Century* 19 July, 1995. Online. Accessed on 4 April, 2005.
<http://www.findarticles.com/p/articles/mi_m1058/is_n22_v112/ai_170 99805/print>

2. Walbert, Buhlmann, *The Coming of the Third Church.* (Maryknowll, NY: Orbis Books, 1978).

3. Andrew F. Walls, *The Missionary Movement in Christian History.* (Maryknoll, NY: Orbis Books, 1996), 68.

4. Tracey K. Jones, Jr., "History's Lessons for Tomorrow's Mission." *International Bulletin of Missionary Research*, 10:2: electronic edition, April 1986, 50-53.

5. Samuel Escobar, *The New Global Mission: The Gospel From Everywhere to Everyone.* (Downers Grove, IL: InterVarsity Press, 2003).

6. Philip Jenkins, *The Next Christendom: The Coming of Global Christianity.* (NY: Oxford University Press, 2002).

7. Dana L. Robert, "Shifting Southward: Global Christianity Since 1945," *International Bulletin of Missionary Research*, 24:2: electronic edition, April 2000, 50-58.

8. It should be noted that while much of the growth of Christianity in the so-called "global south" has, indeed, occurred in the southern hemisphere, much of it has not – for example in Central America, northern South America, much of sub-Saharan Africa and virtually all of Asia where Christianity has grown, lie in the northern hemisphere – and this is cause for some confusion. Thus, for purposes of clarity, I will employ Buhlmann's historically (rather than geographically) rooted moniker of "third church," as well as the ever-useful tag "emerging church.")

9. Larry D. Pate and Lawrence E. Keyes, "Emerging Missions in a Global Church," *International Bulletin of Missionary Research*, 10:4: electronic edition, October 1986, 156-161.

10. Larry W. Kraft and Stephanie K. Kraft, "Evangelical Revival vs. Social Reformation: An Analysis of the Growth of the Evangelical Church in Brazil from 1905 to the Present." (Unpublished master's degree paper. Pasadena, CA: Fuller Theological Seminary, 1995), 24.

11. Ibid.

12. www.ibge.gov.br.

13. This ranking is frustratingly difficult to ascertain with any level of certainty for two reasons. First, of the five largest Evangelical churches in the world, a fairly accurate accounting seemingly can only be made for the USA and Brazil. It is much more difficult in the cases of China, India and Nigeria. Second, definitions and research methodology vary widely. Three of the best sources are Patrick Johnstone's

Operation World Database, David Barrett's *World Christian Encyclopedia* and the accompanying *World Christian Trends,* and the CIA World Factbook. However, there are no standardized definitions, and the researcher ends up with a shopping cart full of domains such as "Christian," "Protestant," "Evangelical," "Pentecostal," "Independent," "Great Commission Christians," etc., often with varying definitions, with huge areas of overlap and with no objective mechanism by which to compare them accurately. My understanding of the data indicates that, while it is difficult to ascertain the exact ranking of the five countries with the largest populations of biblically defined believers in, and followers of, the Lord Jesus Christ, we can determine that 1) China and the USA occupy the first two positions (not necessarily in that order) and, 2) Brazil, India and Nigeria occupy positions three through five (not necessarily in that order).

14. COMIBAM stands for Cooperación Misionera Iberoamericana. It is a partnership of Latin American mission agencies. See <www.comibam.org>

15. Quoted in Oswaldo Prado, "A New Way of Sending Missionaries: Lessons from Brazil." *Missiology: An International Review.* (Vol. 33, No. 1, January 2005), 52.

16. From William D. Taylor, ed., *Global Missiology for the 21st Century: The Iguassu Dialogue.* (Grand Rapids, MI: Baker Academic, 2000), 364.

17. Bertil Ekstöm, in *Modelos Missionários Brasileiros para o Século XXI,* the manual for the 2nd Brazilian Congress on Missions, 9-13 November, 1998, 96.

18. Tim Halls, "The Missionary movement from Latin America." *Latin America Mission* website, 12 November 2003. Accessed on 8 April 2005. http://www.lam.org/view.html?id=265

19. Ekstom, p. 96.

20. According to the AMTB's page on the Infobrasil website. Accessed on 8 April 2005. <http://www.infobrasil.org/amtb/index.htm>. While 1984 seems to be the year that the association began to function in earnest, according to Bertil Ekstöm (in *Modelos Missionários Brasileiros para o Século XXI,* the manual for the 2nd Brazilian Congress on Missions, 9-13 November, 1998, p. 97) the association actually was formed in 1974.

21. <http://www.infobrasil.org/agen/ing/consulta-1996/bra/_resum.htm>. Accessed on 8 April 2005.

22. <http://www.infobrasil.org/agen/ing/consulta-1996/bra/_resum.htm>. Accessed on 8 April 2005.

23. Ibid.

24. As reported in *Modelos Missionários Brasileiros para o Século XXI,* the manual for the 2nd Brazilian Congress on Missions, 9-13 November, 1998, p. 5.

25. And, confusingly, at 139 and 155, depending upon where the data is reported. He puts the number at 132 in the Brazil section of *Operation World,* 139 in Appendix Four and 155 in the *Operation World* Database on CD-ROM.

26. Patrick Johnstone, *Operation World*, CD Version.

27. Ibid.

28. Which, in Brazil's case, is 14.5 churches per missionary. Finland ranks number one at 1.5 churches per missionary.

29. Paul G. Hiebert, *Anthropological Insights for Missionaries*. (Grand Rapids, Michigan: Baker Books, 1985),

30. To be sure, theologies of mission have been developed elsewhere within the broader Latin world, namely, the Spanish speaking world. Notable work has been done by Orlando Costas, René Padilla and Samuel Escobar, among others. Brazilians, however, have little affinity with Spanish-speaking Latin Americans.

31. Paul G. Hiebert, "Critical Contextualization." *Missiology: An International Review* (Vol. 12, No. 3, July 1984), 287-296.

32. See Melvin L. Hodges, *The Indigenous Church*, 1953.

33. In "Back to the Future of Missions: The Case for Marketplace Ministry." Accessed on 11 April 2005. <http://www.scruples.org/web/articles/Back%20to%20the%20Future%20of%20Missions%20VI.htm#_Toc487092753>.

34. Heinz Suter and Marco Gmür, *Business Power for God's Purpose*. (Greng-Murten, Switzerland: VKG, 1997), 19-40.

35. For further study on the theological and historical development of the sacred-secular dualism, see, among others: R. Paul Stevens, *The Other Six Days: Vocation, Work, and Ministry in Biblical Perspective* (Eerdmans & Co., 2000); C.J. Bulley, *The Priesthood of Some Believers: Developments from the General to the Special Priesthood in the Christian Literature of the First Three Centuries* (Paternoster, 2000); and Hendrik Kraemer, *A Theology of the Laity*. (Westminster Press, 1958).

36. CIA World Factbook, online. Accessed on 9 December 2005. <http://www.cia.gov/cia/publications/factbook/rankorder/2001rank.html>. Brazil's estimated GDP for 2004 was $1,492,000,000,000.

37.   Ibid. <http://www.cia.gov/cia/publications/factbook/rankorder/2004rank.html>. The 2004 estimate was $8100 per person.

38.   Ibid. <http://www.cia.gov/cia/publications/factbook/rankorder/2003rank.html>. 2004 estimate.

39.   Ibid. <http://www.cia.gov/cia/publications/factbook/rankorder/2129rank.html>. It was 11.50% in 2004.

40.   Ibid. <http://www.cia.gov/cia/publications/factbook/rankorder/2092rank.html>. It was 7.60% in 2004.

41. In Taylor, William D., Editor. *Too Valuable to Lose*. (Pasadena, CA: William Carey Library, 1997), 149.

42. Oswaldo Prado, "A New Way of Sending Missionaries: Lessons from Brazil." *Missiology: An International Review*. (Vol. 33, No. 1, January 2005), 52.

43. I will not go into great detail here because of numerous outstanding resources now available. A good place to start is Yamamori and Eldred's edited *On Kingdom Business*, Rundle and Steffen's *Great Commission Companies*, and *The Lausanne Occasional Paper on Business as Mission* produced by those of us involved in the Lausanne Forum Business as Mission issue group that convened in Thailand in October of 2004. See: <www.businessasmission.com>

44. Steve Rundle and Tom Steffen, *Great Commission Companies: The Emerging Role of Business in Missions.* (Downers Grove, IL: InterVarsity Press, 2003), 22.

¹ Rundle and Steffen, 41-42.

45. Steve Rundle, "Preparing the Next Generation of Kingdom Entrepreneurs," in Tetsunao Yamamori and Kenneth A. Eldred (eds.), *On Kingdom Business: Transforming Missions Through Entrepreneurial Strategies.* (Wheaton, IL: Crossway Books, 2003), 229-230.

46. Rundle and Steffen, 41.

47. Charles Neal Johnson, *God's Mission To, Within, and Through the Marketplace: Toward a Marketplace Missiology.* (Unpublished Ph.D. dissertation. Pasadena, CA: Fuller Theological Seminary, 2004), 328.

14

Professional Work as Ministry: A Chinese Case Study

Mans Ramstad

Solid Rock was established in the early 1990s, functioning as a ministry co-op with workers seconded from several organizations. Solid Rock now has 26 full-time foreign workers from five countries and 40 full-time Chinese workers. Our purpose, as openly advertised within China, is to provide services for the community in the name of Christ.

The topic for 2005 meeting is "Business as Mission." We need to clarify what is meant by "business." I gather the primary focus is on production and financial profitability in the absence of donations. So at the outset I want to mention this approach would be only one small part of our goal in Solid Rock. We would talk more in terms of legitimacy in the community and "professionalism"[1] than business profitability. I hope you will see the ways in which we embrace the business as mission model, but even more so, the principles we believe are essential to fruitful and sustainable long-term mission – regardless if it is traditional missions, tentmaking, business as mission (BAM) or community development.

Solid Rock is a Wholly Owned Foreign Enterprise, but we function as a non-profit, including paying taxes only on goods and services sold in-country. Our 2005 total budget was just over $1 million USD with five percent of income from sales of products and services.

We have work in the community in the areas of agriculture, health care, education, and rural economic development (small business start-up). While each of these areas function very differently, they share the following:

1. Called Christian workers working in the community in areas they have qualifications and which the community and/or the government welcomes.

2. These areas of work are not "platforms" or "covers." They are valuable and an integral part of ministry and witness.

3. These areas of work give legitimacy and allow us to do ministry in three realms: witness to people in those areas of work, disciple/train believers on a personal level and serve the church on a broader social level.

Our business involvement over the years has involved helping dozens of farmers launch small businesses and we currently have two businesses that are a part of our work that are successful. Much could be said about each of these areas of work and I welcome input and further discussion on this after the session, but I think in keeping with the purpose of this conference, I will move on to the issues of mutual concern, how to do ministry effectively in the modern context.

Philosophy of Ministry

Biblical models, historical models, and sociological models provide Solid Rock a solid philosophy of ministry.

Biblical Models

Priscilla and Aquila: Team work in Society and the Church Planting Axis. In Acts 18 we learn the Apostle Paul was in Corinth, working in the leather business and preaching the gospel. One day Priscilla and Aquila happened to meet Paul, because they were of the same trade. They invited Paul to their home, and showed hospitality to him. This was the beginning of their ministry teamwork.

Joseph: Excellence Axis. "Now Joseph had been taken down to Egypt, Potiphar...bought him . . . . The Lord was with Joseph and he prospered, and he lived in the house of his Egyptian master. When his master saw that the Lord was with him and that the Lord gave him success in everything he did, Joseph found favor in his eyes . . ." (Gen 39:1-4, NIV).

Daniel: Faithfulness, Integrity and Openness Axis. In 605 BC, the young Daniel was taken captive by Nebuchadnezzar into Babylon and given a place of prominence in Nebuchadnezzar's kingdom. Later we read, "Now when Daniel learned that the decree had been published (forced worship of Darius) he went home to his upstairs room where the windows opened towards Jerusalem. Three times a day he got down on his knees and prayed, giving thanks to his God, just as he had done before" (Dan 6:10).

Historical Model

Jesuits in China: Professional Work Integrated with Intentional Witness Axis. After the Rites Controversy of 1715 Catholic missionaries in China were forbidden access to intellectuals and officials, and were not allowed to make converts from among them. Many churches were shut down as well. But there was a Jesuit physician Stephanus Rouset, who had accompanied Emperor Kangxi as his personal physician. Rouset was known to be a very amiable preacher, and during the years when the Christian church was banned in China, many Chinese believers came to his place for healing and prayers.

Sociological Model

One way to describe Solid Rock's status in China is that of a mediating structure.[2] We stand between the government and the people, a gap which historically in China has been very broad. While we are not the government, we respect the government leaders, and are sympathetic to their plans for developing China. We are aware that there are short-comings in the leadership, but we do not find it to be as mitigating to cooperation as some would think. Furthermore, we seek to engage in selected programs which will assist the government leaders in carrying out their objectives, most of which are very noble, but because of lack of resources, years of central planning and a relatively poorly educated populace, have been difficult to carry out.

Second, we are not the people, but we identify with the people. We are foreigners, and can never assume the role of the common Chinese person. But we can get to know the people, empathize with them, understand their passions and frustrations, and seek to carry out programs that will benefit them. In fact, our purpose statement states that we are to carry out programs beneficial for the common people.[3] Enter Solid Rock. Unlike the common people, we have access to the government leaders. And seemingly we have more access to the people than the government does. Having the respect of the leaders, we can communicate the needs and passions of the people to the government. If done in the right way, this information is very helpful to them and they appreciate it. It also helps them carry out their work with a view to the people whom they are called to serve. In this sense Solid Rock represents the people. Likewise, having the respect of the common people, when we come to them with our programs, they see these programs as coming in large measure from their own government. In this way they develop a more positive view of their government leaders and a confidence about the future.

This model actually has precedent in Chinese culture. Historically, China has been a two-class society, the government officials (– *guan)* and the people (– *min)*. These two classes had little contact, with the officials holding power and the people paying obeisance to them. In the Qing Dynasty a class arose known in English as the gentry (– *shen)*. The role of the gentry (derived from the word gentleman) was to carry out public good for the benefit of the people on behalf of the officials. They were well educated and spent little time engaged in common labor themselves. They were instrumental in helping the officials carry out public works like road and bridge building. They had significant responsibility for the people.[4]

Although the reputation of the gentry class in history is mixed, ideally it served a powerful role to bridge the gap between the government and the people.[5] Being foreigners, we could never assume a role as citizens, which the gentry were; and the historical context of the Qing Dynasty was a unique setting in which the gentry class arose. So we would not want to push the analogy too far. But it does serve as an historical example of a mediating structure in Chinese society from which to learn.[6]

Social Identity Axis

These models inform our view of serving in China and of our identity in China. We seek to discern the leading of the Holy Spirit who always goes before us as we seek to serve in Jesus' name. Our approach to serving in China can be summarized as our "Deeper Ways of Serving." (1) We value both professional and spiritual training of those we serve (comes from the Priscilla and Aquila model). (2) We work with the open church (comes from our Daniel model).

We value our public witness and want to help the Chinese church to enter more into society. We also long for Chinese society to grow to understand the Chinese church, which is a part of the church's witness to the gospel. We know from Jesus' own words that we are not to leave the world, but go out into the world, trusting that Christ will keep us from the evil one (Jn 17:14-17; 1 Co 5:9-10).[7] "Live such good lives among the pagans that, though they accuse you of doing wrong, they may see your good deeds and glorify God" (1 Pe 2:12). In this capacity we publicly defend and show our love for the Christian church. (3) We want to help church leaders broaden their ministry involvement. (4) Development in health, education, agriculture, culture, economics, and spiritual life are part of an overall transformation process. One can see this comes from the ministry of Jesus whose preaching of the kingdom of God was similarly holistic.

To summarize, we see ourselves simultaneously engaged in three spheres of ministry:

1. Through our work in society as part of our public witness.
2. Personally, one-on-one, or small group, as the Lord brings people to us. This is following the teaching of 1 Peter 3:15 to be ready with a witness at all times.
3. In the open, public Chinese church.

Spiritual Results

Following are some of the spiritual results. (1) A church was planted. We praise God for this, but we also feel that a church "planted" is not itself the end goal of mission, it is just the beginning.[8] As Gordon Fee has said, "...our gospel is not simply that of 'saving souls'; it is rather, as with Jesus, the bringing of wholeness to broken people in every kind of distress."[9] Planted churches need to be watered and grow to maturity lest they die. (2) Church ministries were expanded. (3) Local staff and their families are learning how to minister in the community. (4) Public witness grows (Ro 8:19-23; Eph 1:22-23; Col 1:19-20). This is important in China, where the gospel has been effectively boxed out of society, the media, education and other public realms. Mission involves a witness to the broader society in ways that may not directly result in the numerical growth of churches. (5) Leadership training.

Lessons Learned

There are many ways to accomplish the mission Christ has left us with and which He now empowers us to do by the presence of His Holy Spirit. The thoughtful practice of mission, under the guidance of the Holy Spirit, and in step with the living and breathing Word of God will give us insights along the way. Here I would like to offer some of the enduring convictions we have developed and lessons learned. I think most of these have relevance for mission done in a variety of ways and are not restricted to what we are doing in Solid Rock.

246   BUSINESS AS MISSION

Legitimacy in the Community. Matt 10:13 provides an enduring principle. Find the "person of peace" (in China a "good man") that God has prepared who will provide a legitimate sphere within which you are able to
minister naturally and freely because people know who you are.

Local Appropriateness. I turn again to Bonhoeffer:

> It is in the context of actual neighbor relationships that we are
> invited to live the life of faith. It is precisely in the unplanned
> and uncontrollable circumstances of our lives that we can find
> God and be found in Him.[10]

Professionalism, Excellence, Integrity. A quality "product," not "business" *per se,* is our priority. Business has been done in missions for centuries–schools, publishing houses, hospitals, etc.–so that is not new. Of higher
priority in terms of successful ways to engage in mission in creative access
contexts is whether the workers are skilled at what they do, are engaged in
society and a healthy, normal member of it, what they offer is welcomed by
the community, and are they accomplishing their purpose. Business as
"production of physical products" is too narrow. Profitability is better, and
that income can come from donations or services sold.

Anything that serves as a false front is lacking in integrity, and anything that is sloppy is lacking in excellence (Phil 4:8). I hope we will support ministry that has integrity and is excellent and faithful, and correct any
ministry that has neither integrity nor excellence. What draws us together in
any form of mission is a call to professional work that has integrity, is locally appropriate, is done with excellence and is faithful to the gospel–both
doing what the gospel calls us to and not doing what it forbids.

Time Commitment. There is no such thing as church planting "on the
fly." I follow the example of Priscilla and Aquila who put together the
pieces and actually built up the "church" which Paul planted. It takes years
invested in the community to build a strong church.

Sustainability. We understand sustainability to include effective local
ownership, leadership and management, financial independence and transformational impact. Sustainability in our medical work means the transfer
of skills and leadership that will endure beyond any given program. Spiritual sustainability means the training and empowering of mature, godly
leaders who can handle the Word of God and lead and disciple people, not
the erecting of some formal structure or building.

We have been asked, "By hiring local people, are you making them dependent on you and they can't survive without you?" My answer is that
among our staff we are training up highly skilled, godly lay workers, not
training pastors. It is our desire that they gain work skills that will make
them qualified for employment in society, and we have examples of people

successfully moving on in just this way. We will not hire people to be pastors, as this undercuts the local church and creates the crippling dependency people fear.

Faithfulness and Commitment. I still believe in the core value of faithfulness, and believe that we need to discern which ministry trends are merely fads and which are viable opportunities from the Holy Spirit. I would like to call people to remember that the work of building godly members for the kingdom of God is long and hard work no matter how you choose to do it. If ministry were compared to baking, there are no microwave ovens.

Critical Contextualization. The phenomenon of globalization is at times masked colonialism, so that the outcome is the Westernization of the developing world. This has fooled us into imagining that English speaking, western style of spiritual formation and worship is somehow the "global form," unaware that it may actually reflect the power and resources of the Western church. A Trinitarian view of globalization would envision a free flow of spiritual resources around the globe under the Lordship of Christ and the freedom of the Holy Spirit. May the West be open to the resources God is giving us through the churches in other lands. To that end, we must remember that effective mission is always locally contextualized and requires learning the local language.

Constructive Partnerships. I appreciate the emphasis in the Business as Mission movement toward cooperation between business and NGOs. Business, agriculture and production is the core of any society. NGOs serve people first. How do NGOs (focusing on people first) and business (focusing on profit first) relate to each other? How can NGOs, who know the language and the community, serve expatriate business people who have value and opportunity to bring to the community?

Experience Crosscultural Ministry. First I am frequently approached by young people who feel called to missions, but who are unwilling to raise financial support and who hope to be engaged in business overseas. My common recommendation to them is to do language study and missions for four years and then go into business.

Focus on People's Basis Needs. Although this may be out of step with current global economic theory, I believe that agriculture, water resources, health and education are extremely fundamental and enduring needs of human societies, not the purchasing of consumer products that make our lives easier. While large businesses are bringing economic growth to China, India and elsewhere, both countries are experiencing dangerous destruction and consumption of natural resources, and staggering disparity between the rich and the poor. So we also have a theological conviction about meeting agricultural, educational and health needs.

Be a Humble Servant. The world needs a "humble theology." Indifference toward the West, and the gospel with which it is associated, calls us to be more humble and less triumphalistic, as we seek to bring the gospel to the world. Serving sacrificially, giving up our rights and comforts, as well as our habits and practices, is a necessary part of any witness.

Conclusion

In conclusion, our experience in China demonstrates the power of meaningful involvement in society and the training up of godly highly-skilled workers for that society. We find it requires deep involvement for a long period of time. We are developing business and want to encourage entrepreneurs and professionals of all types to consider using their area of work or business for kingdom-building purposes all around the world. "So then, think of us first as servants of Christ and as stewards of the mystery of the gospel. The one thing required of such servants is that they be faithful to their master" (1 Co 4:1-2).

Discussion Starters

1. What strikes you as new or distinctive about Solid Rock?
2. Does the focus on professionalism and excellence feel at odds with the humble ministry of Jesus Christ?
3. How does Business as Mission as it is being currently presented differ from the "professional" work by NGOs being promoted in this essay?
4. Funding national workers who want to be missionaries in their own country or elsewhere is a challenge in missions. What are aspects of the approach of Solid Rock that could enhance the potential for such workers being able to realize their dream of doing cross-cultural missions?

Notes

1. I have thought about John Piper's argument in his book "Brothers, We are Not Professionals," in which he argues that the pastoral ministry has been given over to a professional mentality, and along the way lost certain of it's spiritual content. While Christians need to beware of this in all areas of life, I feel his concern is primarily for pastors and a different issue from what I am trying to promote in this paper.

2. The term "mediating structure" comes from Robert Simmons, *Competing Gospels: Public Theology and Economic Theory* (E. J. Dwyer Pty Ltd, Australia, 1995), pp.160-161.

3. Reinhold Neihbur *(Moral Man and Immoral Society,* New York: Charles Scribner's Sons, 1932) decried the poor communication that exists between the church and society because of insistence on using one's own jargon. He coined the phrase "middle level axioms" to describe concepts and terms that the church shares with the world and can be used to enhance communication and mutual understanding.

4. Tong Zonglin, *Long yu Shangdi: Christianity and China's Traditional Culture*, (San Lian Publishers, Beijing, 1992), pp. 187-190.

5. "Missionaries, eager to survive and develop their work, often focused on...their mission compound. They did not personally know the scholars, gentry or the local magistrate around them. Many of the gentry...were the intermediaries between the government and the people...They were in charge of local educational and charity projects...On the local level they exemplified and defended the Confucian tradition. When missionaries penetrated China's interior and began schools, orphanages, clinics and chapels, they were supplanting the role of the gentry unawares" Samuel Ling. 2000. *China Source* (Vol. IV, 1 – Spring), pp. 1-6.

6. One important lesson we can learn is not to be excessively loyal to the government or become mere tools in their hands to accomplish what they want without regard for its appropriateness or morality. The gentry were often used by the government against the people. We must stand firm in our middle position, neither being naïve toward the government, nor antagonizing the government.

7. Abraham Kuyper in Peter S. Heslam's *Creating A Christian Worldview*, The Paternoster Press, Michigan, 1998 reminds us to go out into the world boldly because there is not one square inch over which Jesus Christ does not reign as Lord and cry out, "Mine."

8. Gary Corwin, "Ministry Idolatries," *EMQ*, July 2005, 41(3):278-79. Corwin warns about three ministry idols: (1) the elevation of breadth of participation above quality of contribution as the chief underlying value, (2) the elevation of church planting per se above disciple-making, and (3) a laser-like focus on multiplication and movements in mission that too often neglects the importance of other mandates.

9. Gordon D. Fee, *Listening to the Spirit in the Text*, (Eerdmans, 2000), p. 178.

10. Dietrich Bonhoeffer, *Letters and Papers from Prison*, (Collins Fontana Books, London), 1953.

Part 4

Future Challenges

15

The Future of Business as Mission: An Inquiry into Macro-Strategy

Jay E. Gary

Over the past ten years a *Business as Mission* emphasis has been developing in Protestant world missions.[1] This strategy calls for Christian entrepreneurs to relocate to developing countries and launch new business enterprises that might transform local communities, both physically and spiritually.

Today Youth With A Mission actively promotes the 'Kingdom Business' concept[2] as an entry strategy to unreached peoples. It reasons that Business as Mission can sustain development efforts among the poor, serve as a model for self-help discipleship and provide a means to both send missionaries and support current operations.[3] Others proclaim that communications technology now enables 'Great Commission Companies' to move from micro-enterprise to multinational business, given "The Good News About Globalization."[4] Business as Mission has grown from a strategic field emphasis to a mobilization call in the local church. ACMC, Advancing Churches in Mission Commitment, even has a 'Business as Mission' promotion arm.

The historical roots of Business as Mission can be traced back some eighty-five years to the International Missionary Council.[5] These ecumenical leaders desired to see the laity released for a greater evangelism.[6] As the decades passed, Evangelicals shaped this into a call for lay people to become cross-cultural witnesses or tentmakers.[7] Various marketplace ministries arose in Asia, Europe and North America to reaffirm work as part of the Christian vocation. Many see this as part of a larger movement, a lay renaissance, to recover a more vital practice of the kingdom of God.[8] Its aim is to bridge the divide between clergy and laity, between sacred and secular.[9]

In its current expression, Business as Mission has a ten-year history. What will its future be over the next decade? How might the downside of globalization challenge and reshape our conception of both business and missions over the next half-century? Will business and missions clash, collapse or converge?

Recently, a Lausanne 2004 Forum issue group on Business as Mission put their strategy in world perspective:

> We want to effect radical, holistic transformation of society's economic systems and structures. The reality of globalisation is increasingly having direct impact on people of all nations and cultures everywhere. As Christians we must intentionally seek to align business with kingdom of God purposes at a macro level.[10]

While this affirms the importance of transforming macro-level systems, up until now Business as Mission has been implemented at the micro-level of team and business formation and at the meso-level of community development. Few missiologists have related this new strategy to the future of the world.

Building on discussions of globalization[11] and the world-futures debate,[12] this chapter aims to open conversations of Business as Mission at the macro-level. It will hold business and missions open to critical inquiry from various macro perspectives: historical, ecological and theological. Specifically, it will argue that business and missions: a) should be held in tension with one another in light of the kingdom of God, b) will face unprecedented crises due to the world's present trajectory of overshoot and collapse, and c) will need to recover a global theology of transformation for the 21st century that is biblically based on the apostolic age.

Holding Business and Missions Together

Jesus often held missions open to business by comparing these two endeavors in parables.[13] In the parable of the dishonest manager (Lk 16:1-13). Jesus claimed that the "Children of this age are more shrewd in dealing with their own generation than are the children of light" (Lk 16:8, NRSV). Readers are often surprised that Jesus treats a dishonest manager as the hero. Yet the parable calls us to wisdom, first to self-preservation and then to social charity, in view of the coming kingdom and tribulation.[14]

James, the brother of Jesus, also held these two life-worlds in tension. In James 4:13-5:7, he challenged the presumption of Messianic Jews who had left Jerusalem for the Diaspora over their business plans to make money, given the "miseries that are coming to you" (Jas 5:1). The 'you' in this passage are the wealthy that withheld wages from the poor.[15]

In both of these examples, business and missions are held in tension. Micro-level actions are judged by impending macro-level realities, that is, the apocalyptic crisis of the kingdom of God.[16] Early Christianity did not maintain that consciousness of crisis much past the first-century. Beyond the cruciform period there have been four succeeding paradigms of faith: Orthodox, Catholic, Reformation and Enlightenment.[17] Many now think a postmodern paradigm could emerge after the modern age.[18] This changing of cultures could hardly be compared to the climax of the covenant of Jesus' day,[19] the changing from Old to New Covenant. But the modern world-system, including Business as Mission, certainly faces what Wallerstein calls 'historical choices of the twenty-first century.'[20]

Beyond Limits to Breakdowns

One reason that Business as Mission is so attractive today is that this sending strategy for cross-cultural workers amplifies church mission budgets, at a time when missionary giving has stagnated.[21] The hope is that, through this effort, a new harvest force might be raised up to fulfill the Great Commission. Some advocates of 'Kingdom Business' speak confidently of the "biblical legitimacy of free-market economics."[22] They cite conservative scholars who sanctify Adam Smith's 'invisible hand of the market.'[23] But there is no guarantee that globalization or the capitalist world-system will deliver on its promises over the next half century, even for those most well-off, much less for the world's destitute.[24]

The next half century could just as easily witness the systemic breakdown of both business and missions due to increasing oil shortages, killer diseases, climate changes, water deficits, terror, error and natural disasters.[25] Take your pick!

No one knows for sure what the future will bring. But in our limited knowledge of the future, we do know that some possibilities on the horizon might be more plausible than others. We must act by faith in view of these more certain uncertainties.

To separate the wheat from the chaff, related to the 21st century, this section will explore a) the world futures debate, b) the ethical challenge behind global problems, and c) the current driving forces that might become 'game changers.'

The World Futures Debate

Since the atomic bomb was unleashed to shorten World War II, scholars have intensified debates about disasters that face humanity. These range from thermonuclear war, [26] environmental degradation,[27] overpopulation,[28] food shortages[29] to the energy crisis.[30] But it was not until the Club of Rome published The Limits to Growth[31] that people began to think of these transnational threats as interrelated, with industrial growth as a cause. The Limits to Growth was initially built on computer models that oversimplified non-linear complex systems. But the study did surface three sobering messages: a) that within a century the world would run out of the nonrenewable resources on which growth depends, b) that piecemeal approaches to solving these problems would be insufficient, and c) that 'overshoot and collapse' could be avoided only by limiting population, pollution and curbing exponential growth. Limits became the ideological bulwark to a left-leaning environmental movement. The Global Problematique, a term coined by the Club of Rome, demanded public policy action in the short-run, in order to restore equilibrium to the world-system over the long-run.

While Meadow's *Limits* defined the pessimistic outlook of the world futures debate, Herman Kahn's *The Next 200 Years* defined the optimistic pole. Defending the Industrial Revolution, his outlook was based on "the general statement that 200 years ago almost everywhere human beings were comparatively few, poor and at the mercy of the forces of nature, and 200 years from now, we expect, almost everywhere they will be numerous, rich and in control of the forces of nature."[32] Countering what he called the 'doomsayers' who saw the world as a "finite pie," Kahn presented his case for an "infinite pie"[33] using statistical projections of declining population growth, adequate raw materials and a robust environment. Kahn's optimism, especially related to energy, was based on a confidence in technological progress, and on the transition to solar energy that would sustain a high level of economic activity. Since Kahn, others have continued to argue there are no limits to growth, and any view to the contrary is neo-Malthusian.[34]

The Limits to Growth debate, as well as the methodology of long-range forecasting, is still being debated today. In hindsight, can we say whether either side was right? Only the 22nd century will be able to answer that question authoritatively. Yet one conclusion is sure: "While there may be 'limits to growth' as far as the world's ecosystems are understood, there are no necessary limits to cooperation as human beings seek to constructively organize and respond."[35] The world futures debate[36] has moved from what might happen to how we might transition to sustainability.[37] The debate has now created an interdisciplinary field called 'global change research,' relating insights from natural systems to human systems.[38]

However we define the 21st century, whether as a problem space or a solution space, the future is calling for a civilization response.[39] The exponential growth of population, production and pollution will taper off at some point in the 21st century. The question is, Will this transition to equilibrium come about abruptly through collapse or will it come about gradually through human self-control and natural processes?

Facing Tough Questions

At the end of the day, this is a question of human stewardship. What kind of world do we want our children and grandchildren to inherit? Business as Mission, especially its free-market wing, needs to ask these questions upfront, not post-facto. Can humans, including those most vulnerable among us, survive the unintended consequences of big business and the exponential growth paradigm?[40]

Recently the CIA offered its map of the global future out to 2020. It envisioned a world where the United States would no longer be the sole superpower.[41] As western Christians, can we envision a post-American world like that? And what can be done beyond just protesting the growth paradigm to insure that we create a post-corporate future?[42]

Thirty years ago Jay Forrester, the inventor of memory storage in computers, posed a number of questions to overseas ministry executives, including:

1. Are the churches today acting in a way that will improve or worsen the future of mankind?
2. Should the churches be responsive to short-term pressures, or should they be custodians of the long-term values of society?
3. Because the short-term and long-term objectives are usually contradictory, how is the balance struck?[43]

By and large, these questions were ignored by Evangelicals. Only a few Evangelical gatekeepers engaged in the world futures debate.[44] Others ignored the future of world civilization, or rationalized that any focus other than evangelization was a retreat into Marxist or humanist ideologies.[45] Historically, one can understand concerns to keep the focus on the biblical kingdom, and not its counterfeits. At the same time, succeeding generations of Evangelicals have affirmed that we should not narrow salvation to deal with the after-life, to the exclusion of this life. Therefore, rejecting a naïve apocalypticism, we need to weigh the driving forces of the early 21st century that could put an end to the growth paradigm of both business and missions.

Potential Game Changers

The September 11th terrorist attacks were not just a tragedy for the victims, they were also a *game changer* for how the U.S. carried out its domestic and foreign policy. Some game changers such as the crash of the Twin Towers come to us totally unexpected, like wild cards off a deck. Others can be imagined, but not predicted, as they play out over long cycles. This is the case with the South Asian tsunami, or the Katrina devastation of the Gulf coast. As a scientist, Rees[46] evaluates a swarm of post-2000 threats, including nuclear mega-terror, engineered viruses, super volcanic eruptions or nanotech laboratory errors.

Climate Change

Sometimes we might think that a game changer has emerged suddenly, but looking back we realize it was connected to long-term trends. Most scientists today consider climate change to fall into this category of a long-term trend that must be taken seriously.[47] these mega-trends may be considered distant or inconsequential at first. Later they are hotly debated only to be legitimized through research after passing an event horizon. The recent pledge by the National association of Evangelicals in March 2005 to combat global warming signaled an official political shift towards a previous problem that had barely registered on the Evangelical agenda.[42]

We need to ask: Besides global warming, what other game changers might be on the horizon that would stall, or totally shut down global economic growth? And could these drivers of change shift the focus of both Christian business and Evangelical missions? Two additional game changers, beyond terrorism and global warming, are developed below. They illustrate how even well-off nations are vulnerable.

Peak Oil

One inevitable game changer is the end of fossil fuels or renewable energy. This includes oil, natural gas and coal. Conventional wisdom foresees the end of oil not arriving until the mid or late 21st century. But that is not the moment we should worry about. Investors are privately fixated on the moment of Peak Oil, the moment that industry experts confirm that we passed the half-life of all known oil production. At that point, cheap and abundant oil, the fuel that has spurred our rocket ride of industry growth, will come to an end. Oil prices will skyrocket, transportation industries could falter, and derivative industries such as plastics could stall. No one knows exactly when that moment of Peak Oil will come, but original estimates placed Peak Oil at the year 2000.[49] This matches well with the fact that annual discoveries of new oil resources began to decline in the 1990s. in 1999, U.S. Vice President Dick Cheney said,

> By some estimates, there will be an average of two-percent annual growth in global oil demand over the years ahead, along with, conservatively, a three-percent natural decline in production from existing reserves. That means by 2010 we will need on the order of an additional 50 million barrels a day.[50]

To put a 50 million barrel a day shortfall in perspective, consider this. The entire world's oil wells as of 2005 pump only a total of 80 million barrels a day. And oil demand is expected to double by 2025, from growing countries such as China and India.

A recent documentary interpreted Peak Oil for North America using this title: 'The End of Suburbia." James Howard Kunstler hails this as the death of the America dream, "We're literally stuck up a cul-de-sac in a cement SUV without a fill-up."[51]

Crushing Debt

Another possible game changer or a long-term trend that could break the back of the growth paradigm is the debt and deficits of the West. Ayres, a U.K. economist, points to an ominous long-term debt crisis mounting in so-called 'rich nations,' such as the U.S., Japan and Europe. These public sector debts are mounting due to the growing cost of health services, pensions and various government services such as policing. Add to this burden the percentage of populations over 65 in developed countries, which at present is growing from 15 percent to near 23 percent in forty years. With more people reaching retirement age, a rising tax burden could fall on few and fewer people. Eventually, Ayres claims, "Government revenues will fall – as in Russia today – and the system will change or collapse."[52] Apart from borrowing money, Ayres claims the choice is either pare back government entitlements or raise tax revenues. All western economies have avoided the latter two choices and opted for the first, borrow money to avoid the evil day, with the hope that windfall economic growth might follow. While many of these realities won't play themselves out for decades, the ramifications of public debt will come home to roost well before 2040.

Since September 11th, the U.S. has mortgaged its future on homeland security. During this time the value of the Euro, compared to the dollar, has risen 23 percent. While President Bush began his second term debating the insolvency of Social Security in the 2040s, the world could go off the dollar standard well before 2015. This would be a major game changer, affecting U.S. trade, and raising domestic prices on everything we buy. The exchange rate of U.S. dollars to foreign currencies would further handicap world missions. In proverbial terms, our world is up to its neck in alligators, and it is too preoccupied with other things to drain the tank.

In discussing game changes like terrorism, global warming, peak oil or crushing debt, most people dismiss out of hand any suggestion that the world-system might falter to the point of collapse. The reality of systemic collapse, however, can occur either suddenly or gradually.[53] Despite Holly-wood's portrayal of the sudden, dramatic collapse, as in the movie, 'The Day After Tomorrow,' history is more nuanced. The collapse of complex societies can take decades. Rather than a free-fall, they often follow a grad-ual descent. Collapses spread over time are punctuated by local disasters, matched by intervals of seeming stability.[54] Unless variety and redundancy are built into human systems, the end inevitably comes. It always has.

Admitting Compassion Fatigue

Those who labor daily in the vineyard of missions already suffer from in-ternal church problems, whether evangelism fatigue or mobilization failure. To ask them to carry the additional burden of society's woes could be the straw that breaks the camel's back. Besides, most Evangelicals have been disappointed by End Time predictions, why would they want to jump on another doomsday bandwagon. Better to focus on what we can change, they reason, rather than what we cannot.

The combination of church and societal futures does not have to be a burden. Perhaps it can be an opportunity for integration. Can Business as Mission be a transforming force in this context? Beyond our smaller stories, what larger stories presently govern Business as Mission?

At present, there are three macro-stories explaining globalization. The official story on Wall Street is that capitalism has won; we've passed over the Rubicon and have reached "the end of history."[55] Any crises beyond the Cold War are just bumps in the road. A second variant on this story con-cedes that big business has won, that it is the wave of the future, but it leaves out the poor. That is why business needs missions. Kingdom profes-sionals only need to be recruited in enough sheer numbers to get the poor into business for themselves. The third variant on the story is that capitalism is the enemy. Business is knowingly shutting down all life-systems on this planet. Multi-national corporations and Wal-Marts must be resisted and destroyed at every turn. All that is left is civilization end-games. In this third variant, the only role for mission is liberation theology. But are these three our only options?[56] There is a fourth story that Business as Mission could develop as we shall see next.

Summary

To open up paths for Evangelical thinking, particularly in regards to Business as Mission, this section has explored whether our world is moving beyond its limits to systemic breakdown. We reviewed the origins of the world futures debate, considered the questions it has put to faith, examined driving forces that might become 'game changers' for society, and acknowledged our compassion fatigue. We concluded by looking at three macro stories we use to either support or resist globalization. Is there a better story than just the Good News of Big Business? I believe there is. Business as Mission can look to the Gospel and find there that fourth story.

Toward A Post-Crisis Society

Anytime mission leaders seek to mainstream new innovations, there is always the challenge of keeping the main thing, the main thing. Cut off from any larger story, Business as Mission could end up merely legitimizing hundreds of smaller stories of God's provision. Some might say these smaller stories of globalization are just human stories of artificially creating demand through advertising and then satisfying it through consumption.[57]

Jesus had nothing against smaller stories. He loved telling a good business story as parable. Sometimes it was about laborers getting a full day's pay, even though they were hired in late afternoon. Other times it was about a foolish rich man who socked away all his wealth, but didn't live to enjoy it. But in nearly every case, Jesus concluded his smaller stories with a punch line that connected it to the larger story of his society.[58] This was the deep wisdom of Jesus' kingdom call, a wisdom largely lost on his followers today.

To outline the contours of the fourth story, this section will argue two propositions. First, that Jesus' larger story, the kingdom of God, was an invitation to create a societal future beyond the deadlock of conventional and counter worldviews. Second, that Business as Mission will be effective to the degree that it recovers this earliest Gospel, and uses this post-crisis story to shape the story of 21st century society navigating toward a post-growth economy[59]

The Future According to Jesus

Since the discovery of the Dead Sea Scrolls in 1947, scholars have grown in their appreciation of first-century Jewish history. Rather than just look at Jesus through systematic theology, the "third quest" for the historical Jesus aims to understand Jesus in view of the human and cultural world of Second Temple Judaism, 587 B.C. — A.D. 70.[60]

Notice the end date of A.D. that historians put on late Judaism. This is the dividing line between a Temple-based Judaism and a later Rabbinic Judaism. This is forty years after the crucifixion of Jesus. What was the catastrophe that changed Judaism? It was the fall of both Jerusalem and the Herodian temple. Social historians of that era refer to this catastrophe as the Great Revolt, while military historians refer to it as the Great War of A.D. 66-73. Based on Josephus, the first-century Jewish historian, scholars now estimate that during this seven-year war the Roman Empire enslaved one million Jews and killed another million, including 200,000 by crucifixion.[61]

By A.D. 70, the entire world that Jesus knew and grew up in was "Gone with the Wind." Taking this Civil War analogy further, we might say that Jesus' ministry was clearly ante-Bellum, before the Great War. The apostolic age led by James, Peter and Paul was Bellum, during the war. And the emergence of Christianity distinct from Judaism was post-Bellum. Why are these historical markers important?

During the ante-Bellum period, according to some historians, Jesus was deeply aware of this looming crisis, this coming Great War.[62] This was the impending clash between Jewish zealots and collaborators with Rome that ended in a Jewish civil war.[63] A leading Evangelical theologian, N.T. Wright,[64] develops this story line. Jesus, through his own death, approached the coming catastrophe vicariously. Wright further claims that Jesus expected the course of events by A.D. 70 to vindicate his death and his movement in what I call the post-Bellum reconstruction period.

Working from this trajectory, I have previously argued (see Figure 1) that Jesus saw the future as a dynamic of three paths: conventional, counter and creative,[65] based on Wright's premise that Jesus' agenda for the end of Second Temple Judaism can be discerned from narrative, discourse, and world view analysis.

Conventional Future

For Jesus, this was the mainstream future. This lower line future had the push of the past. It had 1,500 years of Moses, or ancestral law, behind it. It had 250 years of Alexander the Great, or Greek culture, defining it. It had 100 years of Caesar, or Roman rule, enforcing it. This was the official world of Second Temple Judaism, ruled by the Herodians and Sadducees. In other words, the conventional future for Jesus was the present state of Roman occupation projected into the future.

Counter Future

The counter future opposed this official future. It was largely defined by the Pharisees, the loyal opposition to Jewish collaboration with the Roman Empire. The Essenes, and later the Zealots, also shaped this popular resistance to occupation. The counter future claimed that it, rather than Herod, repre-

Future of Business as Mission   263

sented Moses. This future rallied people behind 200 years of Jewish nation-alism, inaugurated by the Maccabeen revolution of B.C. 167.

Jesus weighed these two lower-line futures and found them wanting. Left to their own, Jesus saw these two futures on a collision course. Any Zealot-led counter future would lead to a head on collision with Rome and the collapse of the conventional future. This house of cards, with its mas-sive Herodian Temple would collapse with not one stone left upon another (Luke 19:44; 20:6).

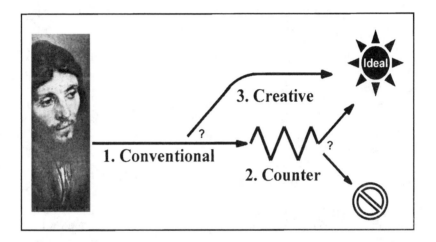

Figure 1. A.D. 27: Three Futures

Creative Future

In view of this impending first-century 'clash of civilizations,' Jesus began to develop a third way, a creative future. This prophetic vision grew out of an intuitive understanding of his fate related to Israel's greatest historical crisis.

As he saw it, death was the only way forward. Either Israel would liter-ally die by the sword in the carnage of the coming Great War, or they could vicariously die to the lower line futures through his death. Those who took no precaution would suffer the carnage of the inevitable Great War. Yet those who followed his way would be spared. They would be raised up in him, and form the nucleus of the New House of Israel.

In contrast with a mainstream or side stream future, this creative path was an upstream future. Jesus saw this high road transcending the lower lines. It would lead to the ideal, the kingdom of God. It would include the ancient covenant made to Israel, but raise it from a one-nation to an all-nation covenant.

If what Wright and McKnight say about Jesus related to his times is true, why does this sound so foreign? The problem is that our theological frameworks have all been focused on the ante-Bellum period, up through the Cross and Resurrection. Only in the last thirty years have historical Jesus scholars begun to realize that the pre-cross to post-cross transformation of the Jesus movement was integrally connected to the Bellum and post-Bellum period of Jewish history.

Therefore, as a transformational leader of this ante-Bellum period, Jesus offered a clear post-crisis path that his contemporaries could follow to both mitigate their society's breakdown and navigate beyond it. He symbolically recreated the threatened institutions of Judaism, namely the Temple, Sabbath, Law, and Land,[66] by revisioning them as internal spiritual realities that would survive the Great War. In other words, world evangelization for the first Christians was an advance invitation to inhabit the 'Age to Come' before the catastrophe.[67] If we accept that Jesus was focused on his world that was at risk, what should be our response to a 21st century now at risk? How could Business as Mission invite people to pre-inhabit a post-crisis world?

A Global Scenario Framework

The key to any forward thinking faith is its underlying framework. While divine foreknowledge of the future is of a different order than human foresight,[68] our generation, like Jesus,' now confronts the possibility of world-system breakdown.[69] How could we apply Jesus' futures framework to the 21st century? Hammond offers three scenarios for 2050, larger stories of tomorrow that call for decisive action today.[70]

Scenario 1: Market World

This 'business as usual' scenario corresponds to Jesus' conventional world. Despite caution about sustainability, this world looks to economic reform and technological innovation to fuel rapid economic growth. The hope is that prosperity will spread from core to peripheral countries. Yet if growth generates more social and environmental problems than the world-system can bear, it can lead to crisis. Two alternatives emerge in Hammond's thinking.

Scenario 2: Fortress World

This crisis-laded scenario corresponds to Jesus' counter world. If top-down growth fails, conflict dominates the international order. Resources are diverted to security and stability, while growing populations outside the walls live in misery and violence. The atrocities of September 11 brought us closer to Fortress world. This scenario can lead to economic breakdown if no other action is taken.

Scenario 3: Transformed World

Before the crisis reaches a breakpoint, Hammond sees a third path of voluntary transformation that can take us toward a post-growth, steady-state economy. This is a world changed by the power of culture, religion and volunteerism, which tempers runaway industrial growth and market-driven consumption. No doubt Hammond's third scenario could come about only through profound revival and social reform, of both business and missions.[71] Like Jesus' creative future, this story calls on people to take decisive action today to create a transformed tomorrow.

Toward the Great Work

How should we talk about the call to invite society into Jesus' creative future? This chapter has argued that Jesus called others to join him in doing the 'Great Work' in his generation, to follow him as he led Israel and the nations toward a post-crisis future. Jesus' Great Commission and Great Commandment supported the Work of God in that apostolic age, as much as David "had served the purpose of God in his own generation" (Acts 13:36). See Figure 2.

By implication, today, the Great Commission ought to be an invitation to follow Christ, to keep his Great Commandment to love others, such that the Great Work is fulfilled in our generation, to insure that humanity will survive itself. Therefore, the Great Commission and the Great Commandment are not isolated mandates; they are part of serving the purposes of God during a historical age.

Unfortunately, this call to the Great Work, this macro-story of new creation and faith for world transformation is not what governs modern Evangelicalism. The larger story of Evangelicalism is that the End of the World is upon us, not the more nuanced End of the Industrial Age.

The Great Commission animates modern evangelists, not the Great Work. Evangelicals are first individualists, not communitarians. God is thought to save the lost out of society into the church, not save society. Rarely is world evangelization even understood or measured in any larger context than personal or congregational piety. Standing at midpoint between church and society, Business as Mission already believes the world of work can be redeemed outside the church.

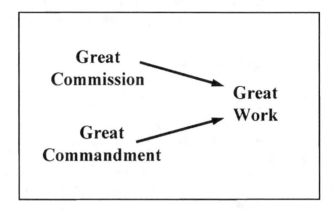

Figure 2. The Great Work Prioritizes Mission

Given its societal orientation, could Business as Mission become a catalyst to accomplish the Great Work? It took nearly a generation of reflection for Evangelicals to resolve that they would hold evangelism and social responsibility together in tension.[72] To ask the descendants of Berlin '66 and Lausanne '74 to reprioritize the Great Commission and the Great Commandment in view of the Great Work is a tall order.

It remains to be seen if Business as Mission can truly move beyond the Gospel of Market World to Transformed World. Evangelicals will need a greater sensitivity to theological, missiological and epistemological issues to reframe their governing metaphors into the 21st century context. Only then would we have what Bosch initially conceived,[73] a global missiology of transformation, to replace a "managerial missiology."[74]

Conclusion

A 'Business as Mission' strategy has recently emerged in world missions, embracing holistic ministry, sustainable development and kingdom values. Seeking to solve the structural obstruction to funding missionaries, Business as Mission aims to enlist both new and mid-career marketplace Christians to start 'kingdom business' among the least and the lost. It's thought leaders in Europe, Asia and North America are as comfortable appealing to economic theory, as they are to Evangelical missiology. Yet their focus has been on the micro-level of team and business formation, or the meso-level of community development, not the macro-level of the future of business over the next six decades.

Building on discussions of globalization and the world futures debate, this chapter sought to start a conversation of how Business as Mission could relate to macro-level forces shaping the future. It has argued six points:

1. That through parables, Jesus held the micro- and meso-life-worlds of business and religion open to critical inquiry from the macro-story of the apocalyptic crisis of the kingdom.

2. That terrorism is the first of many 21st century 'game changers,' possibly followed by climate change and genetic pandemics. These forces will cause the world-system of business to face its own historical crisis related to living beyond its limits, in creation abuse, energy overuse and debt formation.

3. That the growth and consumption paradigm's unintended consequences are unlikely to be solved by the economic theories that created it; and that we may move from Market world to Fortress world to Water world, unless we forge a new path through the woods to Transformed world.

4. That the Gospel of the kingdom was and is an invitation to join a vanguard that will follow Jesus' way out of the exile and crisis we've created for ourselves, and recreate our world from the inside out.

5. That the Great Commission was and is a call, based on the work of God in Jesus Christ, to join a new community that follows the Great Commandment. These two mandates must find their place in the higher order call to the Great Work, which insures humanity will survive its folly.

6. Therefore, Business as Mission will be effective to the degree it recovers this earliest Gospel, and uses this post-crisis story to shape the story of 21st century society navigating toward a post-growth economy.

Could Business as Mission be a catalyst that God might use to help a runaway world? It certainly could, if it keeps pursuing Jesus Christ, the Son of God, who in his earthly life shared our toil, hallowed our labor, and led us beyond the grave.

Discussion Starters

1. Evaluate Gary's premise: "Business as Mission will be effective to the degree that it recovers the earliest Gospel, and uses this post-crisis story to shape the story of 21st-century society navigating toward a post-growth economy."

2. How might game changers like terrorism, climate change, peak oil or crushing debt either stall or shut down globalization? How would this affect both Christian business and Evangelical missions?

3. What can we learn from Jesus' approach to the 1st century, that might help us navigate the 21st century?

4. What does Gary mean by "the Great Work" as a call to mission? Evaluate its usefulness as a macro-story for Business as Mission, in reference to the Great Commission and the Great Commandment.

Notes

1. S. B. Sharon & D. Nordstrom, *Transform the World: Biblical Vision and Purpose for Business* (Center for Entrepreneurship and Economic Development, 1999).

2. T. Yamamori & K. A. Eldred, *On Kingdom Business: Transforming Missions Through Entrepreneurial Strategies* (Wheaton, IL: Crossway, 2003).

3. YWAM Global Leadership Team. (YWAM and Business as Mission, August 2003). Retrieved March 15, 2004 from:
http://www.ywamconnect.com/ubasicpage.jsp?siteid=29315&pageid=328906

4. S. Rundle & T Steffen, *Great Commission Companies: The Emerging role of Business in Missions* (Downers Grove, IL: InterVarsity Press, 2003).

5. W. R. Hogg, *Ecumenical Foundations: A History of the International Missionary Council and its Nineteenth Century Background* (New York: Harper, 1952).

6. J. R. Mott, *Liberating the Lay Forces of Christianity* (New York: Macmillan, 1932); J. R. Mott, *The Larger Evangelism: The Sam P. Jones Lectures at Emory University* (Nashville: Abingdon-Cokesbury Press, 1944); H. Kraemer, *A Theology of the Laity* (Philadelphia: Westminster Press, 1958);

7. D. Green, *Mission Strategy for the 21st Century* (April 2002). Retrieved April 21, 2005, from Tentmaker Information Exchange, http://www.tentmakernet.com/pickenham/intro.htm; R. Siemens, The Vital Role of Tentmaking in Paul's Mission Strategy. *International Journal of Frontier Missions, 14*(3), 121-129; J. C. Wilson, *Today's Tentmakers: Self-support—An Alternative Model for Worldwide Witness* (Wheaton, IL: Tyndale, 1979).

8. P. Hammond, R. P. Stevens & T. Svanoe, *The Marketplace Annotated Bibliography: A Christian Guide to Books on Work, Business & Vocation* (Downers Grove, IL: InterVarsity Press, 2002).

9. M. Volf, *Work in the Spirit: Toward A Theology of Work* (New York: Oxford University Press, 1991); M. Novak, *Business as A Calling: Work and the Examined Life* (New York: Free Press, 1996); H. J. Alford & M. Naughton, *Managing as if Faith Mattered: Christian Social Principles in the Modern Organization* (Notre Dame, IN: Univ. of Notre Dame Press, 2001); W. McGee, J. Plumme & M. Tunehag, eds., *Business as Mission: Issue Group #30*. 2004 Forum for World Evangelization: Sept 29 - Oct 5. Pattaya, Thailand: Lausanne Committee for World Evangelization, 2004, (pre-publication copy, March 2005).

10. W. McGee, J. Plummer & M. Tunehag, M., eds., p.52.

11. S. P. Huntington, *The Clash of Civilizations and the Remaking of World Order* (New York: Simon & Schuster, 1996); T. Sine, *Mustard Seed vs. McWorld: Reinventing Life and Faith for the Future* (Grand Rapids, MI: Baker Books, 1999); P. Singer, *One World Ethics of Globalization. The Terry Lectures.* (New Haven: Yale University Press, 2002); J. H. Dunning, ed., *Making Globalization Good: The Moral Challenges of Global Capitalism* (Oxford: Oxford University Press, 2003).

12. B. Hughes, *World Futures A Critical Analysis of Alternatives* (Baltimore: Johns Hopkins University Press, 1985); B. Hughes, International Futures: Choices in the Face of Uncertainty, (3rd ed.) *Dilemmas in World Politics (*Boulder, CO: Westview Press, 1999).

13. M. A. Zigarelli, *Management by Proverbs: Applying Timeless Wisdom in the Workplace* (Chicago: Moody Press, 1999).

14. K. E. Bailey, (1976). *Poet and Peasant: A Literary-Cultural Approach to the Parables in Luke* (Grand Rapids, MI: Eerdmans, 1976).

15. B. Chilton, & J. Neusner, *The Brother of Jesus: James the Just and His Mission* (Louisville, KY: Westminster John Knox Press, 2001).

16. A. Schweitzer, (1968). *The Quest of the Historical Jesus: A Critical Study of its Progress from Reimarus to Wrede* (W. Montgomery, Trans.). (New York: Macmillan, 1968). (Original work published 1906).

17. H. Küng, *Christianity: Essence, History and Future* (J. Bowden, Trans.). (New York: Continuum, 1995).

18. O. Spengler, *The Decline of the West (2 vols.)* (C. F. Atkinson, Trans.). (New York: Alfred A. Knopf, 1922; D. J. Bosch, *Transforming Mission: Paradigm Shifts in Theology of Mission.* American Society of Missiology series. (Maryknoll, NY: Orbis Books, 1991).

19. N. T. Wright, *The Climax of the Covenant: Christ and the Law in Pauline Theology* (Minneapolis: Fortress Press, 1992a).

20. I. M. Wallerstein, *Utopistics: Or Historical Choices of the Twenty-first Century* (New York: New Press, 1998).

21. J. F. Engel & W. A. Dyrness, *Changing the Mind of Missions: Where Have We Gone Wrong?* (Downers Grove, IL: InterVarsity Press, 2000).

22. Rundle & Steffen, p. 7.

23. R. C. Chewning, J. W. Eby, and S. J. Roels, *Business Through the Eyes of Faith* (San Francisco: Harper & Row, 1990); M. Novak, *Toward a Theology of the Corporation* (Washington, DC: American Enterprise Institute, 1981); M. Novak, *Business as A Calling: Work and the Examined Life* (New York: Free Press, 1996); R. P. Stevens, *The Other Six Days: Vocation, Work, and Ministry in Biblical Perspective* (Grand Rapids, MI: W.B. Eerdmans, 1999).

24. W. W. Wagar, *The Next Three Futures: Paradigms of Things to Come* (New York: Praeger, 1991).

25. M. J. Rees, *Our Final Hour, A Scientist's Warning: How Terror, Error, and Environmental Disaster Threaten Humankind's Future in this Century on Earth and Beyond* (New York: Basic Books, 2003); G. Green, "The End of Suburbia: Oil Depletion and the Collapse of   the American Dream," retrieved March 17, 2005 from http://www.endofsuburbia.com.(2004).

26. H. Kahn, *On Thermonuclear War* (Princeton, N.J.: Princeton University Press, 1960).

27. R. Carson, *Silent Spring* (Boston, MA: Houghton Mifflin, 1962); J. L. Simon, *Hoodwinking the Nation: Fact and Fiction About Environment, Resources, and Population* (New Brunswick, NJ: Transaction, 1999).

28. P. R. Ehrlich, *The Population Bomb* (New York: Ballantine Books, 1968); J. L. Simon, *The State of Humanity* (Cambridge, MA: Blackwell, 1995).

29. A. Peccei, *The Chasm Ahead* (New York: Macmillan, 1969).

30. P. R. Odell, *Oil and World Power: A Geographical Interpretation* (New York: Taplinger, 1971).

31. D. H. Meadows, D. L. Meadows, J. Randers, & W. W. Behrens III, *The Limits to Growth: A Report for the Club of Rome's Project on the Predicament of Mankind* (New York: Universe Books, 1972).

32. H. Kahn, W. Brown, & L. Martel, (1976). *The Next 200 Years: A Scenario for America and the World* (New York: Morrow, 1976, p.1).

33. Kahn, Brown, Martel, p.10.

34. J. L. Simon & H. Kahn, *The Resourceful Earth: A Response to Global 2000* (New York, NY: Blackwell, 1984).

35. D. L. Cooperrider, & J. E. Dutton, *Organizational Dimensions of Global Change: No Limits to Cooperation* (Thousand Oaks, CA: Sage Publications, 1999, p.4).

36. The School of Leadership Studies at Regent University, Virginia Beach, VA, is launching in 2005 the first M.A. in   Strategic Foresight at a graduate Christian university. I will   teach their "LMSF616 World   Futures"   course.   See http://www.regent.edu/acad/sls/academics/msf/courses.htm

37. World Commission on Environment and Development, *Our Common Future* (New York: Oxford University Press, 1987).

38. L. H. Gunderson & C. S. Holling, *Panarchy: Understanding Transformations in Human and Natural Systems* (Washington, DC: Island Press, 2002).

39. R. A. Slaughter, *The Foresight Principle: Cultural Recovery in the 21st Century* (Westport, CT: Praeger, 1995).

40. T. M. Berry, *The Dream of he Earth* (San Francisco: Sierra club Books, 1988).

41. National Intelligence Council. Mapping the Global Future: Report of the National Intelligence Council's 2020 Project: Based on consultations with non-governmental experts around the world. (NIC 2004-13). Retrieved from http://www.cia.gov/nic/NIC_globaltrend2020.html. (December 2004).

42. D. C. Korten, *When Corporations Rule the World* (2nd ed.) (Bloomfield, CT: Kumarian Press, 1995); D. C. Korten, *The Post-Corporate: World Life After Capitalism* (West Hartford, CT: Kumarian Press, 1999).

43. J. W. Forrester, Churches at the Transition Between Growth and World Equilibrium in D. L. Meadows & D. H. Meadows, eds., *Toward Global Equilibrium: Collected Papers* (pp. 337-353). (Cambridge, MA: Wright-Allen Press, 1973, p. 255)?

44. D. E. Hoke, *Evangelicals Face the Future: Scenarios, Addresses, and Responses from the "Consultation on Future Evangelical Concerns" held in Atlanta, Georgia, December 14-17, 1977* (South Pasadena, CA: William Carey Library, 1978); J. Stott, ed., *Evangelism and Social Responsibility: An Evangelical Commitment.* International Consultation on the Relationship between Evangelism and Social Responsibility, *June 19-25, 1982* (Grand Rapids, MI: Lausanne Committee for World Evangelization and the World Evangelical Fellowship, 1982).

45. P. Beyerhaus, *God's Kingdom and the Utopian Error: Discerning the Biblical Kingdom of God from its Political Counterfeits* (Wheaton, IL: Crossways Books, 1992).

46. Rees, 2003.

47. H. Kendall *World Scientists' Warning to Humanity* (Rept.). Retrieved February 8, 2005, from Union of Concerned Scientists: http://www.ucsusa.org/ucs/about/page.cfm?pageID=1009, (1992); T. H. Tietenberg, *Environmental and Natural Resource Economics* (6th ed.) (Boston: Addison Wesley, 2003).

48. L. Goodstein, *Evangelical Leaders Swing Influence Behind Effort to Combat Global Warming (New York Times (New York)*, Late Edition - Final, Sect. A; Col. 1; National Desk, March 10, 2005, p. 16).

49. M. K. Hubbert, *Nuclear Energy and the Fossil Fuels* (Spring Meeting of the Southern District). Retrieved March 17, 2005, from the American Petroleum Institute: http://www.hubbertpeak.com, (March 7-8-9, 1956).

50. K. Aleklett, *Dick Cheney, Peak Oil and the Final Count Down*. Retrieved March 17, 2005, from The Association for the Study of Peak Oil: http://www.peakoil.net/Publications/Cheney_PeakOil_FCD.pdf, (August 12, 2004, p.1).

51. Kunstler cited in D. Green, *Mission Strategy for the 21st Century*. Retrieved April 21, 2005, from Tentmaker Information Exchange, http://www.tentmakernet.com/pickenham/intro.htm, (April 2002, para. 1).

52. R. Ayres, *Turning Point: The End of the Growth Paradigm* (London: Earthscan, 1998) p.43.

53. J. M. Diamond, *Guns, Germs, and Steel* (New York: Spark Pub, 2003).

54. J. A. Tainter, *The Collapse of Complex Societies* (New York: Cambridge University Press, 1988).

55. F. Fukuyama, *The End of History and the Last Man* (New York: Free Press, 1992).

56. R. Theobald, *We Do have Future Choices: Strategies for Fundamentally Changing the 21st Century* (Lismore, N.S.W.: Southern Cross University Press, 1999).

57. B. Goudzwaard, B. Fikkert, L. Reed, A. García de la Sierra, & J. W. Skillen, *Globalization and the Kingdom of God* (Grand Rapids, MI: Baker Books, 2001).

58. J. Jeremias, *The Parables of Jesus* (S. H. Hooke., Trans.). (New York: Scribner, 1955).

59. What is a post-growth economy? This is an economy that has made the transition from growth to value, at the company level (J. Mackey, & L. Valikangas, "The Myth of Unfounded Growth." *MIT Sloan Management Review*, 45(2), 89-92. (Winter 2004) and societal level (H, Henderson, *Paradigms in Progress: Life Beyond Economics* (Indianapolis, IN: Knowledge Systems, 1991).

60. N. T. Wright, *The New Testament and the People of God* (Vol. 1). Christian Origins and the Question of God. (Minneapolis: Fortress Press, 1992b).

61. N. Faulkner, *Apocalypse: The Great Jewish Revolt Against Rome, AD 66 - 73* (Charleston, SC: Tempus Publishing Ltd, 2002).

62. R. A. Horsley, & J. S. Hanson, *Bandits, Prophets & Messiahs: Popular Movements in the Time of Jesus* (Harrisburg, PA: Trinity Press, 1999); S. McKnight, *A New Vision for Israel: The Teachings of Jesus in National Context* (Grand Rapids, MI: Eerdmans, 1999).

63. M. Hengel, *The Zealots: Investigations Into the Jewish Freedom Movement in the Period from Herod I Until 70 A.D.* (Edinburgh: T. & T. Clark, 1989).

64. N. T. Wright 1992a; N. T. Wright, (1996). *Jesus and the Victory of God* (Vol. 2). (Christian Origins and the Question of God). (Minneapolis, MN: Fortress Press, 1996); N. T. Wright, *The Challenge of Jesus* (Downers Grove, IL: InterVarsity Press, 1999).

65. J. E. Gary, *The Future According to Jesus.* Retrieved August 19, 2004, from http://www.christianfutures.com/future_jesus.shtml. (May 24, 2004).

66. E. P. Sanders, (1985). *Jesus and Judaism* (Philadelphia: Fortress Press, 1985); N. T. Wright 1996.

67. In keeping with the Jewish two-age theory of history, Jesus likely used the concept of the 'age to come' to refer to both Israel's post-crisis age after AD 70 and the after-life (G. Vos, *The Pauline Eschatology* (Grand Rapids, MI: Eerdmans, 1952); G. B. Caird, *The Language and Imagery of the Bible* (London: Duckworth, 1980; D. C. Allison, *The End of the Ages has Come: An Early Interpretation of the Passion and Resurrection of Jesus* (Philadelphia: Fortress Press, 1985).

68. B. D. Jouvenel, (1967). *The Art of Conjecture* (N. Lary, Trans.). (New York: Basic Books, 1967).

69. H. Tibbs, Millennium Scenarios. *YES! A Journal of Positive Futures, Spring,* Retrieved August 19, 2004, from http://63.135.115.158/article.asp?ID=862. (1988).

70. A. L. Hammond, *Which World? Scenarios for the 21st Century* (Washington, DC: Island Press, 1998).

71. Micah Challenge. (2004). Mobilising Christians Against Poverty. Retrieved April 21, 2005 from:
http://www.micahnetwork.org/eng/index.php/home/micah_challenge

72. Stott, 1982.

73. Bosch, 1991.

74. Engel & Dryness, p.149; D. L. Miller & S. Guthrie, *Discipling Nations: The Power of Truth to Transform Cultures* (Seattle, WA: YWAM Publishing, 1998).

16

Where Both Business and Mission Fall Short

Ralph Winter

We hear some people these days talking as if "business as mission" will be able to replace—not merely augment—missions. Granted, business-as-mission is different from the kind of tentmaking effort in which people go overseas to "take a job." Business as mission goes overseas owning a business that hires people—and also provides some good service of some kind. Some say the usual tentmaker takes jobs, while "business as mission" makes jobs. However, it is likely not that simple.

Some people think that missionaries only do "church work." True, missionaries do believe that their central strategy must be to bring people under the Lordship of Jesus Christ and into accountable fellowships within the family and small groups as the best basis for business or mission. But missionaries also set up schools, clinics, agricultural ventures and businesses. They are the only workers for whom no human problem is outside their mandate. And one main reason they can potentially pursue any problem is precisely because they do not have to restrict themselves to things that will pay them back for their effort. They don't have to support themselves. They can do many things by that method that businesses cannot do. This is not to say that good businesses are not an essential backbone in every society.

However, every time a new thought gains wide interest there is the tendency to describe it as entirely new and distinct from earlier ideas (and far better). I have noticed this sort of thing since I myself have done a lot of thinking about the emergence of new ideas in mission. The bulletin of the U.S. Center for World Mission is actually named *Mission Frontiers,* and has been published continuously for more than 25 years. The International Society for Frontier Missiology has been around many years, and its associated journal, the *International Journal of Frontier Missions* just now completes its 21st year (see the web site, www.ijfm.org).

There are Many Mission Frontiers

More specifically, I have been writing and adding to a paper mentioning major frontiers (now twelve), which, as I see it, have gained our attention during just the relatively short history of our work at the U.S. Center for World Mission.

But even those twelve frontiers range widely over the general field of missions and, of course, all are frontiers in mission in particular. In that list I include frontiers that are no longer entirely frontiers, such as the massive switch in mission thinking from evangelizing individuals of whatever background to the evangelization of specific people groups. This particular frontier peaked in a sense at the World Consultation of Frontier Missions held in Edinburgh, Scotland in 1980.

Another frontier I mention in that list of twelve is far less well addressed as yet, and has been called "Radical Contextualization." It is closely associated with the even more radical concept of the Gospel expanding now around the world in ways not associated directly with identifiable forms of what we loosely call "Christianity." This more radical frontier I have called "Beyond Christianity." Others call it "Insider mission."

Other frontiers mentioned in that paper touch on the way we train leaders in mission lands, the rarely considered interface between Christianity and science, and the perplexing confusion about the works of Satan today. Those works include clever disease germs, which display unexplainable intelligence. Furthermore, they continue their deadly work unnoticed theologically and are thus almost totally un-assailed from any theological or Christian point of view. People in Calvin's day did not know about germs.

New Frontier: "Business as Mission"

My purpose here, however, is to turn specifically to what could be considered a thirteenth frontier of thinking: "Business as Mission." Although the idea is certainly not altogether new, the mounting and widening discussion of the idea is new—witness the new swirl of related books and conferences. No doubt "Business as Mission" can legitimately be called a "new" frontier in mission awareness and thinking.

This sphere interests me greatly, in part because some of my own experiences involve business activities. During grade school I delivered papers early in the morning. I was paid by the people I served for doing what they were willing to pay for. While in high school, I worked one summer in a heating company spray painting on the night shift. My pay came from the people I served since I was doing what they were willing to pay for. Another summer I worked for the Square-D Electric Company, first as a mechanical draftsman, then later in its quality-control department. Again the customers being served paid for that service. After the war I was hired to do a topographical survey of the Westmont College campus. I did what they wanted me to do. While in seminary I worked as a civil engineer for an engineering company. Those who paid for this activity were being directly served. However, during my 50 years in missions I have rarely been paid by the people whom I directly served—a distinctly different dynamic.

Nevertheless, as a missionary in Guatemala I initiated 17 small business endeavors that others ran. I enabled seminary students to earn their way while in school. More importantly, that then gave them a portable trade after graduation, allowing them to serve beyond the confines of their own acreage. Most earlier pastors were tied down to the soil, so these 17 "businesses" were all portable (as with the Apostle Paul). These registered businesses were also the first ever in which mountain Indians became the registered owners.

Two other missionaries (from other missions) and I started the Inter-American School, which is thriving to this day. I helped very slightly in the founding of an Evangelical university, which today has 30,000 students and has provided almost all the judges in Guatemala.

At Fuller, while on the faculty, I was urged to set up a publishing activity, which is called the William Carey Library. It has been operating for 35 years, sells $1 million worth of books a year, and is now wholly owned by the U. S. Center for World Mission. I also helped set up the self-sustaining American Society of Missiology, not to mention the U. S. Center for World Mission and the William Carey International University. Both of the latter involve many essentially business functions.

The history of missions is full of other examples. The Moravians went out to establish new villages with all of the trades necessary to a small town. They planted what is today the largest retail company (a kind of Sears Roebuck) in Surinam. William Danker's book *Profit for the Lord*, which may well be the classic text on business-as-mission, tells how Swiss missionaries planted a chain of hardware stores in Nigeria. Those stores not only fulfilled a much-needed function but also displayed an attitude toward customers that was a marvelous Christian testimony. And, of course, every church or school that is planted on the mission field, and is self-supporting, is like a business in the sense that it renders a service and is provided for by those whom it serves. If you add up all such "small businesses" on the mission field (churches and schools), it would run into millions of businesses. This is "Big Business" no matter how you look at it. In fact, I read yesterday that there are "over 500,000 pastors" in Nigeria alone, who are essentially—even if only part time—in that kind of "business."

Now let's look more closely at the general question.

What is Business?

Business is basically the activity of providing goods and services to others on the condition of repayment to cover the cost of those goods and services. This is not to say that businesses never do anything that does not at least indirectly assist their efforts in image building, public relations or something of that kind. However, businesses that use profits in ways that add nothing to the business would seem to be very rare. Businesses, in fact, that try to do that would, it seems, inevitably run into conflict with their customers' interests, employees' interests, or stockholders' interests. Why? They are jealous if any considerable proportion of the gross income is diverted by the owners to private interests of no concern to customers, employees or stockholders.

Note that business typically involves a concrete understanding between two parties (the customer and the company) and comprises what is essentially a two-way street: the company gives the customer something and the customer gives back something previously agreed-upon. Missionaries, by contrast, serve people from whom they do not necessarily expect to receive anything previously agreed-upon.

However, mission work is, in one sense, actually a business. Donors and supporters of missionaries are, in a sense, the customers paying for a service they wish to see rendered to a third group. The missionaries are providing the services for which the donors are "hiring" them. Note that the ultimate beneficiaries of the missionaries' labors, and of the donors' payments, are needy people in foreign lands who receive aid of some sort without paying for it. Incidentally, when those final recipients get something for nothing it is hard for them to believe what is happening and they often impute lesser motives to the missionaries.

But missions are not like businesses in one unfortunate way. I refer to the simple fact that most missionaries are not adequately managed and face temptations to slack off or, more likely, to overdo. Most humans cannot survive under those circumstances. Missionaries are for the most part highly dedicated people. That does not mean they will inevitably be good managers of themselves.

Sooner or later it may dawn on the ultimate recipients that someone wants to help them without asking payment, as in Jesus' case. Is there any better way to communicate God's love?

Of course, it is equally true that a goodhearted and hard-working businessman may be providing a very beneficial service out of genuine love, not just as a means to earn a living. That is equally true, but to the customer, not equally obvious—altruism is so often missing from the marketplace that suspicions will rule.

What Types of Business?

You can well imagine that some business-missionaries will go overseas and start a business that will be owned and operated by citizens of that country. Others will plant a business or a branch of an international business, owned by the business/missionary, which is an activity that truly serves the people, and is itself therefore a type of ministry. Others will not only plant a business but will expect to support other work from the profits.

Still others may not have the capital necessary or the required expertise to set up a business but can only take a job in the foreign land. Not everyone can buy 20 tons of castor oil at a time, as described in an excellent book I will mention below. The biggest problem I see with Christian college courses on business-as-mission is simply that the average student taking that course may be enamored of this new approach but not be wealthy enough to swing it, even in his own country, let alone amidst all the increased hazards and bureaucracy of foreign lands.

However, just getting a job in a foreign land is what is more often thought of when the phrase tentmaker is used. Ironically, Paul the Apostle was not that kind of tentmaker. He essentially owned his own business. He evidently on occasion supported both himself and others with him, although they, too, may have helped him in his leatherworking tasks. He also accepted gifts from churches so as to cut down on his need to do leatherworking, that is, he apparently valued his other ministries more highly than his leatherworking as a ministry to customers. Thus, he fits all of these patterns except the one we most often associate with tentmaking, namely becoming an employee in a foreign country. In other words, he made tents but was not what we call a tentmaker!

How is the Business Viewed by the Customer?

I firmly believe there is ample room for businesses owned by believers who work with Christian principles. Those principles, however, may not always be clear to everyone. I mentioned earlier a hardware chain founded by Swiss missionaries. It astonished people by the fact that if a customer bought something that had the wrong specifications or that did not work he could exchange it or get his money back. Thus, for a business to be effective mission, it needs to be perceived by onlookers as a service, not just a way for businesses to make money for the owners, although, frankly, most onlookers will still suspect the latter.

Here in America, of course, all businesses loudly proclaim their desire to serve the customer. We get used to that. We do not really believe it. Businesses in many overseas situations don't even claim to be working for the customer. Neither the customer nor the business owner views the money received as simply a means of continuing the service rendered, but as a contest to see who gets the best end of the deal.

It is also true that no matter how altruistic an owner is, what pulls down many a business or ministry is the very different attitudes of the employees. The owner may have high purposes. The employees may not.

Furthermore, once a business starts overly siphoning off "profits" (whether to increase the owner's wealth or to help fund some Christian work), the business may be unable to withstand competitors who plow almost all profits back into what they do, either to refine it or to lower their prices below what the Christian-owned business—with its extra drain on profits—can afford to offer.

One of our board members, Ted Yamamori, has edited an excellent book entitled *On Kingdom Business, Transforming Missions through Entrepreneurial Strategies*. In several chapters, the various authors wisely question businesses run by missionaries as a "front" or a disguise for mission work. And they should. To "see through" such disguises is not at all difficult for governments or private citizens. It is questionable whenever "business-as-mission" is simply a clever disguise.

We also read that "micro-enterprises" have their problems. If one woman in a village gets a micro-loan enabling her to utilize a sewing machine, she may produce more for less and be better off. At the same time she may simply put a number of other women out of work in that same village, which is not the most desirable witness.

Special Circumstances with Unreached Peoples

Most of the chapters in Yamamori's book do not distinguish between the attitudes people have where mission work has been long established, and where it is just beginning.

Consider this example. When I first went to Guatemala, as I neared the Mexico-Guatemala border it occurred to me that the border officials of a predominantly Catholic country might not welcome a Protestant missionary. It also occurred to me that, since my most advanced education was in the field of anthropology (not theology), I might get through the border with less hassle if I presented myself as an anthropologist.

I had to give up that idea the moment we got out our passports at the border and I noticed that mine (back in those days) plainly labeled me a "missionary." As it turned out, when we got out of the car at the border station, our two little daughters (ages two and three at that time) worked their magic, wandering around among the desks of the customs officials and charming everyone with their blond hair. We had no difficulty getting into Guatemala.

Two years later I experienced an "aha" moment when I found myself down at the capital renewing my passport at the U.S. Embassy. For a brief moment in that process the thought again flew through my mind: "Now I can change my designation from missionary to anthropologist." But instantly, I recoiled at the thought. After two years in Guatemala I had learned that, in even the tiny mountain villages, over the decades people had learned the difference between a missionary and an anthropologist. Anthropologists are often possessed of the idea that culture is completely relative, so it does not matter how you act. Mountain villages had seen anthropologists whisk in for a few weeks and go out again, leaving behind a reputation of totally immoral behavior. Missionaries, by contrast, came and stayed—for years on end—and were accorded the very highest respect. If I were in a mountain town and needed some cash, as a missionary I could write a simple IOU on a scrap of paper and borrow five dollars from anyone, believer or not. Moreover, the rural towns of Guatemala, even if solidly Catholic, almost always chose a Protestant believer to be the town treasurer.

Thus, in much of the world, even governments with formal restrictions on mission work know the difference between missionary personnel and others. Even where formal government barriers exist, if there has been any long-standing missionary work, there will likely be an ocean of good will among the people toward missionaries.

However, forget all that if you seek to work among a truly unreached people. In such cases you may wonder how you can ever gain the trust of the people. Whatever you do, business or missionary, will be subject to suspicion. Any good deed, no matter how generous, will be interpreted as somehow to your benefit. The constant question in the people's minds for perhaps years will be "What's he up to now?" Even in Guatemala, where I had instant respect due to the missionaries who came before me, the people were quite surprised when we returned for our second five-year term. Knowing a bit about the affluence of the society from which we came, they were more likely to wonder why we would want to come back than to discern good will when they saw it.

No Matter What

In any case, "no matter what," every society needs many basic functions and services. Whether as formal businesses or as an aspect of standard mission work, all societies need certain things. They need a banking system. They need fully reliable channels of raw materials and finished products. Curiously, they need guidance in the production of many things they have never seen and for which they can see no use. Think of all the seemingly bizarre novelties coming out of South China these days! And now rural people in the remotest spots around the world can use cell phones to find out what the prices are in a distant market.

Yet in all of this there is absolutely no substitute for honesty and reliability. Honesty is so rare that the absence of integrity alone is the chief drag in many societies. There will always be room for integrity and good will, for the one who keeps his word.

In the growth of our young republic, when westward expansion was rapid, connections between suppliers and buyers East and West were tenuous. Two Evangelical businessmen in New York, Arthur and Lewis Tappan, founded a company to compile a list of businessmen west of the Appalachians, mainly those encompassed by revival—people whom they could trust. Today that company is called Dunn and Bradstreet.

J. C. Penney, in the early days, attempted quite successfully to found a business-in-mission. A devout Christian, Penney sought to deliver at the lowest price what people truly needed. A mother in Nebraska could send her two children down to the J. C. Penney store with a note for the store-owner to outfit them for the fall school term. She did not have to worry that they would come home with things they did not need.

In the early days of IBM, any salesman would be fired who ever over-sold IBM machinery or services to any company beyond their real needs. As a result, companies no longer put out competitive bids because they could trust the advice and wisdom of the IBM salespeople. Indeed, at IBM even the highest executives had to get out and do sales work once a month in order to stay close to the customer. IBM became strong because it truly served.

Thus, there will always be a tension, real or suspected, between business services and business profit. In one sense, when a customer pays for a good or service, he turns those funds over to a business owner who might do well to consider those funds as held in trust. That money is needed to buy more goods of the kind just sold, to pay wages to the employees serving the customer, and to keep the owner in food and lodging. Those funds may also be needed to pay the equivalent of interest on any business loans that are making the enterprise possible. Certainly, customers' payments ought to be spent on improving the service rendered. The funds the customer gives ultimately and most legitimately should be used to benefit the customer, to maximize the service rendered. It ought not be a question merely of how much a business can "get" for something it is selling.

Now what if the product the customer is paying for is scarce or unique and a high price can readily be charged? The income beyond cost can effectively be spent in improving the product or streamlining the service. Can it legitimately be diverted to a Christian ministry unrelated to the customer's interests?

Polarization

Here at our Center in Pasadena we also have a university, the William Carey International University. The latter is committed to what we term "International Development." This phrase refers to any and all types of contributions in a society, religious or secular, that contribute to the building up and healthy development of that society. This is what beneficial businesses are doing. This is also what missions are doing. The latter more often renew hope and vision, while the former deal with more concrete things, the essential stuff of daily life. At times, the missions are more heavenly minded than they are of earthly good. Businesses are sometimes the opposite, of genuine earthly good but with no thought whatsoever for eternal values. This is an unfortunate polarization.

In our own midst, we sense this same polarization. We have three staff families in India. One has started a business that is owned and operated by Indians. In the second, the husband has held an academic position in a university there and still is able to witness among a wide range of intellectuals that church people in India could hardly touch. The third is working with church leaders on a curriculum with mission vision, even though the husband has an advanced degree in science.

All this can be confusing. Right on our campus we have a university devoted to development, mainly run by missionaries without business experience. Some people may find it hard to understand why it exists because they don't understand the full spectrum of missionary concern as exemplified by the broad perspective of William Carey after whom the university is named. Even in Yamamori's book to which I have referred to earlier I sense this same polarization.

When I was in Guatemala I lay awake many nights pondering the problem of a vast mountain Indian population that had cut down all the trees for fuel and heat, eaten every animal form of life for food, and tilled every square inch of flat (and even very steep) land. Among these dear people were thousands of faithful believing (and slowly starving) Christians.

For my own thinking process I wrote a paper entitled "The Future of the Rural Man." I showed it to a State Department official who happened to be visiting a missionary friend out in our area of the mountains. He showed it to the U.S. Embassy in Guatemala City and suddenly I got invited down to the capital to talk it over with about twenty of the U. S. Agency for International Development (USAID) workers assigned to Guatemala.

When I was done with my presentation, one man asked me what I would do if they allocated $10,000 to my work. I told them that what my people needed were raw materials light enough to be imported economically, the capital to buy those materials in advance and to pay for essential equipment, the know-how for which their patience and hand skills were appropriate, and reliable connections to outside markets. I realized that they could never get out of poverty selling to each other (why do the microenterprise people not see this?) Thus, I said, if given $10,000 I would use it to place ads in the Wall Street Journal seeking multinational businesses to discover the potential labor market these Indians constituted. I never saw any of their money.

I perceived at that time a subconscious polarization between five different spheres:

1. USAID type (money-giving) agencies. They have often worked as if they can solve any problem by throwing money at it.

2. The commercial world. Whatever people say, this is a substantial backbone to any country, but which is an activity not expected to be altruistic.

3. Political people at the State Department level. For these people governmental reform is the most vital matter.

4. Peace Corps people. They were assigned a variety of good things to do, such as starting chicken farms. In Guatemala they were instructed to have nothing to do with missionaries.

5. Finally, religious agencies. These entities, like my own Presbyterian mission, were involved in building schools and conference centers, doing Bible translation, church planting and literacy work, founding hospitals and medical clinics, and even fielding full-time agricultural specialists, etc.

An Example

The Peace Corps man, who lived in a village near where I worked, always avoided me. But once I found myself going up a steep narrow street and saw him coming down. I instantly knew that we would at least have to exchange a greeting. I had heard that his two-year term was soon to end and wondered what he had understood of what I was doing. When he approached I stuttered out a hello and asked him how the chicken farm was going. "Lousy," he complained. "I don't think it will continue when I leave." I knew he had put his heart into it, so I asked him what was the problem. He snarled, "You can't trust these Guatemalans. When I leave each month to go to the capital for our Peace Corps briefing, the egg production drops on exactly those two days. No, you can't trust these Guatemalans."

By this time I had been in Guatemala for almost ten years, so I took some offense. I found myself replying, "Look, you want to find an honest Guatemalan? That's the business I'm in. I can find you an honest man in any village of Guatemala." By then every village in Guatemala had at least one Evangelical congregation of humble people whose lives had been renewed because of a heavenly hope and a new earthly Master for whom deceit and dishonesty were detestable.

I could tell he didn't believe me. Maybe I exaggerated a little. Nevertheless, mission work still has an inherent advantage. The diversity, mutual antagonism, and lack of coordination of the earnest efforts of the agencies I have listed above is a real burden and hindrance to development and hope. This burden and barrier is really only nearly erased when you get into the world of the religious agencies, particularly the standard missions. By "standard missions" I don't mean the specialized religious relief and development agencies. They also cannot be effective in most cases unless the religious agencies get there first and generate honest people. All agencies need enough renewed people to create the minimal integrity required to manage the essential developing infrastructure of a country.

Not even in this country do we have enough renewed people of that kind. I am disappointed with the amazingly popular (and good) book—Rick Warren's Purpose Driven Life—which is entirely devoted to all the good things church members can do in helping their local churches in their after-hours time. I can't find one word about the quality or focus of the believer's work during their forty-hour week. Not even in this country are there very many visible Christian businesses, for that matter.

But there is one more consideration.

The Cultural Mandate?

A number of people these days refer to the Genesis "Cultural Mandate" which was given to Adam, note, before the Fall. This way they feel they can rightly and reasonably justify earnest Christian efforts in just about any good business which is essential to the growth and welfare of society. These people also speak of what is called "The Evangelistic Mandate," which arose of necessity after the Fall, and was intended to advance the Kingdom and thus redeem the fallen creation.

However, these are not complementary mandates. They are sequential. The cultural mandate came first, and assumed no emergency. The cultural mandate is like what happens in peacetime. But, when an emergency strikes (such as a tsunami or war), while cultural (read domestic) activities cannot totally cease, they will be radically modified. As I look back on my experience during the Second World War, I remember both civilians and servicemen being totally caught up in the war. I vividly recall that even domestic activity was extensively bent and refitted to support both the true essentials of society as well as the war effort.

The gasoline being burned up by war vehicles on land, armadas of ships and submarines at sea, and hundreds and even thousands of fuel-burning planes in the air, did not leave enough gasoline for anything but truly essential use at home. You could be fined $50 ($500 today) for going on a Sunday drive with the family if that trip did not include some war-related or crucial civilian-related purpose. Nylon stockings vanished in favor of parachute cords. Coffee totally disappeared as a non-essential.

What I am saying is that, while the vast array of activities that can be included in a business or Cultural Mandate are good and important—and while the Cultural Mandate has never been rescinded—after the Fall of Adam the Cultural Mandate is no longer enough. Nor can the Evangelistic Mandate be purely "heavenly-oriented." After the Fall it is no longer merely a matter of getting people prepared for heaven, it is a case of preparing them both for heaven and for all-out, knock-down, drag-out war against the powers of darkness and evil. A wartime emergency, both physical and spiritual, still exists and must be dealt with on a wartime basis or the glory of God will continue to suffer.

Two Mandates or One?

It is impelling that both mandates should be merged into a single "Military Mandate," which, in this life, in the story of a re-conquering Kingdom of God, may well be the only mandate we should be concerned about. A Military Mandate logically includes all the essential civilian functions. It must also include fighting evil and the works of the devil, which is essential to the "re-glorification" of God. This is in addition to true reconciliation of humans and the new life of Christ within them and whatever is necessary to accomplish that redemptive and recruiting function.

The Second World War definitely unified these two mandates. When the Allied forces were poised to invade the continent on D-Day, they were, of course, seeking to liberate the French, Belgians, Dutch, etc. from the oppression of Nazi occupation. But that could not be their only purpose. To do that they first had to track down and defeat Hitler and destroy his evil empire. In fact, defeating an evil empire was no doubt more prominent in their minds than liberating Paris.

Today in business or missions, then, we cannot simply go out to do good to people in need. People do not just happen to be poor. They are oppressed. Yes, by humans, but also by intelligent, evil powers behind both social and biological evils. Human societies are riddled with graft and corruption and greed and unscrupulous operators of all kinds, for whom human life is meaningless. Furthermore, all poor populations, more than anything else, are dragged down and decimated by intelligent evil attackers too small to see with the naked eye.

A Major Example

This latter dimension—disease—looms so large and is so unnoticed that it can be employed as a major example of the interplay of mission and business. I am familiar with this dimension because it forced its way into view for me during the last eight years due to cancer taking my first wife and now plaguing my own existence.

Missions and businesses are both good at helping out when people get sick. In fact, money from sick people is very nearly the single resource of the largest industrial complex in this country next to education, namely the medical/pharmaceutical complex. But virtually nowhere is any substantial and serious thought being given to a crucial activity for which sick people are not paying, that is, the eradication of the very pathogens that haunt most human societies on the face of the earth. Even in the U. S.A, these deadly but tiny terrorists kill millions per year, dragging down nine out of ten Americans to a premature death. Note that in this arena we can find no insights in Luther or Calvin's writings or theology because they did not know about germs.

But, in any case, where there is no income there is no business. The medical/pharmaceutical complex thus gravitates 1) to artificial substances that can be patented and sold at a very high price, and 2) to medicines for chronic diseases that ensure that customers will be long term. That is just "good business." This means that market remuneration will not as effectively support an effort to seek outright cures or especially to seek to eradicate the causal pathogens.

Only a donor-supported "mission" can deal with those things. That sort of "mission" can be found in the Carter Center, which is attempting to eradicate five major diseases, and also in the nearly unique Howard Hughes Medical Institute. The latter, unlike most universities and even the National Institutes of Health, is not dependent on funding and bonuses from the pharmaceutical industry.

Lamentably, most of the research done by universities and our government is extensively subsidized (and in effect controlled) by outside commercial interests. Thus, the flow of funds to all the world's efforts focused on eradicating pathogens amounts to pennies when compared to the energies expended when humans notice and must pay for help with their illnesses. It simply is not "good business" to create medicines for poor people.

So, therefore

If we wish truly to glorify God in all the earth, we need to realize that we cannot go on allowing people to believe that our God is not interested in defeating the Evil One. The Bible plainly states that "The Son of God appeared for this purpose, to destroy the works of the Devil" (1 Jn 3:8). Only that way can France and Belgium be truly liberated. Only that way can we do as Paul described in his mandate to Agrippa: "To open [peoples'] eyes and turn them from darkness to light, and from the power of Satan to God" (Acts 26:18).

Unfortunately, I do not see the mechanism of business being of any great help in this. And, while I see missions focusing on both earthly and heavenly blessings, I do not see any significant effort—mission or business—aimed specifically at the defeat of the works of Satan, beyond rescuing humans from their spiritual problems. Our Christian mission is certainly not significantly recruiting them for war and the casualties war expectably entails. In this case, I refer to everything from auto accidents, diseases, addictions, marital distress—you name it—things that we do not usually attribute to an intelligent enemy, but which drastically curtail effective ministry.

We seem to assume that the world is simply the absence of good rather than the presence of both good and dynamic, intelligent evil. Is there even one substantial Christian mission (or even secular or Christian business) in the world focused specifically on the eradication of pathogens that tyrannize the entire world to this day? They both are failing.

Realistically, in a given country either sluggish or lagging Gross Domestic Profit (GDP) is more likely the result of disease than any other single factor. We are almost blind to that fact, even when we ourselves get sick. During ten years in Vietnam we lost ten American soldiers per day. In Iraq we are losing ten a day. But in this country due to cancer and cardiovascular disease alone we are losing 300 times that many per day. In other words, our losses due to heart disease day by day equal the death rate of 300 Vietnam or Iraq wars. Meanwhile, note that while we poured billions of dollars into Vietnam and are pouring multiple billions into Iraq, not one percent of the money spent on patching up heart patients is focused on deciphering the now clear evidence that infection is the initial and major factor in heart disease.

Yet, what is our "business" under God? Is it good enough for us to traverse the globe with good but relatively superficial remedies? Or, does our mandate derive from the larger, Biblical purpose of defeating the intelligently designed works of the Devil and in that way restoring glory to God (which, incidentally, benefits man)?

Is This War?

Is it good enough simply to make people feel secure in this life and hopeful about eventually getting out of this sin-filled world and safely through the pearly gates? Right now that is the main thing the church is doing. In stark contrast are those tasks like restoring creation, restoring God's glory, rediscovering Satan's works, and deliberately destroying his deeds and deadly delusions. Are we trying to win a war simply by caring for the wounded? The fruits of evil—sickness, poverty, illiteracy, and inhumanity—draw our attention away from the roots of evil.

This is a "wartime" and Biblical perspective, yet that fact has apparently evaporated into the thin air of the current mood, which is defined by an artificial and inadequate (albeit pervasive) "peacetime" mandate. The Biblical mandate is "the Gospel of the Kingdom," — meaning the extension of that "Rule" against opposition. It is not merely a "Gospel of salvation." The Gospel of the Kingdom is the central matter of God's "will being done on earth as it is in heaven." It is a mandate that is distinctly larger than getting along in this life with the help of business, and getting to heaven with the help of missions. God's glory is at stake, and His glory is our main business.

Comments On Questions

This perspective heals forever the artificial breech between "evangelism" and "social action." Those are two different things when you have a basically humanistic outlook in which human eternal life is more important than restoring glory to God. Millions of thinking people today are not as impressed by promises of eternal salvation as they are by the faith-destroying evidences of outrageous evil in a world supposedly controlled by a loving and all-powerful God. It is no doubt theologically true that "This is the best of all possible worlds," but this world of rampant infanticide, global prostitution, endemic corruption, ever-present sickness and suffering is clearly and loudly not "The best of all ideal worlds."

Thus, the gap between "what is" and "what ought to be" is the definition of mission. If we do not extol and work toward God's "ought to be," as well as "what is," we falsify one of the two and undermine our evangelism.

Do we need to go back to our knees in prayer? Yes, but we cannot consider that enough. Prayer is as essential to our sense of direction as oxygen is to the lungs. But breathing is not a weapon of warfare, it is a condition of action. Telling God what we want Him to do or what we want Him to help us do is not the only or best use of prayer. We might as well twirl a prayer wheel. I don't feel that prayer is thus best described as a "a weapon of warfare." Prayer is an essential condition of, and a conditioning for, action on God's behalf. Prayer itself should tell us to do more than pray.

Spiritual warfare? If spiritual warfare does not mean we must fight the evil one on the physical, laboratory level it is not much more than beating the air.

Why is not caring for the sick enough? Here is a fictional account. A missionary in the mountains of Guatemala discovers that four out of five babies are dying before their first birthday. Dysentery, requiring re-hydration is indicated. He assists the people to install IVs in every hut. Now only three out of five die in their infancy. But, one of those survivors grows up and goes down to the capital city and returns some years later with a university degree. In his mountain village he seeks out the now-gray-haired missionary. "Why did you not know that the best solution would have been to clean up the water supply—isn't that where the dysentery is coming from?" "Sure, I knew that," the missionary replied, "but that is not the business I'm in. I need to demonstrate God's love and get these people to heaven. Putting IVs in every house was a much more visible testimony of God's love than ridding the water of pathogens the people don't know about or believe in." The young man shot back, "So for the last 20 years you have let two out of five babies die and in doing so you have proven to me that your God does not care about the heartache and suffering caused by the deadly pathogens in contaminated water? All he can do is get people into heaven?"

290 BUSINESS AS MISSION

1. Provide scriptural references for Winter's three mandates: Cultural, Evangelistic, and Military. How does the Great Commission justify a proactive effort to eradicate pathogens?

2. How might a business be viewed from the different standpoints of the consumer? a mission organization? a governmental agency?

3. What are some of the barriers to combating the "tiny terrorists" in the medical/pharmaceutical complex, and in mission organizations?

17

Suits or Sandals: Making Business as Mission Work

Sue Russell, Carla Hausman, Sarah Vinateri

Business as missions is gaining the attention of the Christian community as a way of reaching people for Jesus Christ. Many are replacing the traditional missionary tent-maker model of missions for one in which business-people form companies as a means of doing missions. While some authors have focused on helping business people realize their role in the Great Commission (Tsukahira 2003, Swarr and Nordstrom 1999, Chewney, Eby, Roels 1990), the most recent focus is on what is called kingdom entrepreneurship and Great Commission companies. These involve setting up businesses with the purpose of mission (Yananori and Eldred 2003, Rundle and Steffen 2003).

Several people discuss case studies that illustrate the success of these companies (Yamamori and Eldred 2003, Danker 1971). Others provide principles on how to start these companies (Rundle and Steffen 2003). However, very few address the types of people and skills necessary to succeed at these enterprises. Some note that Great Commission companies require a specific type of person, someone who is bivocational, a missionary and business person, and each of these requires a different skill set (Sudky 2003, Tsukahira 2003). As Rundle (2003) notes, "Kingdom entrepreneurship is a missionary strategy that combines the skills of a businessperson and missionary" (p.225). However, we argue that not only do missionaries and businesspeople have different skill sets, but they have been trained to work in fundamentally contrasting ways. This can lead to conflict when they work together in a Great Commission company.

In order to address the contrasting differences in work styles a comparison between business and mission environments is presented. The basis for this comparison is a study conducted in the School of Intercultural Studies (SICS) and the School of Business (SB) at Biola University using Lingenfelter's (1996) grid/group model. In order to discuss the potential conflicts between missionaries and businesspeople we will explore how people trained to work in mission and business environments perceive labor, productivity, exchange, leadership and values. We then explore how these differences could lead to conflicts between missionaries and businesspeople desiring to work together.

Lingenfelter's Grid/Group Model

For the purpose of this chapter, we will use the grid/group model to compare and contrast two different social environments, the business environment and the missions environment. Lingenfelter's grid/group provides questions to analyze these social environments in terms of grid and group, allowing the user to place his particular social environment within one of the four structures of sociocultural interaction. It is not meant to be an absolute measure of grid and group but rather to aid people in comparing and contrasting the interests, interaction, and expectations of people from distinct social environments. The grid/group model provides insights into potential areas of conflicts when people from two different social environments work together, in our case, those trained in business and those trained in missions.

Grid describes the degree that a social environment has role specialization and distinctions. In order to imagine the concept of grid, think of directories on computers. Some people like to make fine distinctions in their directories and have several subdirectories under each main directory. For those with several distinct subdirectories only certain material goes in each subdirectory. For instance, Sue's computer has a directory labeled "Teaching." This directory has subdirectories for Acts, linguistics, applied linguistics, and anthropology. It further divides the Acts subdirectory into directories labeled lectures, student outlines, exams, grades. Each of the directories determines the type of material placed in them. Personal letters are not placed in the "Teaching" directories, rather, they go in the directory designated personal letters.

Generally, high-grid social environments are associated with hierarchy. Just as on Sue's computer several subdirectories are organized under a directory, so roles in society often are organized in hierarchical fashion. For instance, the organizational structure of Biola University is high-grid with specialized roles organized in a hierarchy. For instance, there are Vice Presidents for academic affairs, facilities, finance, and advancement. Responsibilities within the university are divided accordingly under each of these Vice-Presidents. Under each of these Vice Presidents are Directors and/or Deans that head various departments and schools.

In a high-grid social environment, status may be either achieved or ascribed. At Biola, status is achieved through either education, successful work, or a combination of both. Ascribed statuses are those that are given at birth, for example the caste system in India. The greater number of role distinctions in the society, the more constrained individuals are in their relationships with one another. Often roles define the relationship people may have with one another. For instance, at Biola the Dean of the School of Intercultural Studies cannot hire a psychology professor. Nor would I feel free to walk into the office of the President of the university without an appointment, as I do with my fellow professors.

In contrast, a social environment that is low-grid has very few role distinctions and very few specializations. The most basic role distinctions may be those of young/old, men/women. In this kind of social environment, people are known for who they are and their character, rather than by the role distinctions. Relationships tend to be made on the basis of the person rather than role.

The concept of group is more intuitive. Group is the degree in which the participants in a particular social environment constrain the behavior of an individual. For instance, in a high-group social environment, the social group has specific criteria for membership and distinct boundaries of who is in the group and who is not. It has collective goals and activities, and the survival of the group takes precedence over the individual. The group endures beyond the individuals who belong to it, constraining their behavior and relationships.

In a low group, social environment relationships are instrumental in nature. People may form groups to complete activities, but they generally participate because it meets their personal agenda rather than that of the group. Individuals in a low-group social environment are free to manipulate resources for their personal gain. Competition rather than cooperation best characterizes low-group social environments.

The combining of grid/group into a matrix produces four distinct structures for sociocultural interaction: Individualistic, low grid/low group; Bureaucratic, high grid/low group; Corporate, high grid/high group; Collectivist, low grid/high group (Figure 1).

In order to compare and contrast the mission environment with the business environment four students, two from the school of business and two from the SICS interviewed professors and personnel from their respective schools using questions based on the grid group model. Although both schools are part of the same institution, the SB's environment was higher grid than that of the SICS. The SB reflected a corporate environment, where as the SICS reflected a collectivist environment (Figure 2). The difference in grid between the two schools reflected the areas of potential conflict that could arise with those trained in business and those trained in mission sought to work together.

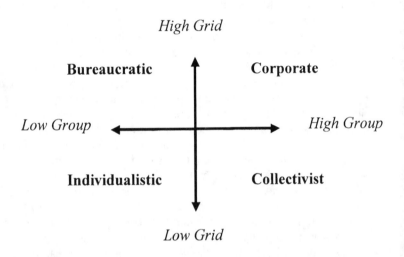

Figure 1. Four structures of sociocultural interaction
(Source: Lingenfelter 1996:45)

Environmental Scans to Identify Conflict

The following section examines how students operating in a collectivist (mission) environment differ from those operating in a corporate (business) environment in five different areas: property, labor, exchange, authority and conflict. It then provides examples of actual conflicts reflecting the difference that arose while the students from the SB and the SICS worked together on this project and the implications of these conflicts for business as missions.

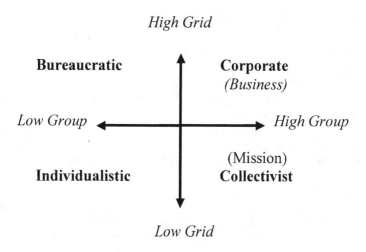

Figure 2. Business and Mission Social Environments

Conflict and Cooperation

There are several areas in which there are potential conflicts between those working from a mission environment and those working from a business environment. In this section we examine how the two different environments perceive and implement ideas about property, labor, exchange, authority and conflict. For each of these we first present the perceptions of the business environment, then the perceptions of the mission environment concluding with possible areas of misunderstanding leading to conflict.

Property

The conflict between the business environment and the mission environment is reflected in their differences in grid. In a high grid environment, such as business, property has symbolic value, in a lower grid environment property has transactional value. In the business environment, property becomes a symbol of status and self-esteem. In the SB, those who lacked offices felt unimportant in comparison to those who had offices. Having their own building is an important goal for the SB, not just for the space it provides, but also the symbolic value it would give to the program. In contrast to the business environment there was much more negotiation for obtaining property in the mission environment. In the SICS, although property is assigned based on seniority, people may gain property through negotiation and by demonstrating a need.

When business and mission people attempt to work together, differences in perception of property can cause conflict. For instance, the business people may want their own building for the symbolic presence that it will provide in the country. However, missionaries may desire to use an existing building that will serve the function of the corporation. Another area of conflict could be the use of buildings. People operating from a business environment tend to desire to preserve property. They want a building to be used for the purposes for which it was designed to preserve it for future use. A person operating from a mission environment would want to invest the property and use it to expand its ministries. Business people could easily perceive missionaries as careless, and missionaries could perceive business people as selfish.

The students experienced conflict over property when they were approached to co-author the paper with their professor and present it at a conference. The SICS student readily wanted to work on the paper together, the SB students did not have time to work on it. However, when the SB students heard that their business professor was presenting at the same conference, the paper gained more status and they desired to join in its publication. The change in the symbolic value of the paper made it a desirable project for the SB students. It would have been easy for the SICS students to think of the SB students as opportunistic, and the SB students to think that the SICS students as groupies for wanting to work with their professor.

Table 1. Different views on property between business and mission

Incident	Problem	Conflict	View of Other
Labor	Property	Interested in prestige Interested in working togethe	Opportunists Groupies
Building illus-tration	Property	Used for business Resource to loan out on weekend	Selfish Irresponsible

Labor

There are several areas in which people that have studied in a business environment and those that have studied in a mission environment could have different perceptions about labor. In the high grid business environment, labor is organized by role. The first priority for hiring professors in the SB is their ability to perform a certain role. Professors in the SB are motivated by performing their role well, i.e., being a good professor. In the SB, labor is evaluated by a standard that is set by the department. For instance, professors are expected to have at least eight hours of office hours. In most high gird business environments, productively is measured by the quality of the product that is produced in a certain timeframe. Students in the SB are expected to achieve a certain level of competence.

Within the mission environment labor is organized by task or goal. Mission personnel are able to choose the tasks that they want to accomplish and there are flexible standards that cater to the needs of individuals. Professors are able to negotiate off-campus time to work on projects that achieve individual interests, for instance writing a book, research. Labor is also scheduled by these goal considerations. In the SICS, although eight office hours are expected each week, there may be rescheduling or cancelled without prior notice if the professor is working on a project or has something "come up." Labor in the mission department is centered on personal interests rather than just being "good professors." In the mission environment productivity is gauged by effort or an achieved goal. In the SICS there is a greater emphasis on experiential learning, becoming and learning, than achieving a professional standard.

There are several areas that differ in perception as to how labor affects the ability for mission and business personnel to work together. While business people want to work by schedule and gauge productively in terms of products produced in a determined timeframe, mission people work according to goals and gauge productivity in terms of the effort put into achieving those goals. One of the conflicts Sue experienced on the field was that the consultant working from a business model expected the translators to be in their office eight hours per day. The translators, however, felt that once they accomplished the assigned number of verses they were required to translate for the day they were free to use their time to accomplish personal interests. The consultant demanded that the translators be in their office eight hours per day, and he would provide a bonus if they went over their quota of verses.

This is another area where the SB and SICS students had conflict. The students agreed to meet at a certain time to work on the project. The SICS students showed up late but with the understanding that they would stay until the task was completed. However, the SB students had only scheduled a certain timeframe that they could work on the project. When the SICS students showed up late, it provided less time to work on the project.

Another conflict that arose out of difference in perception of production was when the project should be turned in. Although there were deadlines for each project, there was also flexibility. The SICS students interpreted that flexibility as time to allow them to insure the quality of the data, even if it meant turning the project in late. The SB students viewed the deadlines as nonnegotiable and desired to turn the project in on time even if it all the data had not been collected.

Another area of conflict between mission personnel and business personnel was in the area of roles and job descriptions. In a business environment work is designated by role within the corporation. Elaborate job descriptions define the duties of a particular role. In a mission environment work is often defined by group interests. People may do jobs and assignments that are not part of their job description because they are interested in the project or because it benefits group good. For instance, in the mission that Sue worked with, each new person assigned to the branch was given "group work." This often was work that needed to be done for the benefit of the group but was outside the role for which a person was trained. For instance, Sue did bookkeeping, cared for the facilities and archived survey data as part of her group service. None of these jobs related to her job title as a translator. In the SICS there is room for people to take on work in the department that is for group interest. For example, Sue is interested in the MA anthropology program so she worked to get the program through the committee process even though that is not her role as an undergraduate professor.

The SICS students operated on an egalitarian model. They would help each other with their tasks with the goal of getting the project done. The SB students worked independently on their assigned portions of the project and did not confer with each other. They maintained the role that was assigned to them.

Mission personnel may have difficulty when work is assigned based on the interest of authority. For instance many SICS students would find it unusual for the Dean to order them to do something even though it is in his right to make decisions concerning work assignment. Most of the course load and assignments are negotiated. Mission personnel in a business environment would have to learn to be under authority of their boss and be willing to put aside personal interests for the corporate goals set by those above them.

When the students worked together, SICS students did not feel the need for a leader, but felt that each person would do their fair share and that work could be negotiated. Everyone would do everything. However, after the first couple of assignments, one of the SB students took leadership and began to assign roles to each of the students. The SICS students resented when the SB students made unilateral decisions without discussing those decisions with them.

In each of the above examples it would be easy for people operating from the expectations of the different environments to judge the other. For people operating on a schedule it would be easy to think of those who are task oriented as slackers because they are not in the office eight hours per day. In the same way it would be easy to judge those who had to meet a production schedule as inflexible and uncaring (Table 2).

Table 2. Different views on labor between business and mission

Incident	Problem	Conflict	View of Other
I'm late	Efficiency	Follow the time schedule	Unbending
		Complete the tasks	Slackers
Late paper	Productivity	Must meet production schedule	Inflexible
		Quality before schedule	Finicky
Leadership	Needed role	Delegate assignments	Rigid
		Ask for volunteers	Flakey
Conferring	Stuck to role	Stuck to role	Uncaring
		Share the work	Unprofessional

Exchange

Exchange is another area where differences in grid could lead to misunderstandings between business and mission trained personnel. In a business environment exchange is done between superiors and inferiors according to the corporate hierarchy. Asking someone in a higher position for a favor puts the asker in debt to the one who is able to provide the resources. Employees are expected to provide deference to those who are higher on the corporate ladder. In the SB the distinction between faculty and staff is clear; each have a very different function in the department. Each can make different kinds of requests of the dean. In the mission environment this distinction is blurred. For instance, in the SICS the staff member taking notes at a faculty meeting often provided input into the discussion and felt free to openly disagree with faculty.

Another difference in how exchange is perceived is in the process of asking. In a mission environment, asking is negotiating. For instance in the SICS any faculty member can bring a request to the dean. Although the institution provides the dean with control of resources, asking is not a superior/inferior exchange. For instance when a professor wanted to receive a course reduction, the negotiation was based on the hours department assignments required. Although there is a recognized hierarchy, people do not have to ask through the "official" chain of command. Any faculty member can negotiate with the dean. People are able to negotiate as equals, and the outcome is based on the needs of department and personal interests rather than on role.

There is potential conflict when mission trained people work in a business environment. Mission trained people would feel free to go around a "chain of command" and ask people they know for a favor or request rather those that are their direct supervisors. Those who are trained in a business environment could see this as going "over their heads" and be perceived as a lack of respect for their position. Another potential conflict could result if mission oriented people did not provide the appropriate deference to their bosses and tried to negotiate work or other responsibilities. In a business environment this would be perceived as inappropriate because it is the boss's role to give what is appropriate.

There are two ways that the difference in perception of exchange affected the students working together. In the SICS department there is less formality between students and professors. A student may approach a professor with a question or request without being indebted for the transaction. The SICS students felt free to approach the professor at any time with questions about the project. The SB students, however, would always ask the SICS students to ask the professor because of the relationship that they had with the professor. Similarly, the SICS students felt free to ask anyone, including the dean, to provide information for their project. However, the SB students generally would not approach a professor directly for information but went through a mediator, the secretary, to obtain information about the department. It would be easy for the SB students to think that the SICS students were too casual, and the SICS students to think that the SB students were too formal.

Table 3. Conflicts about exchanges

Incident	Problem	Conflict	View of Other
Social debt	What to do	Used go between	Timid
		Go directly to professor	Casual
Chain of command	Gather data	Ask secretary	Formal
		Ask anyone	Forward

Authority

Perhaps one of the greatest areas of difference between business and mission trained personnel is in the area of authority. In the business environment there are distinct chains of command. Power and authority are in a separate hierarchy where decisions are made centrally. Leaders delegate jobs and distribute the power to those under them as seen fit. The larger the corporation the more layers of managers there are between the central decision-making body and those that carry out the work. Leaders in a corporate structure are able to make decisions independently of those that work under them. For instance, the dean of the SB has ultimate decision-making power in his school. The faculty has freedom to operate within the sphere of power delegated to them, but the dean has recognized authority over them.

In the mission environment the power of the leader comes from the power allocated by members of the group. In a mission environment, those who exercise independent power tend to alienate their subordinates. In the SICS the dean seeks support of the department *before* implementing new programs or making major decisions. For instance, although the dean was in favor of creating an MA in anthropology, the whole department had to approve it before it could be implement. Because the SICS is part of Biola's institutional chain of command, the dean could exercise independent power, however, he chooses to negotiate and achieve consensus before implementing a decision

In working together in business as mission, there is great potential for misunderstandings between mission trained and business trained personnel. Business people in authority would expect to be able to make independent decisions and delegate power to those under them. Mission trained personnel would perceive that they were not being treated as an equal. In some cases they may seek to undermine the decision by joining with others. Missions personnel who do not respect the chain of command may be perceived by business personnel as "doing an end run."

One of the areas of conflict for the students was over authority. One of the SB students began to take over leadership of the group and assigning roles. The leader also took responsibility for the master copy of the assignment and made independent decisions about the formatting and final look of the project. The SICS students were annoyed because they were not involved in the decision making process. It would be easy for the SICS students to view the SB students as bossy, whereas the SB students could view the SICS students as lacking strong leadership.

Table 4. Differences in conflict

Incident	Problem	Conflict	View of Other
Write up	Conflict	Go to professor Rewrite it ourselves	Tattletale Chicken

Conflict

Conflict is another area of potential misunderstanding between the two groups. Most of the misunderstandings would arise from a difference in perception of authority and hierarchy. In a business environment, conflicts are normally resolved by going through the formal chain of command. People are able to power a decision and make people implement that decision by going through formal channels. Rather than working things out between each other, an individual may use the power and authority of the chain of command to make an individual do something they might not have otherwise done. In this type of structure the person in the chain of command has the authority to implement the decision against the will of those under him or her. In a formal business structure there is an institutional process for resolving conflicts, i.e., procedures and places for handling conflict. For instance, the matter may wait until a meeting or a formal appointment.

In a mission environment, conflicts tend to be resolved through informal networks. People will seek to negotiate the outcome directly with those involved in order to create a win-win situation. The situation will not wait for a formal meeting or appointment, but will be resolved when people can get together. The decision would not be based on institutional rules, but rather what is best for both parties.

The difference in decision making and conflict resolution has the potential to create tension in business as missions. For instance, if a Chair attempts to use a formal process to resolve conflicts in the SICS, this is seen as inappropriate and impersonal. By using only the formal institutional processes, those in authority will not be trusted and decisions will be resented. Using a chain of command would be seen as bypassing any attempt to negotiate an outcome that would benefit both parties. In contrast, someone from a business environment could perceive the attempt to negotiate an outcome outside the formal process as an attempt to usurp the power and authority of their position. It could also be perceived that bypassing the formal procedure would create an exception that they do not want formalized.

There was also a difference in how the students handled conflict. In one case one of the members of the group submitted work that did not fulfill the assignment. Students could have used a formal procedure, i.e., tell the professor, however they chose to avoid conflict by rewriting a portion of the assignment and handing it in. The SB students, however, did approach the professor formally about a conflict within the group. It would be easy for people operating from different environments to judge one another or even spiritualize the differences in how each approach the conflict.

Conclusions

Business as missions has the potential to reach people for Jesus Christ in areas of the world that have been traditionally closed to missions. However, those trained in missions and those trained for business have been trained for fundamentally different working environments. This can potentially lead to conflicts and misunderstandings as we attempt to merge these people into a single entity However, understanding the perceptions and expectations of people trained in these two different environments help avoid potential conflicts and misunderstandings enabling each to learn from the other.

Discussion Starters

1. Which of the four social environments best describes you or your institution?
2. What kind of conflicts have you had in the past when working together with someone?
3. Have you ever described someone's behavior in terms of the conflicts described in these quadrants?
4. How would you resolve some of the conflicts described in the chapter?

Notes

1. Peter Tsukahira, "The Integration of Business and Ministry," in *On Kingdom Business*, Yamamori, Tetsunao and Kenneth A. Eldred eds. (Wheaton, IL: Crossway Books, 2003), pp.117-126.

2. Sharon Benteh Swarr and Dwight Nordstrom, *Transform the World*. (Kona, HA: The University of the Nations, 1999).

3. Richard Chewney, John W. Eby, and Shirley J. Roels, *Business Through the Eyes of Faith* (San Francisco, CA: Harper & Row, Publishers, 1990).

4. Tetsunao Yamamori and Kenneth A. Eldred, *On Kingdom Business* (Wheaton, IL: Crossway Books, 2003).

5. Steve Rundle and Tom Steffen, *Great Commission Companies* (Downers Grove, IL: InterVarsity Press, 2003).

6. William J, Danker, *Profit for the Lord* (Grand Rapids, MI: William B. Eerdmans Publishing Company, 1971).

7. Thomas Sudky, "Strategic Considerations in Business as Mission," in *On Kingdom Business*, Tetsunao Yamamori and Kenneth A. Eldred, eds. (Wheaton, IL: Crossway Books, 2003), pp.153-168.

8. Steve Rundle, "Preparing the Next Generation of Kingdom," in *On Kingdom Business*, Tetsunao Yamamori and Kenneth A. Eldred eds. (Wheaton, IL: Crossway Books, 2003), pp.225-246.

9. Sherwood Lingenfelter, *Transforming Culture* (Grand Rapids, MI: Baker Books, 1996).

10. The basis of this discussion is from data collected by Kellen Logan, Amanda Moropoulos, Sarah Vinatieri and Carla Hausman for Anthropology 403, Economy, Society and Values, Biola University. Examples are used with permission of the authors.

18

Microenterprise Projects and Business Training

Joseph Kilpatrick

The church has an enormous task of taking the good news throughout the whole world as a testimony to all nations. It cannot afford poor management of people, waste of resources, sloppy business principles and practices, or loss of opportunities to reach and teach people in need (1 Co 14:33, 40). Every moral and ethnical tool, method, and technology backed with all the skill and training that is available must be used to accomplish this sovereignly given task. Church leaders, pastors, administrators, teachers and missionaries must realize that good business principles, when used properly, enhance ministry and increase its effectiveness in meeting the needs of people. These business and management principles can assist missions and church leadership as they guide their outreach and training programs to reach established goals and objectives.[1]

While traditional strategies for supporting missions projects and ministries have contributed to raising people out of spiritual darkness and economic poverty, yet too many of the world's population still live in poverty, financial bondage, and spiritual darkness. Meanwhile, too many national churches abroad languish without spiritual victory or financial resources to launch advances to evangelize and disciple their communities for Christ. Others wait or struggle along depending on donated money from the developed nations. Is it possible that these people truly posses the desires to improve their economic condition in life and to expand the ministries of their churches? Could such desires and needs be touchpoints for Christian businesspersons and business/missions students and educators to share the love and message of Jesus Christ as now being done with teaching English (TESOL), medical missions, and relief and development projects?

The purpose of this chapter is to propose that Christian colleges and universities, Christian mission agencies, Christian businesses, and others should partner to help fulfill the Great Commission through developing microenterprise projects and teaching business principles, methods and stewardship from a Christian worldview to national believers in less-developed and developing countries.

A Theology of Business

No doubt some critics of the integration of business and missions may rightfully argue that some businesses, especially large corporations, are corrupt, unethical, and have exploited others. Some are quick to apply Scriptures such as "Render unto Caesar…" (Mt 22:21); "You cannot serve God and mammon…" (Mt 6:24); and "The love of money is a root of all kinds of evil" (1 Ti 6:10) to justify complete separation of business and ministry, money and the church, dollars and salvations, and so forth. True, a positive view of business and economics is lacking by many people today. Obviously, some business executives and entrepreneurs have abused their positions and privileges through greed, selfishness, and opportunism for personal gain. Corruption and unethical practices date back to the early days of humans on earth. While these few make the headlines, the vast majority of business people are moral, ethical, and dedicated to providing services or products that help meet the needs and wants of their customers.

Scripture is not silent on money and business affairs. Howard Dayton, President of Crown Financial Ministries supports this point when he says,

> Jesus talked much about money. Sixteen of the 38 parables were concerned with how to handle money and possessions. Indeed, Jesus Christ said more about money than about almost any other subject. The Bible offers 500 verses on prayer, fewer than 500 verses on faith, but more than 2,350 verses on money, management, and material possessions![2]

Obviously, God considers the management of business affairs and money to be important spiritual functions. However, it is understood that business practices are not a substitute for spiritual qualities required for church and missions leadership. Wise men learned long ago that God does not bless what is used as a substitute for doing his will and work in His way. On the other hand, He will bless creative supplements when they are used with a pure heart and right motives. Many things in life are neither right nor wrong in themselves. The intent of the heart determines their moral value.[3]

In his excellent chapter "Christ and Business: A Typology for Christian Business Ethics," Louke van Wensveen Siker expands on H. Richard Niebuhr's classic study, *Christ and Culture*. Christians over the centuries have dealt with what Niebuhr calls "the enduring problem of the relation between the authorities of Christ and culture." Working from Niebuhr's five typologies of Christ and culture, Siker purports five views of Christ and business. These five categories will provide a uniquely theological way of identifying various approaches in Christian business functions and ethics. Niebuhr's reinterpreted five types are summarized below:

1. *"Christ Against Business"*

   Here extreme views of radical Christians who stress the presence of evil in culture and business so that they can see Christ only in opposition to it. Thus, business is inherently evil and should be shunned by followers of Christ.

2. *"The Christ of Business"*

   At the opposite end of the spectrum one finds the position of cultural Christians, who see no basic contradiction between the demands of culture and the demands of Christ. They assume that God's aims and the aims of business are essentially in harmony. Despite some corruption and unethical behavior in business, they see themselves as agents of Christ to make disciples, make money, and make changes to improve culture.

3. *"Christ Above Business"*

   Another less optimistic, yet widespread Christian approach to business is the assumption that business life needs to be elevated by means of authoritative, external guidelines set forth by Christ.

4. *"Christ and Business in Paradox"*

   With this viewpoint, dualist Christians are highly sensitive to the fallenness of culture, yet at the same time they feel called to participate in it as it has been preserved by God for a purpose.

5.   *"Christ, the Transformer of Business"*

> The conversionist Christian sees the serious evil in the
> business world, but seeks the conversion of the human
> spirit and subsequent social action while they work from
> within business hoping for actual, historical transformation
> of business life.[4]

Personally, I support the "Christ of Business" approach. Business people should use their God-given talent, time, testimony and resources to help obey the Great Commandment and fulfill the Great Commission. No longer should Christian business people and business students sit on the sidelines in the worldwide battle for people's minds and souls, lamenting that "we are just business people—we are not missionaries." To the contrary, they should capture every opportunity to win, teach, build, and send others whom God has placed in their sphere of influence, both at home and abroad. No, there is no difference in the sacred and the secular in Kingdom work. Every bush is a burning bush and all ground is holy ground. God-called and God-gifted business people with influence, networks, financial resources, and years of valuable experience in business are waiting for missions agencies to utilize them in the harvest fields.

Cases for Business-Missions Ministries

Great Commission Companies

In recent decades global missions have been influenced by such movements as medical missions, relief and development efforts, and tentmaking professionals working in restricted access countries. Little, however, has yet been said about the new missions opportunities created by today's globalized economy. Nor has much been documented about the role that corporations and businesses can have in the missionary enterprise. Economist Steve Rundle and missiologist Tom Steffen offer a new paradigm for the convergence of business and missions—the Great Commission Company (GCC). These companies intentionally create businesses in strategic locations, pursuing profits while remaining unabashedly Christian in their purpose. By establishing authentic businesses that employ local workers among the least-reached peoples of the world, they contribute to the economic health of the immediate community and also provide avenues for both physical and spiritual ministry.

Rundle and Steffen studied five examples of GCCs giving keen analysis of their principles and practices. Although changing the names and locations of some of these companies for security purposes, detailed facts of their profit-making operations showed their impact on their customers and employees. One of these company's mission statement was "to make money, to build people, and to create eternal value." Another's sought "to provide one-time and ongoing spiritual, emotional and physical support to missionaries and church organization of like faith worldwide, and to provide opportunities for missionaries and laypeople of like faith to work in various trades related to acquiring, renovating and providing low-to-moderate-income housing as a community ministry." [5]

The authors believe that in an era where multinational corporations have global influence and impact, the GCC opens up new possibilities for missions-minded entrepreneurs and business people who want to change the world to the glory of God.

Microenterprise Projects

Latin America The Latin American Mission has pioneered numerous microenterprises and job creation projects in Latin America. LAM's board chairman, Willard W. (Butch) Dickerson explains,

> While recognizing that there are a multitude of legitimate forms and shapes of missionary service, for me personally, given both my professional work experience and my understanding of current world conditions, being involved overseas in microeconomic/job creation projects like the ones in Costa Rica and Colombia has opened many new avenues for effective and fruitful missionary endeavor. Many of my former and present business-oriented Christian colleagues and contacts are also finding meaningful missionary service by becoming involved in a variety of business enterprise projects. As doors for former methods of missionary activity close, many new doors of opportunity for involvement through economic and business participation are opening. As much sense as it makes for Christians with business experience and skills to be involved in economic activity overseas, we must not lose sight of the fact that such commercial activity is not an end in itself. It is rather a means of assisting individual Christians and churches overseas to build the body of Christ and to fulfill their roles more effectively as ambassadors and missionaries.[6]

With financial assistance of Latin America Mission's Economic Development Fund and through missionaries with special gifting in areas of business and management, many people are being reached for Christ and discipled. In countries where unemployment is considered problem number one, evangelistic outreach requires a social context. What better way to present the gospel than creating businesses that give people work? The Apostle Paul instructs us to "work with your own hands, so that your daily life may win the respect of outsiders, and so that you will not be dependent on anybody (1 Th 41-12).[7]

LAM's microeconomic activities abroad include the following projects:

1. The programs of Union Biblica in Lima, Peru include a ministry to street children through an indoor soccer court, camps, high school ministries, a program for the deaf, medical services, and the production of devotional books used throughout Latin America. Over 75% of their budget (U.S. $500,000) is generated by 14-income-generating projects such as a public parking lot, the rental of commercial office space, the rental of a large auditorium, a fleet of 20 taxis, a fleet of 65 motorcycle taxis, a river taxi boat, a carpentry shop, silkscreen project for t-shirts, a shoe factory, a water purification plant for bottled water, and handicraft exports.

2. The Loreto Hydro Dam project, built by HCJB World Radio, the Ecuadorian and missionary staff, volunteers and staff from various places around the world, provides electrical power to HCJB Radio with excess power being sold to the area governments for thousands of dollars per year beyond HCJB's current needs.

3. Through LAM's Office of Promotion and Social Development, some larger churches in Latin America have started a revolving loan program to provide capital or micro-loans to develop small businesses. With the loan comes administrative and accounting training. A committee drawn from the church and professional community approve applications and monitor training, financial statements, loan interest and principal payments. With the help of this credit and training, church members have started businesses as jewelry manufacturing and sales, fish farms and retail stores, printing operations, etc. Training programs consist of classes about business development, accounting, marketing and employee management. Some of these businesses have grown to where they are now able to employ other members of the church, thereby multiplying the job creation effects of the micro-loan program.[8]

India Setting up a business run by women who live in the slums is improving the lives of many people in Bangalore, India, one of the fastest-growing cities in the world. A small center established to teach women to use sewing machines and to make something people will want to buy—in this case, tea towels—has given people a new sense of self-worth. The women's interaction proved as important as their acquisition of new skills.[9]

Bulgaria Ken Vander Weele of Opportunity International reports from Bulgaria that unemployment is as high as 80 percent in some parts of the country. His program provides capital at reasonable rates of interest to trustworthy people who will try to establish new enterprises, and it gives them the technical training and consultative advice that will enable them to succeed. For example, he helped establish a dry cleaning store with tailoring services that now has become a business that designs and manufactures clothing. He has also helped to open a restaurant just outside the only remaining state-run factory.[10]

Ghana The African Christian Microenterprise Development (ACMED) held a conference in Nairobi, Kenya in February 2003. The theme was "Building God's Kingdom through microenterprise development. The purpose of the conference was to define the vision for ACMED organizations in terms of how they can effectively contribute towards wealth creation and poverty reduction in Africa through the promotion of microenterprise development and Kingdom building. One such project is the Sinapi Aba Trust in Northern Ghana. It has been putting Christian microenterprise development into practice. They have seen the local church benefiting both financially and in terms of commitment and fellowship, which in turn brings more people into the Kingdom.[11]

Other Microenterprise Projects The list of microenterprise and cottage industries is limited only by the creativity, knowledge, skills, and financial resources of nationals who are willing to improve the impoverished conditions of their families, churches, mission programs, schools, etc. Other examples include the following: sewing machines and selling clothing, exports of native arts and crafts, fish farms, cow / goat / water buffalo farms, vegetable and poultry farms, imports and exports, Internet sales, bakeries, beauty salons, woodworking, metal works, upholstery shops, bean bag manufacturing, secretarial and photocopy services, colporteur book sales, and other small businesses.

Teaching Opportunities

The National Foundation for Teaching Entrepreneurship uses a suitable means of planting seeds that encourage entrepreneurship that may come to fruition in later life. It is an action learning approach, which is an excellent vehicle for teaching business studies, especially to under-privileged groups. Just as students are clambering to learn English, young graduate students and business people are just as anxious to learn business, information technology, the Internet, the free market system and international trade. When I was in a certain Eastern European country a few years ago, I met with a group of men on a Bible translation project. They were not kidding when they asked me to go home and get my family and return to teach business in their local university. They explained how the Russian teachers were being called home and all that the business students knew was the Communist's centrally planned economic system and authoritarian managerial style. "We want to learn how business is done in the West. We can get you and your colleagues a professorship position in our universities," they pleaded.

Of course, similar positions are available in China and other less-developed countries. On my trips into China, the people I worked with did not know me as a missionary, but a "foreign educational expert," a position they highly respected. However, numerous other opportunities exist to teach overseas with the potential of reaching even more locals if we sponsor and conduct our own business training seminars teaching them from a Christian worldview. Also, we can teach at Bible studies and chapel services in various business establishments. Crown Financial Ministries (discussed below) has one such model deserving serious consideration.

Tentmakers

Global Opportunities Ruth E. Siemens, tentmaker and founder of Global Opportunities, answers on her Web site the question *What are Tentmakers?* She explains that "Tentmakers are Christian professionals who work in secular jobs in order to reach another people with the gospel by integrating work and witness." She further elaborates,

> *Tentmakers* are missions-motivated Christians who support themselves in secular work as they do cross-cultural evangelism on the job and in their free time. They may be business entrepreneurs, salaried professionals, paid employees, expense-paid voluntary workers, Christian professionals, or funded research internships, or exchange and/or study abroad students. They can serve at little or no cost to the church.[12]

International Fellowship of Alliance Professionals One outstanding tentmaking program is the International Fellowship of Alliance Professionals (IFAP) sponsored by the Christian and Missionary Alliance. IFAP's purpose statement is to utilize to the fullest extent Christian and Missionary lay professionals for worldwide evangelism and discipleship with emphasis on restricted-access areas and areas deemed strategic to Alliance ministries. The reasons given for IFAP explain that well over half of the unreached peoples in our world live under governments that refuse entry to missionaries with regular visas. IFAP was established to mobilize lay professionals in C&MA churches to reach the unreached nations and peoples through living and working among them. IFAP does not appoint or send Alliance professionals, but rather serves as resource to and liaison for such individuals. Some IFAP members are employed by North American companies, organizations, or government agencies operating overseas. Others work for agencies, schools, or companies belonging to the host country.[13]

Short-Term International Teams

In 2002 Crown Financial Ministries, Gainesville, Georgia, launched a new international program titled Freedom Xperience. This new endeavor is part of Crown's major objective to teach by September 2015 over 300 million people–30 million Americans and 270 million people internationally–to handle money from God's perspective. Crown's work of teaching God's financial principles is centered in the Great Commission of Mt. 28:19-20: "...teaching them everything I have commanded you."

Freedom Xperience can be described as a plan to partner the work and the excitement for what God is doing in our nation and people's lives and what God desires to do in the lives of the people of the world. This is accomplished through the four main purposes of Crown's short-term international teams that consist of: Spontaneous Growth Teams, Catalytic Event Support Teams, Follow-up Teams and Targeted Teaching Teams. Team members undergo intensive training on how to teach stewardship to pastors and business leaders abroad.

At the pastors' event, each pastor will be thoroughly trained and then asked to sign a covenant to train 100 people over the next 10 years. The pastors will also be given all the materials necessary to train their congregations. The business leaders will also be thoroughly equipped and resourced as they commit to train staff and customers in their businesses or practices. As the local church promotes a healthy view of money and possessions, the church becomes the storehouse God intended. Those in poverty, both physically or spiritually, will be blessed. The church will be able to give bread and water as "daily bread" and "living water." Men and women become free from slavery of materialism in order to serve Christ, not money. Moreover, people come to know Christ. It is estimated that over 19,000 came to know the Lord in a personal relationship through Crown's ministries this past year. Freedom Xperience offers 1-3 week trips to the numerous countries annually.[14]

Business Student on Short-Term Missions Trip In 2003 one of Toccoa Falls College's junior business majors, Aaron Cox, participated in a FX03 short-term trip to India. Afterwards Aaron writes,

> My first contact with Crown was in a college class at TFC called Business for Nonprofit Organizations, which used Larry Burkett's *Business by the Book* as a textbook. The class also required us to interact with Crown's Web site to learn more about this ministry and read their articles. Soon after that semester a representative from Crown came to our college to speak about a new Crown program called Freedom Xperience or FX03 for short. This was the trip I had been waiting to find for I didn't

want to go on a typical student mission trip to do construction, VBS or youth camps.

I went to India that summer with FX03 for a month to hold four conferences teaching God's financial principles. The trip changed my life. I came back a different person. Through the entire experience with Crown I would learn that I shared many of Crown's goals. Not only did I find the idea on the trip, but also I found my life's calling during the trip. I now desire to help fund the Great Commission by ministering to people through their finances by teaching what the Bible says concerning how we should handle our money. I would also like to do this internationally. So when I decided I wanted to do an internship this summer, I didn't have to look far. I knew that I would enjoy working this summer as a volunteer at the Crown Ministries' headquarters in Gainesville, GA.[15]

Field Treasurers and Business Managers

As a young child, I knew that God had His hand on me for a special work. When I was a senior in college, majoring in accounting and working my way through college as a payroll/cost accountant at a local manufacturing firm, I attended an area-wide missions rally one Sunday afternoon. Following the service, the guest speaker, a missions executive from my denomination's foreign missions division, held a question-and-answer session. I remember raising my hand and asking, "Does our mission board need someone like me with an accounting degree and gifts for business?" I was disappointed with his answer: "Almost 98 percent of our career missionaries are ordained ministers having gone to Bible school or seminary and pastoring a church for at least two years. We do make exceptions for a few nurses, doctors, printers, and technicians, but have no business people on the field."

A year later I attended a Saturday night service sponsored by Wycliffe Bible Translators. Afterwards, I approached the guest speaker and asked the same question I had asked my denomination's representative. My heart leaped with excitement when I heard him describe their need for business managers, purchasing agents, administrators, accountants and auditors, etc. That conversation flamed a latent calling and engraved on my mind that there was a place of ministry for business-trained people on the foreign mission field.

A few years later I was hired as the Finance Secretary (comptroller) for my denomination's foreign mission's division, a position I held for eight years. During that time I traveled to various countries setting up financial books, auditing publishing operations, helping missionaries straighten out their financial books and reports, and speaking in Bible schools on stewardship and handling money God's way. Seeing the need for helping the missionaries, I put together some job descriptions and set out to various cities in the U.S. to interview candidates for positions of field treasurer and institutional business managers overseas. What a joy to see these young business couples going off to the mission field. But what about my 10-year old dream? Then it seemed that the Lord said, "It is time for you to take a step of faith and go yourself." A unique need in Europe had surfaced in the board meeting for a business manager who could direct the publishing of a distant education college and finances of a Bible college nearby. I jumped on the opportunity. The next morning I anxiously entered my Executive Director's office with my completed application for the European position in one hand and my resignation as controller in the other. Faith and courage sprang up and I boldly presented my documents and intentions. God confirmed that this was the right decision and my wife and I enjoyed three years of ministry in Europe. Amazingly, that Executive Director invited me to become his Administrator to replace the retiring missions executive who had visited my church nearly 15 years prior.

I served as Administrator for five years before returning to the field, this time to Hong Kong and then to Miami, to continue with my calling to church ministries, missions administration, publishing and education. Later, the Lord arranged for me to assist Dr. Bill and Vonette Bright, co-founders of Campus Crusade for Christ International, for nearly five years as their General Editor and Publisher for New Life Publications. In all, the Lord gave my wife and me 28 wonderful years in denominational and parachurch missions work before directing us to Toccoa Falls College where we train and equip future business leaders to serve in professional positions in ministry and business organizations.

Business-Missions Ministry Opportunities

Collegiate Curriculum

Christian Colleges and Universities should design new interdisciplinary curriculum programs to serve more effectively their students and partnering ministries. For years I have carried a burden for seeing our business administration majors become more engaged in missions and international ministries during college and after graduation. Finally, after several months of brain-storming, negotiating and committee meetings, the Academic Affairs Committee of Toccoa Falls College approved a new Cross-Cultural Business Administration Major jointly sponsored by the School of Business Administration and the School of World Missions. Dr. Fred Smith, Director and Professor at Toccoa Falls College's School of World Missions, describes the program,

> The Cross-Cultural Business Administration major is an inter-
> disciplinary degree that mixes missiological principles with
> business principles to prepare students in the area of interna-

tional business with knowledge of cross-cultural principles. This will enable the student to enter creative access countries (CACs) with a marketable skill. This could be as an accountant (upon completing further studies), developing a microenterprise business, or serving as "tent-makers" with a multinational business or another organization requiring these skills. The graduate from this degree could help develop economically viable community projects that would enhance the living standard of the community and financial resources to support the Lord's work. This degree establishes the foreign worker in an acceptable role in communities that disparage professional religious workers."[16]

Our goal is to prepare students in the areas of general and international business with knowledge of cross-cultural principles that would enable the student to reach the following objectives:

1. To enter creative access countries (CACs) with a marketable skill, which is the ability to earn a living outside of the traditional missionary support role. Such roles could include accountants, business managers, production supervisors, sales representatives, human resources specialists, or similar professional positions upon completing graduate studies. Although not a novel approach, numerous doors of opportunity still exist for expatriates to serve as "tentmakers" while working for multinational corporations. Those serving with nonprofit and nongovernmental (NGOs) organizations in areas of economic development, relief, and microenterprise projects, help lift impoverished people in less developed countries out of poverty and financial bondage. Viable community projects enhance the living standard of the community and provide financial resources to support the Lord's work.

2. With the knowledge, skills, and Christian worldview acquired from this joint missions-business degree, graduates could also aspire to serve as field treasurers and business managers for denominational mission boards and parachurch agencies. Others may serve as church business administrators, accountants, auditors, controllers, managers, marketing representatives, or other positions in financial development, medical missions, relief and feeding programs, Christian publishing and retailing, and inner-city ministries.

3. Thirdly, graduates will be encouraged to join with an established team in church planting or unreached people group outreaches. This could include serving as the accountant / treasurer / administrator for the team, helping the team

> open a new track of ministry to the community in developing microenterprises or job training programs. Trained persons with these gifts and stature will supply local credibility and leadership to the team.

The new CCBA major at TFC is jointly sponsored, supervised, and promoted by the Schools of Business Administration and World Missions. Courses will be taught and administered by the respective faculties for the two schools per course pre-fix codes. Students must select membership and an advisor from the school that suits their employment and/or graduate school interests.

Students pursing the CCBA major will take the following courses in the 133-hour program in addition to 30 credit hours of Bible and 30 hours of general education courses. The missions and business courses selected for the major are listed below:

School of World Missions

- Cultural Anthropology
- Gifts, Guidance, Goals
- World Religions
- Cross Cultural Communications
- Strategy of Missions
- Ethnography
- Field Internship (Required)
- Religious Belief Systems
- Sociolinguistics
- Anthropology Research Project
- Missiological Research Project

School of Business

- Microeconomics
- Principles of Accounting I
- Principles of Accounting II
- Introduction to Business
- Business Finance
- International Business
- Principles of Manageme
- International Management
- Principles of Marketing

In view of the specific nature of this major it is recommended that the student select open electives, rather than a minor, choosing from the following courses to total 15 hours:

School of World Mission

- Church Planting & Development
- Training and Discipling
- Applied Anthropology

School of Business

- Business for Nonprofit Organizations
- Information Systems
- Human Resource Management

Other Recommendations

1. Strategic alliances, joint venture partnerships, and other means of coordination among our mission boards/agencies, Christian colleges and universities, and Christian businesses doing international business are needed to sponsor short-term missions trips, summer internships, study abroad programs, microeconomic development, microenterprise projects and business/stewardship training seminars.

2. Business school graduates need information about employment, ministry and career opportunities with mission boards/agencies (both in the home office and field assignments) and as expatriate employees and tentmakers with multinational corporations and NGOs.

3. A faculty chair could be established and funded for a director of the college/university's overseas microeconomic development and related business/management/stewardship training programs. A retired executive with international business experience could make a tremendous contribution here.

Conclusion

"...it is he [God] who gives you the ability to produce wealth..." (Dt 8:19).

Although this chapter places emphasis and urgency on the mission executives, Christian college and university educators and students, and Christian business people, the nationals in foreign lands must share in the responsibilities. I believe that we will find them willing to improve the impoverished conditions of their families, churches, mission programs, schools, and so forth. Often, all they need is a helping hand from fellow-believers in developed countries who already have the knowledge, skills, training, degrees, and resources needed to help them. Many members of our national churches have a desire to start or improve a business. Most of them want to follow God more fully, but are buried under unemployment, poverty, lack of credit, and lack of knowledge to start or expand a business in today's competitive, global environment.

One mission executive, entrepreneur, and educator who has given his adult life to the ministry of economic development for the glory of God is David R. Befus, President of Latin American Mission. He shares his calling and burden,

> God called me into this ministry of economic development. When I started on my doctoral program, I had no idea that I

would also have the privilege to work in international consulting with a prestigious international company, and also see what the world looked like from the vantage point of projects with the World Bank, government agencies, and multinational companies. This experience and the doctoral education were applied in jobs with World Relief and World Vision, which provide me with the opportunity to work in Africa, Asia, and Eastern Europe. I had no idea how different some of these contests were from Latin America and how necessary it was to contextualize methodologies to fit the environment. Now I am back where I started, at the Latin American Mission, where business has long been an acceptable tool for the ministry of the Church. I hope that my experiences and ideas about economic activity will result in more effective proclamation of the Gospel, and encourage Christians to communicate hope in action. May God call others, as he has called me, to the ministry of promoting productive economic activity.[17]

Another such author and educator who shares the burden of the theme of this paper is Tom Steffen, Professor of Intercultural Studies at Biola University. He expresses that burden this way,

> The purpose of this [Steffen's] book is to challenge assemblies, agencies, and academia – at home and abroad – to work together in creative partnerships to fulfill the Great Commandment and the Great Commission through well-trained cross-cultural Christian workers. The need for creative partnerships has never been greater than it is today. Resources around the world, human and financial, are in short supply. Stewardship faithfulness demands that expatriate and non-Western pastors, missions committees, missions executives, educators, and trainers on the formal and nonformal levels pull together rather than pull apart.[18]

"Work together in creative partnerships...pull together rather than pull apart." The Schools of Business Administration and World Missions at Toccoa Falls College are committed to working with other schools, mission boards/agencies, NGOs, and businesses to train cross-cultural workers to go to the whitened harvest fields with internships, summer short-term trips, and career positions to use microenterprise and economic activity to share the Good News and build the Kingdom. Our mission statement at Toccoa Falls College is "to glorify God through seeking and developing Christian servant leaders who will impact their world with the love and message of Jesus Christ." We stand ready and committed to partner with others to help fulfill the Great Commission through developing microenterprise projects and teaching business methods and stewardship from a Christian worldview to national believers throughout the world for the glory of God.[19]

Discussion Starters

1. What Christian colleges and universities have interdisciplinary curriculums in business and missions? Who is on the cutting edge of interfacing business, business-education, and missions to minister to the less fortunate in developing and less developed countries?

2. What schools or agencies offer international internships, study abroad programs, summer projects, and short-term trips abroad whereby educators, students, and business persons can get vicarious experience in setting up and improving microenterprise projects in addition to teaching biblical stewardship principles?

3. Who are the missions and nonprofit organizations that are using microeconomic and community projects to befriend people and share the love and message of Jesus Christ?

4. What U.S. and Canadian agencies recruit and/or place Christian business people with multinational, nonprofit, or nongovernmental organizations? What web sites provide interested persons information on tentmaking, job opportunities overseas, and short-term missions trips for business students and business people?

5. What businesses in the developed countries share the burden of raising the economic conditions of the people of less developed countries of the world and would be willing to sponsor, or better yet, to participate in joint microenterprise projects and teaching seminars abroad?

6. Who is in the best position to serve as a depository of information and catalyst of resources and needs to help facilitate the activities of Christian business and/or missions schools, missions agencies, business people, and national churches?

7. "Where are the counterparts to venture capitalists, investors, entrepreneurs, in the ministries of world missions? If we see doctors, English teachers, theologians, well-diggers, educators and similar professionals involved in world missions, why not trained business people who encourage profit-seeking business enterprises?" "Why shouldn't we encourage Christian entrepreneurs to use their skills to raise the living standard of poor Christians and their unbelieving neighbors? And why shouldn't we expect them to make a profit while doing so? Why shouldn't we encourage them to do their work for the health and growth of Christ's church internationally and in our own urban centers?"[20]

Notes

1. Joseph W. Kilpatrick *Church Business* (Springfield, MO: Global University, 1987), p. 21.
2. Howard Dayton *Your Money Counts* (Gainesville, GA: Crown Financial Ministries, 1996), p. 8.
3. Kilpatrick, pp. 20-21.
4. Louke van Wensveen Siker "Christ and Business: A Typology for Christian Business Ethics" (1988) in *Beyond Integrity: A Judeo-Christian Approach to Business Ethics*, Second edition, by Scott B. Rae and Kenman L. Wong (Grand Rapids: Zondervan, 2004), pp. 55-59. Richard Niebuhr's book, *Christ and Culture*, was originally published in 1951 by Harper & Row, New York.
5. Steve Rundle and Tom Steffen *Great Commission Companies: The Emerging Role of Business in Missions* (Downers Grove: InterVarsity Press, 2003), p. 210.
6. Willard W. Dickerson "Ambassadors for Christ in Business" *Latin America Evangelist*, Vol. 84, No. 2 (July-October, 2004): 4.
7. David R. Befus "God's Provisions/People's Need" *Latin America Evangelist*, Vol. 84, No. 2 (July-October, 2004): 3.
8. Mark Stedman OPDS—A Model of Micro-credit at the Service of the Church *Latin America Evangelist*, Vol. 84, No. 2 (July-October, 2004): 12-13.
9. Max L. Stackhouse "Microenterprise Revolution" *The Christian Century*, Vol. 112, Iss. 20 (June 21, 1995), pp. 629-632.
10. Max L. Stackhouse, pp. 629-632.
11. Makonen Getu "First African Christian Microenterprise Development Conference" *Transformation*, 20 (July 2003), pp. 129-133.
12. Ruth E. Siemens, Global Opportunities, 24 February 2005 <http://www.globalopps.org>.
13. International Fellowship of Alliance Professionals, 26 February 2005 <http://cmalliance.org/missions/serve/ifap.htm>.
14. Freedom Xperience, Crown Financial Ministries, 26 February 2005 <http://www.freedomexperience.org/>.
15. Aaron Cox *Crown Financial Ministries Internship Portfolio*, (Summer 2004).
16. Fred Smith "School of World Missions" *Toccoa Falls College 2005-2006 Catalog*, p. 78.
17. David R. Befus *Kingdom Business* (Miami: Latin America Mission, 2001) pp. 9-11.
18. Tom A. Steffen *Business as Usual in the Missions Enterprise?* (La Habra: Center for Organizational & Ministry Development, 1999), p. 8.
19. The author wishes to acknowledge the following article that contributes greatly to a collegiate perspective on microenterprise development programs and business education: Ron Webb "Business Education and Microenterprise: a millennial marriage" *The Journal of Biblical Integration*, (Fall 1999), pp. 187-203.
20. Gary R. Corwin "Wanted: Venture Stewards" *Evangelical Missions Quarterly*, 36 no. 3 (July 2000), pp. 286-287.

Conclusion

"And He gave some as apostles, and some as prophets, and some as evangelists, and some as pastors and teachers, for the equipping of the saints for the work of service, to the building up of the body of Christ . . ."
(Eph 4:11-12, NAS)

Business as mission is back with a bang! In fact, it never really left. The biblical and historical foundations of the BAM approach are embarrassingly evident. From Abraham to Paul to the Moravian Brethren, to William Carey, to today's tentmakers, God has used the marketplace as the *primary* conduit for his gospel and church. How could we have missed it? How could we have gotten so far off track? How is it that the role of the professional witness (the clergy) usurped God's call upon his people (the saints) for his mission on earth (Eph 4)?

This volume speaks to those among us who wonder how we might best serve our Lord on commission to disciple all nations. It should be an encouragement to professional as well as marketplace witnesses. Equippers — missionaries, missions agencies, church leaders — can re-focus their strategies to equip and empower the workers (cross-cultural and indigenous) to fulfill their roles in the Great Commission. Marketplace saints can be released to invest their lives in God's mission to all peoples.

In fact, the BAM story is one of intense cooperation between the equippers and the saints. The Evil One's myth of separation of sacred from secular is being exposed. The legacy of "today's tentmakers," as J. Christy Wilson referred to them, is alive and well. Politically correct fears concerning the ethics of creative access missions strategies will not stand. Civil disobedience for the sake of the gospel and the oppressed continues.[1] Legitimate platforms for life and work among the least reached of our world are making an impact. Motives for BAM are maturing beyond our first thoughts of fund raising to more strategic considerations such as building sustainable bridges for the gospel that will stand long after we move on.

BAM is not an easy path to follow. When you return to a mindset and culture that inseparably connects your work with life and witness, there is no escape, no time-out from God's mission. Every minute in the marketplace is an opportunity to shine the light of Christ. Every entrepreneurial brainstorm has God's mission tagged to it. Every business decision is accountable to the supreme CEO. This is how it has been. This is how it should be. This is BAM!

What does the future hold for BAM? With a foot planted in "the ministry" and another in "the marketplace," I can't wait to see it. Whom will God raise up as the next Moravian Brethren—a church on mission among the nations through the marketplace? Will one of my students step up and lead the way for a generation of 21st-century tentmakers? Which missions agencies will "get it" and capitalize on this new wave of "flat world," global CEOs for Jesus? What world-changing partnerships will we see between ministry and marketplace leaders? How will the third world church invest in BAM in a way that glorifies God? When will we see an indigenous church planting movement that so impacts its people that their standard and quality of life will be transformed and God-honoring?

Thank you Lord for letting us watch you at work. Thank you for letting us work on your team, for your company. Thank you for serving as our supreme CEO. Lead and guide us as we equip and serve alongside others in this great venture of BAM.

Mike Barnett
Columbia International University
May 2006

---

[1] For a discussion of the ethical implications for creative access and BAM see this author's chapter 8 in Michael Pocock, Gailyn Van Rheenen, and Douglas McConnell's, *The Changing Face of World Missions: Engaging Contemporary Issues and Trends*. Grand Rapids: Baker Academic, 2005.